Project Appraisal for
Developing Countries

Project Appraisal for Developing Countries

Robert J. Brent
Fordham University

HARVESTER
WHEATSHEAF

New York London Toronto Sydney Tokyo Singapore

First published 1990 by
Harvester Wheatsheaf,
66 Wood Lane End, Hemel Hempstead,
Hertfordshire, HP2 4RG
A division of
Simon & Schuster International Group

Printed and bound in Great Britain by
BPCC Wheatons Ltd, Exeter

British Library Cataloguing in Publication Data

Brent, Robert J.
  Project appraisal for developing countries.
  1. Developing countries. Economic development. Projects.
  Assessment
  I. Title
  330.9172'4

  ISBN 0-7450-0422-9

---

1 2 3 4 5 93 92 91 90

To my parents, Josephine and Lukas

Contents

Preface

The chief practitioner of project appraisal is the World Bank. The fundamentals of their approach are explained in *Economic Analysis of Projects* (L. Squire and M. van der Tak, 1975, hereafter denoted by S & T). Their account is entirely theoretical, very condensed (everything is covered in 147 pages), and has many omissions. It is my belief that the field of project appraisal would not be so misunderstood if one had available a much clearer and fuller expression of the analysis presented in S & T. To this end, this book aims to interpret, expand and evaluate their methods. The hope is that it will help to unify the field by providing a clear structure to which future research can be added in a logical fashion. It is expected that, at some time, S & T's text will also be read. However, this book is much wider than S & T's text, which comprises the first two parts of Chapters 1–8. In the third part of Chapters 1–8, numerous challenges to the ideas of S & T are presented, especially through recommending the inclusion of the 'numbers effect'. Moreover, in Chapters 9–13, extensions to S & T and a discussion of alternative methodologies are covered.

The book is based on my years of teaching Project Appraisal for Developing Countries at Fordham. This course is open to all levels of the Graduate School, spanning the MA, PhD and IPED (International Political Economy and Development) programmes. Although use of mathematical notation is widespread, the only mathematical requirement is a knowledge of arithmetic. (Any points that require higher levels of mathematics are included in the appendices.) Other prerequisites are Intermediate Microeconomics and a Development Economics course. The course is therefore geared to advanced undergraduates and first-year graduate students where economics is a major component of the programme. It is hoped that the book will make the material accessible to a much wider audience, including policy-makers and practitioners in the field.

To help make the material more accessible, the book has been written with the following features:

(1) The book has a very narrow focus. It concentrates on S & T's methods, and illustrates these by going into depth with just a few applied studies which are referred to a number of times. All the existing texts (apart from S & T) suffer from the lack of a clear focus. What is the point of showing that a particular estimation method is consistent with a dynamic optimisation approach? If the dynamic optimisation method were consistently used as a basis for deriving all the parameter estimates (which is not the case), then this approach would be useful for academics in the field. But it would not be useful for a reader trying to learn the subject for the first time. In addition to introducing unconnected theoretical arguments, most of the texts present a whole list of alternative ways of estimating a particular theoretical concept. These additional options confuse rather than illuminate matters for the general reader. So, a limited focus is an advantage and not a drawback.

(2) Applied material is included that corresponds with every theoretical concept presented in the text. The applied emphasis of the book is reinforced by problems in each chapter relating to actual case studies. Also a complete project appraisal is carried out in the final chapter (based on data presented in Chapter 8).

(3) Every step in the construction of a formula is outlined and even the simplest of substitutions is demonstrated.

(4) All chapters are split into three parts. The main concepts and their applications constitute the first part. The degree of difficulty varies across chapters because the level of complexity of the concepts used by S & T varies. But in each case the presentation is set at the lowest level that gets the material across to the reader. The second part involves the problems. These range from simple calculations, which reinforce those already made in the chapter, to problems that deal with limitations and possible extensions of the theory. The third part is headed 'Discussion'. It is in this part that controversy is introduced. This is usually more advanced, but is presented only after the essential aspects of the subject have already been covered. A reader can omit all discussion sections yet still obtain a basic understanding of the principles of project appraisal. As a consequence, all my own work on the subject appears in the discussion sections. One does not have to accept any of this to appreciate S & T's approach to project appraisal.

(5) The book is not a series of topics, for it forms a unified course. All chapters interrelate, and there is a logical order in which they are included. Together the chapters form a complete picture of project appraisal. Chapters 1–8 constitute Part One, which gives the essentials of the S & T approach. Chapters 9–13 constitute Part Two. This deals with further issues in project appraisal.

The structure of the book follows that of my one-semester project appraisal course. One chapter is devoted to each (two-hour) class. The main features of the S & T approach are covered in the first eight classes/chapters. From then on, the reader can tackle a practice project appraisal which focuses on understanding the essentials of the S & T approach as is currently formulated. (The practice project appraisal constitutes the mid-term examination for my course.) The extensions to S & T methods that take place in Chapters 9–12 are covered on the basis of the earlier understanding of the essentials. (The essay questions in Chapter 13 are the type that appear in the final examination for the course.) This two-part set-up has two main pedagogic advantages. The reader is faced with a well-defined problem, i.e. how S & T would evaluate a project, rather than trying to uncover the 'best' way of doing a project appraisal; and the instructor has some flexibility to add or delete material from the second part of the book. A ten-week course can supplement Part One with any two chapters from Part Two.

I would like to thank the following: Fordham University who gave me a semester off from teaching in order to write the book; Professor Jerry Miner who arranged my visit to Syracuse University for the spring semester of 1987, and did everything to make my visit productive and enjoyable; six sets of graduate students at Fordham who took the course (especially Joan Combs Durso, who suggested that I write the book in the first place, and James Boyce, who helped me clean up the final copy); Professor Robert Millward who taught me my first course in public expenditure economics; and most of all, my wife, Elizabeth, and sons, Adam and Matthew, who had to put up with an absent husband and father while I devoted time to the book.

PART 1

The essentials of the S & T approach

1

Introduction to project appraisal

1.1   Introduction

The first task is to define the general subject area. Then we will identify
the particular approach that will be used as the guide for this book.

1.1.1   The definition and scope of project appraisal

The area which covers the subject matter of this text is cost–benefit
analysis – a social assessment of the cost and benefits of public investment decisions. Cost–benefit analysis as applied to developing countries
is called project appraisal.
     The basic difference between cost–benefit analysis as applied to
developed countries and that contained in project appraisal is in terms
of the emphasis given to market values. In developed countries, market
values are assumed to be the correct starting point for the measurement
of social values. The market values may need to be supplemented when
there is a change in the market price of the good affected by the public
investment. This causes additional effects to be considered (termed
'producer and consumer surpluses'). Or else, the market values may
need to be imputed when a formal market does not exist, either due to
complete market failure ('public goods' such as defence) or because the
project involves intangibles (such as aircraft noise that accompanies the
building of an airport). When there are large indirect ('external') effects
one tries to scale up or down the market valuation. Nonetheless, in all
these cases market prices form the point of departure.
     But, in the context of project appraisal, market prices may not be

used for social valuation even when they are available. There are two main reasons for this: first, as explained in greater detail below, there is the presumption that the market imperfections are on too large a scale in developing countries to make them remotely reliable, and second, development economists are not so ready to assume that the individual preferences underlying the market values are to be the ultimate arbiters of social values.

Project appraisal has therefore concentrated on finding an alternative starting point to market prices. The determination of these alternative social prices (called 'shadow prices') form the centrepiece of any project appraisal methodology. The fact that project appraisal directs itself more at the fundamentals of what is required to evaluate a public investment explains an important distinction of practice. Cost-benefit analysis tends to be a more fragmented literature. Each application often deals with only one aspect of a particular public investment and attempts to provide an original contribution to measurement. There is very little attempt to connect contributions. Project appraisal, on the other hand, tries to unify principles. Social valuation parameters are first established and these are subsequently used for all parts of the entire evaluation.

There are two main comprehensive approaches to project appraisal: the Little and Mirrlees (1974) method (denoted by L & M) and the UNIDO (1972) approach. As explained in the preface, this book will provide a systematic exposition and critique of the L & M method, as interpreted by Squire and van der Tak (1975) of the World Bank – hereafter referred to as S & T. The World Bank are responsible for making the largest number of project evaluations, so an elaboration of the thinking, if not the practice, of two main representatives of the World Bank is vital to an understanding of the heart of project appraisal.

The appraisal itself is the third stage of what Baum (1970) calls the World Bank's 'project cycle'. First, a project needs to be identified. This involves serving repeater loans, or using 'piggyback operations' (extending an appraisal from the main project, such as a dam, to consider possible projects that may feed off from the main project, e.g. a power-generating project) or sending out a mission especially to detect potential projects. The second, preparation stage requires checking that the project is feasible. The technological capability must exist, and financial cost estimates must produce numbers that are commensurate with a rough estimate of expected benefits. This is the stage when alternative versions of the project are considered, in terms of technology, scale or site location. Then comes the appraisal itself. It was never the case that the World Bank provided 100% of the financing. This meant that an appraisal always contained a financial as well as a social analysis (it being assumed that other bodies providing the finance would only do so if they expected a financial profit). The fourth and final stage relates to the World Bank's supervision of the project, once it has been approved. They wish to ensure that the project is carried out as planned (as well as seeing that the loan is repaid). It is because this last stage often leads to the identification and preparation of new projects that the four stages can be understood to be a self-renewing process (a 'cycle'). A discussion of the significance for project appraisal of the existence of the three stages other than appraisal will be given later in the chapter.

1.1.2 The basic cost–benefit model

Prest and Turvey in their survey of cost–benefit analysis define the basic model as the aim to 'maximise the present value of all benefits less that of all costs subject to specified constraints'. This breaks down to four interrelated questions:

1. What are the relevant constraints?
2. Which costs and benefits are to be included?
3. How are they to be valued?
4. At what interest rate are they to be discounted?

The answers to these questions depend on the assumptions one is willing to make about the economic and political environment in which the investment decisions are being made. In the rest of this section we will present the set of assumptions on which most analysts involved with project appraisal agree. The next section will outline S & T's particular framework.

(1) The aim is to maximise net social benefits:

$$\text{social benefits} - \text{social costs} \tag{1.1}$$

The main way that constraints are treated is by scaling up or down the benefits and costs. For example, if Kenya is interested in the 'Kenyanisation' of the economy, one could multiply by some factor greater than 1 the benefits of projects that hire African workers.

There are two main constraints that are generally supposed to apply to developing countries:

(a) The savings level is considered too low. This is a constraint because general income levels are too low to generate adequate savings. Only in the long run can the government promote the

growth of income that will remove the constraint. In the mean-
time, any consumption that is produced by a project is given a
penalty (scaled down).

(b)   The government's ability to tax to affect the distribution of income
is limited. The ratio of taxes to national income in developing
countries is about half that of developed countries. Apart from
this being a symptom of the low-income, low-savings constraint
just mentioned, it does mean that many sectors of the economy
are outside the tax system. This restriction on the tax system may
have a multitude of origins. Widespread illiteracy prevents the
completion of income tax forms. Political forces may oppose taxes
on land, the main source of wealth in a developing country. Irrespective of the cause, the constraint on the tax system means
that if the government is concerned with the distribution of income, any benefits that go to the poor should be given a premium
(scaled up).

(2) A policy of maximising the net benefits in the abstract is meaning-
less unless one states the objectives. Dickey and Miller (1984) have
defined a project as follows: 'Projects are the basic building blocks of
development. They usually are defined to be the smallest unit which
can be analysed and assessed as an independent entity.' It would follow
then that the objective for project appraisal should be 'development'. In
the 1960s, raising the rate of economic growth was taken to be the single
indicator of development. When it became clear in the 1970s that those
countries that achieved a fast rate of growth did not necessarily expand
economic and social opportunity for all, a second, social objective was
added. The redistribution of income accompanies the desire for economic growth as the twin goals of development. The vehicle for combining the two objectives is to use distributional weights, i.e. the scaling
process for incomes mentioned in point 1. Mathematically, this is akin
to using a weighted rather than an unweighted average. It is weighted
net benefits (the income distributionally weighted growth of output)
that one is now trying to maximise.

(3) The valuation of the output effects comes in two stages. Firstly, one
needs to measure all the inputs and outputs of the project in physical
terms. Then one needs to put a monetary value on the inputs and outputs. The first stage is basically the same for a government interested in
development as for a firm trying to maximise its profits (revenues minus
financial costs). It is the second stage that is different. The differences
are ones of omission and commission:

(a)   Society may get benefits not in the form of revenues, and costs
(forgone opportunities) not of a financial nature. An example of

the former is education, which is alleged to spin off benefits to others in terms of reduced crime. An example of the latter is air pollution emitted from a factory chimney.

(b) Private firms may include revenues that are not benefits to society (such as employment subsidies) and count as financial costs items (such as sales taxes) which do not reduce the opportunities for society.

Because market prices may not be 'right' from society's point of view, they must be replaced in a social cost–benefit analysis by shadow prices – prices that do not actually exist and are only used in the accounting of benefits and costs. Hence they are also called 'accounting prices'. Market prices would be the right ones only if the economy was run under perfect competition and there were no external effects. In these circumstances:

$$\left.\begin{array}{l} \text{Market price} = \text{Marginal costs} \\ \text{or} \\ \text{Marginal social value (MSV)} = \text{Marginal social cost (MSC)} \end{array}\right\} \quad \textbf{(1.2)}$$

It is thought that market prices are much worse reflections of social value in LDCs (less developed countries). L & M (Chapter 2) give ten reasons. Here we will just mention five.

(a) Market prices usually rise at a much more rapid rate in LDCs. One cause is the fact that price adjustments are easier in some sectors than others. For example, in Kenya the price of maize and meat is controlled by the government, but car prices are not. This distorts relative prices, the main factor that allocates resources in an economy.

(b) Because of the greater inflation rate, the domestic prices in LDCs move out of line with foreign prices, causing currency overvaluation. This can be corrected by altering the exchange rate, but this is seldom done. To prevent the rise in imports that would follow from their prices being lower, governments often impose restrictions on imports (quotas and tariffs). These restrictions place a gap between market and social prices.

(c) Wages in LDCs are considered to be institutionally set and not determined by market forces. For example, unskilled labour may earn much more in urban areas than can be explained by the higher costs of living in towns. According to the Third Kenyan Development Plan, the average wage was five times larger in the

urban areas. In these circumstances, market wages do not reflect forgone opportunities.
(d)   The distribution of income is usually more unequal in LDCs. For instance, Musgrave and Jarrett (1979) reveal that the lowest 40% of income earners received 10% of income in Kenya and Brazil; while the relevant percentages were 19.7% for the United States and 18.8% for the United Kingdom. How does this relate to the issue of market prices? The answer is that market prices reflect one's ability to pay, as well as one's willingness to pay (the usual definition of benefits in the cost–benefit literature). If there is great inequality, consumer preferences are imperfectly reflected in market prices.
(e)   Capital markets in LDCs are typically fragmented. There are widely different interest rates charged in different sectors of the economy. An integrated market would charge an equal rate of interest whenever the risk was judged to be the same.

With all these domestic market imperfections, project appraisal focuses on the international trade market. L & M use the world price for a particular good directly, while UNIDO combines the prices of many traded goods to form a shadow exchange rate, and then applies this to the particular good. Again, adjustments will need to be made to the world price (when goods are not traded, or when an LDC dominates a particular market). But the foreign market sets the standard for the shadow prices.

(4) The final issue relates to what discount rate shall be used to find the present value of benefits and costs. It has been argued (under point (e) above) that one cannot rely on market rates to obtain a single rate for discounting purposes. Because of this (and other more fundamental reasons), the MSV of capital is not equal to the MSC of capital. But which rate should one use, the MSV or the MSC? In cost–benefit analysis, the choice is between the social time preference rate (the MSV) and the social opportunity cost rate (the MSC), or some combination of the two. In project appraisal, both concepts have a distinct role to play. When one rate is chosen as the social discount rate, the other is used to calculate the shadow price of capital.

1.2   S & T's methods

We begin our analysis of S & T by covering parts of Chapters 1 and 6. For reference, any equations that are from S & T have an asterisk alongside the numbering on the right.

The fundamentals of any project appraisal method are contained in the identification of the set of individual factors that are considered to be most important, and the way that these factors are integrated to provide an overall assessment. How S & T deal with these two aspects of an appraisal will now be discussed.

1.2.1 Identification of the key factors

A number of considerations were mentioned in the previous section covering the basic cost–benefit model. S & T focus on six of these: shadow prices for outputs and for inputs, domestic market imperfections, distributional issues, the savings constraint and the social discount rate. These six considerations give rise to four key ingredients:

(1) When inputs and outputs are revalued at social rather than market prices, then an economic efficiency outcome is obtained. Let E be this efficiency, real resource outcome. In the S & T framework, E is expressed in terms of world prices.

(2) However, some resource effects have their initial impact on the home economy rather than on the foreign market. Since these effects are expressed in domestic prices, they need to be converted into terms of the shadow prices: β is this conversion factor and reflects the fact that many domestic market imperfections need to be excluded from domestic prices to form the social price equivalent.

(3) S & T combine the distributional issue and savings constraint into one parameter, ω, which is to be attached to any additional consumption, C, that is generated by the project. Additional consumption has two dimensions. In the first, there is a benefit derived by the group that actually does the consumption. This benefit is greater the lower the income (consumption) of the group involved. This is the distributional issue. The second dimension of consumption is a loss, in that extra consumption implies a loss of savings. The more binding an economy's savings constraint, the greater will be the significance of this loss. In fact, ω is the ratio of the benefits to the costs of the extra consumption. The more redistribution is desired relative to the value placed on savings, the higher ω will be.

(4) The final ingredient is the social discount rate.

Each of these ingredients will be examined in detail throughout the book. At this stage of the exposition, it is useful to see how they will fit together. This account of the integration of the factors will be elaborated in Chapter 3.

1.2.2 Integrating the key factors

Although there are four key ingredients, to see the overall picture it is simplest to set the social discount rate equal to zero. (Alternatively, one can assume that the project lasts only for one year.)

The starting point is the real resource outcome of a project, given by E. That is, E is the net benefits given by equation (1.1) when benefits and costs are measured in economic terms. A social evaluation involves adjusting E for the value of any extra consumption, C, that takes place. Let the additional consumption that takes place be undertaken by the private sector. The remainder, $E - C$, goes to the public sector. Because E is measured in world prices, and C is in domestic prices, the two are not directly commensurate. However, by applying the scaling factor β to C, which corrects for domestic price distortions, both would now be in world price terms. The impact on the public sector can then be denoted as $E - \beta C$. The part that goes to the private sector, C, has a distributional and savings effect. The relative importance of the two effects is contained in the parameter ω. Thus, $C\omega$ is the private-sector impact of the project. The social outcome, S (the effect on society as a whole), is the sum of the impacts on the public and private sectors:

$$S = E - C\beta + C\omega \qquad (1.3*)$$

Equation (1.3) contains two terms in C. The first, $C\beta$, represents the loss to the government of not having the consumption resources available to them. These resources cannot be disposed of as the government sees fit. On the other hand, the private consumption does have some social significance. It affects both the distributional objectives and the saving constraint; $C\omega$ is, then, the social gain provided by the consumption. The net social effect of the extra private consumption would then be $C(\omega - \beta)$. If the social gain of the consumption is greater than the loss, then the project would record a social value greater than the real resource effect E. However, S & T implicitly assume that the savings loss will be greater than the distributional gain. So they rewrite (1.3) in a way that expects C to cause a net reduction to E:

$$S = E - C(\beta - \omega) \qquad (1.4*)$$

One must not confuse the negative sign attached to extra C in (1.4) with a quite different situation whereby private consumption was actually reduced by the project. In the case study that is to follow, the tractor project led to a land-ownership reorganisation whereby most small farmers lost their farms, and hence their main source of income. In this case, private consumption as a whole actually fell and $- C\omega$ is its social significance. At the same time, there was a large addition to public-sector resources, and $E + C\beta$ is the real resource gain. The appropriate social criterion when C falls is therefore:

$$S = E + C\beta - C\omega \tag{1.5}$$

The difference between the two formulations (1.3) and (1.5) highlights the core of project appraisal methodology. The efficiency effect is added to, or reduced by, project impacts that affect the distribution of income and the level of savings. The combined effect of these impacts can be favourable – in which case one adds to E to find S. Or else the impacts can be unfavourable, thereby reducing E. The case study shows that it is quite possible to have a project that produces a positive efficiency outcome, yet to have a quite different social outcome. But the reverse situation is also quite possible, i.e. a positive S with a negative E. It all depends on the signs and sizes of E and C, and the magnitudes of β and ω (which are always positive in sign).

1.3   Measurement practice

Let us immediately attach some numbers and significance to the criteria just presented. There are three ways of evaluating projects: financial, economic and social. Each of these will be illustrated in the context of the case study of tractors in Pakistan by Tyler (1979). First we supply some information about the project and Tyler's evaluation.

The World Bank had previously made a financial and economic appraisal of the introduction of tractors in Pakistan. These appraisals had come out strongly in favour of the project. As the tractors were used to increase crop yields on large (high income) farms, causing large-scale unemployment on small farms, Tyler wanted to see whether a social evaluation would have given a different assessment. Tyler worked with a number of alternative parameters. Here we present just one (extreme) set of values that he considered. This set highlights the differences among the three main kinds of project evaluation. For simplicity (to abstract from discounting), we will assume that we can ignore the initial capital charge for the tractors. All inputs and outputs, and their values, were the same in each year. Thus, if the project were judged positive by any criterion in one year, the same judgement could be made in all subsequent years.

The inputs and outputs that accrued to the project in each of seven years were valued as follows (here, and throughout the remainder of this chapter, all figures are in thousands of rupees):

	Value of outputs	Value of inputs
At market prices	4,020	1,987
At world prices	2,662	1,132

1.3.1   A financial appraisal

Let us first place ourselves in the position of the private farmers in Pakistan. They judge whether the tractor imports are worthwhile according to the financial profits that result. Profits are the difference between the revenues from the extra output that is generated by the tractor and the costs associated with the use of the tractor. Both the additional output and the associated costs are valued at market prices. In Pakistan, the additional output was worth 4,020 and the costs were 1,987. The financial profit was therefore 2,033 in each year. As the profit figure was positive, the farmers as a whole were willing to import the tractors.

1.3.2   An economic appraisal

Now let us view matters from the position of a traditional economist. The concern here is with the validity of market values as indicators of the 'true' worth of resources. This true worth, or shadow price, differs from the market price because of the existence of distortions, which make prices differ from their competitive levels. The chief reason that the shadow price figures were lower than the market price figures in Pakistan was because of an overvalued exchange rate, i.e. the official (market) price of dollars in terms of rupees was higher than that implied by the demand of Pakistan's exports relative to its imports (US exports). The main inputs (tractor fuel and fertilisers) and the main output (the crops) were traded (imported or exported). So both sets of domestic values (for inputs as well as outputs) were lower when effectively revalued at a lower exchange rate. The real resource benefits of the tractors were therefore 2,662 and the real resource costs were 1,132. The net economic effect, the economic efficiency outcome E, was 1,530 per annum. Since E was positive, the earlier World Bank evaluation based on the traditional economic approach also endorsed the import of the tractors into Pakistan.

1.3.3 A social appraisal

Finally, let us take the position of the Pakistan government that feels responsible for all individuals in the economy. The overall size of the economics gains (E) is important. The economic effect, 1,530, will be the starting point for the social evaluation. But how these gains are distributed is also important. The distribution effects centre on the extra consumption C from the additional output from the tractor project. The social importance given to distribution relative to E is reflected in the weight $(\beta - \omega)$.

The tractors were most efficiently utilised on large farms. Production on the small farms was therefore replaced by that on the large farms. As a result the small farmer was made unemployed. Consequently, there was actually less consumption (by 432) after the project than before it was instigated. This makes equation (1.5), where C enters negatively, the appropriate social evaluation framework rather than equation (1.3), where C enters positively.

Since small farmers had low incomes even prior to the project, their lost consumption was given a high distributional weight. With savings not highly valued, this implied a high value to ω which, averaged over all groups affected, was 8.06. The social disadvantage of depriving a poor group from consuming would reduce the economic gain by 3,482 (obtained by multiplying 432 by 8.06). That is, $-C\omega = -3,482$. On the other hand, the reduced consumption meant that more resources were at the disposal of the government and could be invested. However, the gain is not all of the 432 reduction in consumption. Consumption is measured in market prices, whereas all the other effects (E and the distributional loss $C\omega$) are measured in shadow prices. A value of 0.67 was used for β, to scale down the gain from the reduction in consumption to make it comparable with the other effects. The social gain from the reduced consumption freeing resources for the government would then be 289 (0.67×432).

The social outcome for the tractor project in Pakistan would be determined as follows. The reduced consumption makes the poor worse off (in social terms) to the extent of 3,482. This exceeds the 289 gain from the reduced consumption because the government has more resources at its disposal. The net distributional effect is negative and equal to $-3,193$ ($289 - 3,482$). Because a social outcome is just the sum of the efficiency gain of 1,530 and the distributional loss of 3,193, the social impact of the tractor project would be $-1,663$. As the social 'profit' is negative, a government concerned with efficiency and distribution would not have agreed to import the tractors into Pakistan. (As stated earlier, this result was just one of the possibilities considered by Tyler. The other possibilities, and a full discussion of all the implications of the Pakistan tractor project, will be presented in the final chapter.)

1.4 Problems

Here we explore some of the social implications of the Pakistan project just illustrated. The aim is to anticipate some of the issues covered in the next section, i.e. the role of compensation tests, and the need for some consideration to be given to the number of losers caused by a public project.

Background information

The changes brought about by the Pakistan tractor project are summarised in Table 1.1. The income figures are in rupees. There is an important point to bear in mind when you try to interpret Table 1.1. Farmers/workers who existed before the change, but do not appear after the tractors have been introduced, became unemployed.

Questions

(a) Who had the highest income before the change, and by what percentage did their income rise? By what percentages did the other groups' income change? What, then, was the impact of the tractors on the distribution of incomes? How does project appraisal attempt to deal with these distributional changes?

(b) In section 1.3 we saw that 1,530 (thousand rupees) extra was generated by the project to the overall size of the gains (the efficiency effect). The consumption of the poor decreased by 432, which meant that the consumption of the rich increased by 1,962 (assuming that the government did not get any of the resources). If it were feasible (if the infor-

Table 1.1 Distribution of income before and after the tractor project in Pakistan

| | Before | | After | |
	Number	Average income	Number	Average income
Big farmers	202	8,990	202	27,153
Small farmers	879	1,923	0	0
Full-time workers	2,236	1,404	912	1,404
Casual labour	660	844	1,156	844

mation was available and programmes were inexpensive to administer) how could one ensure that the programme had some gainers, but no one would lose? Do you think it is feasible to ensure that there are no losers for every beneficial social change that takes place in any economy?

(c) How many people gained from the tractor project, and how many lost? Do S & T's methods allow for such differential impact of numbers of gainers and losers? If the losers had the same level of income as the gainers before the change, would using distributional weights allow the evaluation to acknowledge the large number of losers?

1.5 Discussion

In this section we will briefly explore the origins of the S & T methodology. We hope to make clear why the S & T methodology is so important, and thus worth building a new book around. With this as background, we can then examine what objectives S & T do and do not include in their analysis.

1.5.1 History and genesis of project appraisal

At root, the history of project appraisal involves the search for a consistent set of rules for managing a mixed economy. The principles of a privately run, competitive economy are well understood. Markets allocate resources in line with consumer preferences. In the process, privately owned firms maximise profits. Market prices link the consumers and producers, and the system functions in a decentralised way. Equally well understood are the principles of running a command economy. The system is highly centralised. Planners' preferences dominate production decisions. Resources are commanded to the publicly owned firms to ensure that the planners' targets are achieved. What was not understood was how to deal with economies where government-run, publicly owned firms coexist with a private sector run on competitive lines.

The first step in the process of developing the economic theory of the mixed economy came with the Lange–Lerner rules for running a decentralised planned economy that appeared in the 1930s. The central planners would still set the output targets. But, instead of having the resources commanded for them, the managers of the publicly owned enterprises would decide the input decisions themselves. Their decisions would be guided by the rule that they would set price equal to marginal cost, this being a necessary condition for economic efficiency. Since this rule would have resulted if perfect competition had existed, the Lange–Lerner rule was clearly an important requirement for the coexistence of privately and publicly owned firms.

The idea of economic efficiency was central to welfare economics, which was the branch of theory developed to justify a social change (or public involvement) in the private economy. The concept, due to Pareto, judged a situation efficient if the change led to a situation whereby someone gained and no one lost. To ensure that no one lost, compensation should be given from the gains. This led to the idea of compensation tests, which stated that for a change to be efficient, the size of the gains should be sufficient to cover compensation to the would-be losers. Clearly, actual compensation was a strong requirement. So, the 'new welfare economics' of the 1950s suggested a modified compensation test. The Kaldor–Hicks test for a potential improvement was that the gainers should be able to compensate the losers and still have some left over. But the compensation need not actually take place.

A major drawback of this simple test was the possibility that these losers may be on low income. To accommodate this possibility, authors such as Weisbrod and Marglin suggested that low income losses should be weighted more highly than high income gains. The alternative compensation test was that the weighted gains must be greater than the weighted losses. As will be pointed out in section 1.5.3, even this compensation test is hypothetical, in that there still may be losers from the government involvement. However, this view did establish that distributional influences should accompany the concern for economic efficiency as joint objectives of government policy. Attention then focused back on how the gains and losses were to be measured.

With both the private and public sectors pricing at marginal cost, the correct way to measure the gains and losses (of small changes) seemed to be to use market prices. This ignored one problem. What if the private sector for any reason did not run on perfectly competitive lines, and thereby did not price at marginal cost? How should the public sector price its output? This class of problems was the concern of the 'theory of the second best' that appeared in the early 1960s. One of the implications of the work by Lipsey and Lancaster was that if any other sector of the economy did not follow the efficiency rules, then the government continuing to price at marginal cost would not ensure efficiency. An impasse was reached in welfare economic theory.

The impasse was broken by a theorem by Diamond and Mirrlees in the late 1960s. They showed that if optimal commodity taxes existed, then the public sector should continue to seek productive efficiency. The implication was that the public sector could continue to price at marginal cost. Attention was then given to the issue of what happens if non-optimal taxes existed, and the whole field of optimal taxation took off in the 1970s. It is important to appreciate exactly what was the optimal taxation literature's contribution to an understanding of how to run a mixed economy. The central idea is as follows: the public sector can pre-empt resources for its own use, and it can then run its affairs efficiently; what is left over goes to the private sector. Since the private sector is to be run on market lines, consumers must choose to buy the remaining goods, given their budget constraint. The budget constraint is a function of income and the prices of the goods. This means that the government must use its instruments of control (e.g. income and commodity taxes) to ensure that consumer budget constraints are at the required levels. To sum up: in a planned economy, the government maximises its objectives subject to the total goods available (determined by the production function). In a mixed economy, the process is the same, except for the fact that it must also satisfy consumer budget constraints.

Using the Diamond–Mirrlees theorem as a point of departure, L & M in 1968 wrote their pioneering manual of project appraisal for developing countries. They interpreted the theorem as follows. In an LDC, the foreign trade (import and export) sector should be considered as part of the public sector. In line with the theorem, the public sector should be efficient and price at marginal cost. The prices that determine the costs for imports and exports of an LDC are the world prices. Thus, world prices should be the shadow prices. Although constructed differently on the surface, the second major approach to project appraisal developed by UNIDO in 1972 ultimately shared this shadow-pricing rationale. It did, however, emphasise distributional matters more than the manual. Consequently, when the revised version of L & M's manual was published in 1974, it now conformed to the welfare economic requirement that distribution and efficiency be the twin objectives of government policy.

The fact that the L & M approach focused on productive efficiency in trade led some to believe that this methodology was just another way of arguing the virtues of free trade. L & M's work therefore quickly became caught up with the protectionist debate in LDCs. While one could justify the use of world prices in terms of the gains from trade, this was not central to the approach. What was vital was that the trade prices be determined independently of the market imperfections and distribution of income existing in the domestic economy. The trade prices could be treated as fixed parameters and lead to no domestic price repercussions. One returns to the price-taking property that is characteristic of perfect competition. In any case, it was not necessary to remove protectionist barriers to use the methodology. The approach allowed a country to have tariffs, yet ensure that public investments were evaluated in isolation of the distortions caused by the tariffs.

S & T's book was written just after the two major contributions to project appraisal by L & M and UNIDO. It is basically a synthesis and simplification of the two approaches (though strongly favouring L & M). This is a major contribution in its own right. S & T's book also has the advantage of providing the most systematic and comprehensive inclusion of distributional issues into project appraisal. It is a secure base from which the future literature of project appraisal can develop.

Nonetheless, S & T's book does have some major deficiencies. The exposition is much too condensed, and there are no applications. The chief task of this book is to remedy these deficiencies. In addition, we wish to provide a critique of S & T's methods. The critique is largely from the perspective of what Stewart (1978) would call the 'details' of the methodology. However, there will be some novel elements; and in the next section (and in Chapter 3) there will be an attempt to justify the general methodology itself. Note that it is necessary to fully understand a methodology before one can appreciate its strengths and weaknesses.

1.5.2 S & T's social objectives

According to the welfare economic theory behind cost–benefit analysis, society is to be concerned with the size of the pie (economic efficiency) and how it is to be shared out (income distribution). Development economics has set its goals for society as economic growth and income distribution. S & T, in their attempt to link the two fields to form the area of project appraisal, assign the growth objective to correspond with 'economic efficiency'. This correspondence is a logical one. But the notions are distinct. Economic efficiency is a static concept (looking at resource availability at a point of time) while growth is dynamic (looking at how resource availability changes over time). Although this distinction is not acknowledged by S & T, it is somewhat accommodated by the way they formulate their distribution weights, as we now see.

The concept of a growth rate relates changes in a variable over time to its existing level. Thus, the growth of consumption would divide the time rate of change in consumption (due to the project) by the level of consumption. S & T value all changes in the level of a group's consumption by reference to the average consumption level. Thus S & T are effectively dividing by consumption levels to obtain their weights. A numerical example may help clarify the point. Say the average consumption level in country A is 100, while it is 200 in country B. For the sake of argument, assume that this difference occurred because the past growth rate in country B was faster than in country A. A group that is poor may have a consumption level of 20 in country A and 40 in country B. S & T would give the poor group in each country the same distribution weight, as they both consume the same percentage (20%) of average consumption. The difference in the growth rates did not affect the weights. Formally, as explained in Chapter 3, S & T are using a 'relative inequality aversion' formulation for the distribution weights. (That is, the same percentage consumption difference in two countries produces the same distribution weight, irrespective of the difference in average consumption levels in the two countries.)

Apart from the dynamic–static difference in interpretation of the efficiency concept, S & T's objectives are those of modern welfare economics. No special allowance is given to particular individual or group interests that are not of a distributional nature. The scaling parameters β and ω are set in advance at the central level and are to apply to all appraisals. The World Bank often initiate a research study to determine the national parameters that are to be used for future studies, e.g. the study by Mashayekhi (1980) for Turkey. In these cases, there is less scope for an analyst to bring in personal prejudices or outside influences.

However, there are many, such as Stewart (1978), who would question whether S & T's intended objectives were the ones that actually guided project appraisal in practice. There are two main charges that need a successful defence. The first charge is that the institutional procedure involved in the project cycle provides ample scope for non-social objectives to influence appraisal outcomes. The second charge is that there seems to be empirical evidence that this ample scope was exploited, and other factors actually determined the outcomes.

(1) As pointed out earlier, the appraisal of the project comes after the initiation and preparation stages. If, as Baum claims, the World Bank only appraise projects for which the host country is willing to provide some internal finance, then one has to accept that political and other groups must have some input in the decision-making process. Nonetheless this does not necessarily mean that the project objectives are not those indicated by S & T. It is useful to characterise the process as proceeding in two steps. First, the ruling political forces in a country will have their input by deciding which projects are to be appraised. Guided by narrow self-interest, these groups are unlikely to put forward projects that are socially the most beneficial. But, once the projects reach the appraisal stage (the second step), the decisions are

made purely on the basis of the social objectives. In formal terms what is being suggested is that political forces decide the opportunity set, while the selection from that set is on the basis of the social objectives. The chosen projects will be the most beneficial socially of those being considered.

This is an example of the use of one of the most fundamental procedural principles of cost–benefit analysis. That is, the decisions are to be made on the assumption that constraints (financial, developmental, political, etc.) are binding. The analyst then tries to maximise net benefits given those constraints. The process is termed one of 'second-best' optimisation; there are other constraints additional to the production constraint, provided by the availability of resources. Of course, one may still expect political and other groups to attempt to influence the second step. But, for a number of reasons (which will be presented in Chapter 3 concerning the use of distributional weights), one can argue that they are unlikely to be successful in their attempt. Here it is only necessary to point out that there does exist the fourth stage of project appraisal. The World Bank are involved also with the supervision of the project once it has been approved. Efforts are made to ensure that the project is carried out as planned. Note that such supervision is rarely carried out for cost–benefit evaluations in developed countries.

Stewart would prefer that the constraints be removed, rather than setting up project appraisal rules to avoid the distortions caused by the constraints. Even if one accepts this position, one must still adopt the rules if, for any reason, the constraints will not be removed while the project is in existence.

(2) An empirical study of the actual determinants of World Bank loans was carried out by Frey and Schneider (1986). They regressed a number of social, economic and political variables on the average per capita commitment by the World Bank over the period 1972–81. They found that political factors were significant determinants, like whether the LDC was an ex-colony or whether it had a 'capitalist climate'. This result would seem to question the usefulness of the S & T objectives for an appraisal. But no contradiction would be implied if one accepts the existence of the two-step process just presented. It was acknowledged that political factors probably would decide the opportunity set, while S & T's objectives would determine the choice from this set. Since actual choices are a mixture of objectives and opportunities, the existence of political factors does not preclude the existence of the social objectives. What is vital in this interpretation is whether S & T objectives appear as significant determinants of World Bank loan decisions, in addition to, rather than instead of, the political factors. Unfortunately, Frey and

Schneider did not test explicitly for all the S & T objectives. In particular, no income distributional variable was included. But both per capita income and the growth rate were significant. So economic efficiency, in both its static and dynamic forms, was represented in the list of determinants. Moreover, the savings and taxation constraints assumed by S & T would imply that surpluses in the budget and the balance of payments should be significant influences; and they were. Note that Frey and Schneider effectively used a 'reduced form' equation to make their estimates. In such an equation, where both objectives and opportunities interact, it is no simple matter to determine what the expected signs should be on the two surplus variables.

1.5.3 Alternative social objectives

Looked at from a welfare economic theory perspective, there are two main considerations that have been omitted from S & T's objective function. The first consideration is now a standard part of modern welfare economic theory. The second consideration is not standard, though there are good reasons that it should be.

An allowance for in-kind income redistribution

When the government decides to build a project, say a dam for irrigation, beneficiaries receive assistance in a particular way. Assistance is given in kind and not directly in cash form. It has been argued that this is one of the fundamental reasons that public expenditure is used as a policy instrument in the first place (see Brent, 1984a). The details of this argument will be developed a number of times in this text. For instance, Chapter 3 explains how S & T's formulation of distributional weights can be extended to consider this in-kind dimension. Here, it is only necessary to emphasise that ignoring in-kind considerations is a major omission from S & T's work that needs to be remedied.

A three-objective social welfare function

(Much of the following is based on Brent, 1984b.)

It has always seemed probable that policy-makers have more than efficiency and distribution in mind when they make public policy decisions. Economists in the public choice school (like Frey and Schneider) would consider that the missing factor is the personal preferences of the policy-maker, whether to gain prestige or whether to obtain votes to get elected (or re-elected) to public office. These personal preferences clearly do play a role. But the previous sub-section explained how social welfare maximisation and narrow political factors can coexist in the project appraisal decision-making process. That is, it was assumed that political factors influence the selection of projects to be considered, while the choice from among this set is guided solely by the objective of social welfare maximisation. It is within the domain of the social welfare maximisation part of the decision-making process that the omission is thought to exist.

To help introduce the main idea, we can consider the following situation. Suppose there is a self-financing clean-up public project that improves the surroundings for a particular individual. If that person feels very strongly about the environment, it may be that on efficiency grounds the project is very successful. If, in addition, the individual has a low income, the project would be judged even more favourable. Nonetheless, one cannot help but question whether the project was in any way a *social* improvement, when only one person in society is involved. Should we not write into the welfare function some regard for the number of people who are affected? Many critics of past development performance seem to be asking this same question. How one inteprets the 'miracle' in Brazil depends largely on how one views the fact that there were whole sections of Brazil that did not gain by the large economic growth which the country experienced in recent times. (See, for example, the comments and reply in the March 1980 volume of the *American Economic Review* to the article by Fields, 1977.)

The original motivation for including a numbers effect as a third social objective in public expenditure analysis came from an empirical study of UK government railway closure decisions (Brent, 1976). The aim of the study was to estimate the implicit distributional weights behind past government closure decisions. But, when one came across the data in the files that the decision-maker actually used to make the decisions, the numbers affected were allegedly of prime concern. The results confirmed this. The number of people who were to be left with no viable alternative means of public transport was a significant determinant of whether an unremunerative railway line was to be closed.

In addition to this empirical result, there is a theoretical reason, given in Brent (1986a), for wanting to include the numbers effect as a third factor. It has been shown (in a poverty context) that no social welfare function based solely on efficiency and linear distribution weights (as recommended in Chapter 3) can be sensitive to the number of losers (the number of persons in poverty). The numbers effect is an additional factor to the other two. An important implication of this theorem is that one cannot say that the numbers effect is just a proxy for the efficiency objective.

If social welfare is to be determined by more than efficiency and distribution, it is important to know how it fits in with the welfare economic base behind cost–benefit analysis. The foundation stone of this analysis is the idea of a compensation test. A project makes society better off if there are sufficient gains such that the losers can be compensated, and there is still some positive amount left over. This is the standard criterion and is basically what S & T use. However, it does ignore the possibility that for real world projects it is almost impossible administratively to arrange for compensation for all. Almost always, there will be losers. It seems logical to acknowledge this, and include the number of uncompensated losers as a separate factor in the cost–benefit criterion.

The final step in the process of including the numbers effect is to interpret what a three-objective social welfare function is meant to represent. A 'good' project is one where efficiency and distribution are furthered. One should choose projects where this good is 'greatest'. From this it is a simple matter to consider the other part of the famous maxim, that the greatest good should be for the greatest number. The three-objective social welfare function could then be interpreted as giving concrete expression to Jeremy Bentham's social philosophy.

Even if one does not wish to express the matter in Benthamite terms, the numbers effect should still be recognised as a separate element. It is interesting to note that there is already someone in the World Bank who thinks of project appraisal in terms of the numbers effect. Ray writes: 'The proposition that the greater the number of beneficiaries the better the project, is taken by many as a truism' (1984, p. 129). However, because he views matters in the standard (efficiency and distribution) way, he fails to give separate consideration to the numbers effect and tries to treat this as a distributional issue. The context in which he was discussing the numbers effect was for a land resettlement scheme in Kenya. The problem was similar to the Pakistan tractor project, but in reverse. In Kenya, a large number of small farmers were to replace a few large farmers. It is important to look at the effect that the change in size of a farm has on productivity. This is an efficiency effect. It is also correct to try to allow for the fact that the group of farmers gaining have low incomes – a distributional effect. But the fact that there were a large number of gainers, and a few losers, should be recognised as a third dimension and warrant its own scaling parameters. Why and how the numbers effect should be incorporated into project appraisal will be a recurring theme. It will be considered whenever the discussion deviates from explaining and illustrating the S & T project appraisal methodology, which is the main subject matter of the book.

2
Investment criteria

2.1   Introduction

S & T cover the whole topic of investment criteria in five pages of their text (Chapter 4). In a sense this can be explained by the fact that they have nothing distinctive to say on the subject. The chapter that is presented here will also be reasonably standard. However, more space will be allocated to this material than was devoted by S & T because it is such a basic part of project appraisal. An additional reason for the further coverage is that, later on, we shall assign a practice project appraisal, and some guidance is needed to carry out this exercise. S & T only state some of the main results. We shall try to fill in some of the missing words of explanation and give numerical examples. A fuller analysis of the theory is covered in Irvin (1978, Chapter 1) and the details of how to make the calculations are contained in Gittinger (1984). S & T present the material in an entirely verbal fashion, so it will be necessary to introduce some new notation. This will not duplicate any symbols that appear in S & T's text.

To understand a procedure, it is often best to look at what happens at the end; just as when one learns to play chess, the moves only begin to make sense when one understands how to end the game, i.e. the 'checkmate'. In this chapter the focus is on the decision rule which determines whether to go ahead with the project once it has been appraised. Central to the use of the decision rules is the process of discounting – using a rate of interest to find the current value of an annual outcome. In the first chapter we considered only a single-period outcome, or a recurring annual outcome with no initial capital costs. This chapter will include multi-period outcomes. It will be assumed that the discount rate has been previously determined. (Chapter 4 deals with the determination of the discount rate.) The first task is to explain how to use this discount rate to collapse the multi-period outcomes to a single current outcome. Then it is a matter of showing how the decision rules decide, on the basis of the single outcome, whether to accept the project.

It is helpful here (and we will be following this approach throughout the book) to refer to how a private firm would deal with the topic under review. A private firm is guided by financial profits when making its investment decisions. To allow for the fact that the size of the financial profit is often related to the size (scale) of the initial capital expenditure, it is usual to express the profit as a rate of return (on the capital expenditure). The percentage rate of return can then be compared with the cost of capital (also expressed in percentage terms). In a competitive economy, the cost of capital is the market rate of interest. The investment rule for a private firm reduces to a comparison of the rate of return with the market rate of interest. The firm will continue investing until the rate of return on the last project equals the rate of interest.

Public and private investment decision rules are similar. Providing the goal is redefined to be seeking 'social profits' rather than financial profits, the decision rules are designed to allow for the same sets of circumstances.

2.1.1 The process of compounding and discounting

Let us assume that the project results in one unit of social net benefits today. The government could then invest this one unit at an interest rate r. The value next year of today's one unit would then be $1 \cdot (1 + r)$. In the second year, it would be worth $1 \cdot (1 + r)^2$, and so on. In any future year, t, the one unit would be worth $1 \cdot (1 + r)^t$. That is:

$$Future\ value\ in\ year\ t = (1 + r)^t \cdot value\ of\ 1\ unit\ today \quad \textbf{(2.1)}$$

The $(1 + r)^t$ term in (2.1) is called the 'compounding factor'. For example, if r is 6%, the compounding factor for one unit would be 1.06 next year ($t = 1$) and 1.123 in the second year.

Discounting works in the reverse time direction to compounding. It asks the question, if the project results in one unit of social net benefits in the future, what is its social value today? 'Value today' appears on the right-hand side of (2.1). Thus, if one divides the future value by the compounding factor, one obtains the value today.

$$Value\ today = Future\ value\ in\ year\ t/(1 + r)^t \quad \textbf{(2.2)}$$

The term $1/(1 + r)^t$ is called the 'discount factor'. It is the reciprocal of the compounding factor. So one unit next year, when the rate of interest is 6%, is worth $1/1.06$ $(= 0.943)$ units today. The year after, $t = 2$, the same one unit would be worth $1/(1.06)$ $(1.06) = 0.890$ in today's values. Clearly, the further away the future period, and the higher r is, the lower will be the value today.

2.1.2   Defining and applying the main investment criteria

There are three main investment criteria: the net present value, the internal rate of return, and the benefit–cost ratio. These will be examined in turn.

The net present value criterion

The project will lead to a stream of social net benefits throughout its life (T years). Each year's net benefits will have a value today. The net present value (NPV) criterion simply sums the stream of annual future net social benefits (S) in today's value terms.

$$NPV = \sum_{t=0}^{t=T} S_t/(1 + r)^t \tag{2.3}$$

where S has been defined in Chapter 1 – equation (1.5) – to be

$$S_t = E_t - C_t(\beta - \omega) \tag{2.4}$$

The decision rule (the rule that decides whether a project should be accepted or rejected) is that one passes all projects where $NPV > 0$, when discounted at the appropriate discount rate r. For in today's value terms, the stream of social net benefits would be positive.

To help show how to calculate the NPV, we will refer to the appraisal of the Morocco Fourth Agricultural Project made by Cleaver (1980). The study was designed to assess, using the S & T methodology, the implications of the price distortions that worked against agriculture. The project was to provide finance through Morocco's Agricultural Credit Bank to farmers to extend their own activities. There were a number of components in the project, involving all aspects of agriculture, including the purchasing of machinery and farm stock. The analysis revolved around five typical sub-projects (called 'farm models') which could, in principle, be replicated. The shares of the total budget allocated to the five model groups were fixed in advance. The aim was to see how socially (and privately) valuable the sub-projects were.

One of the component models was the purchase of a tractor to be used for land preparation on farms of between 60 and 120 hectares. The tractor investment was expected to last ten years and the rate of interest was 6%. All the steps for making the calculation of the NPV are shown in Table 2.1 below. The social net benefits, and today's value amounts, are all in terms of the Moroccan currency, dirham. For comparison purposes, the table also shows what the NPV would be if the discount rate were 48% rather than 6%.

The method is to see what one unit of social net benefits would be worth in any year (in today's value terms) given the interest rate, and then multiply that figure by the actual amount of S in that year. The sum for all years that the project is expected to last produces the NPV. The discount factors can be found by substituting 0.06 for r in equation (2.2), for each of the ten years ($t = 1$ for the first year, and $t = 10$ in the last year). Or else, as was done here, one can simply look up a set of tables which provides the discount factors (Gittinger, 1984, has a set of tables which also has detailed instructions on how to use them). Note that in Table 2.1, the first year's S value was discounted. This follows the common practice cited by Gittinger (1984, p. 157) of regarding the period when the decision is being made (just prior to the beginning of the project) as period zero (strictly, the last day of the zero-th year). Year 1 (the last day of year 1) would be one year away into the future. Any effects occurring then must be discounted.

The Moroccan tractor project was clearly a socially profitable one. The positive NPV using the 6% interest rate indicates that if it were considered on its own, it would have been accepted.

Table 2.1 Calculating the NPV for tractors in the Morocco Fourth Agricultural Project

Year	Social net benefits (S)	Discount factor at 6%	Today's value at 6%	Discount factor at 48%	Today's value at 48%
1	−45,353	0.943	−42,768	0.676	−30,660
2	16,490	0.890	14,676	0.457	7,536
3	25,585	0.840	21,491	0.308	7,880
4	29,090	0.792	23,039	0.208	6,051
5	25,690	0.747	19,190	0.140	3,597
6	25,305	0.705	17,840	0.095	2,404
7	20,750	0.665	13,799	0.064	1,328
8	20,750	0.627	13,010	0.043	892
9	20,750	0.592	12,284	0.029	602
10	20,750	0.558	11,579	0.020	415
		NPV at 6% =	104,136	*NPV* at 48% =	45

The internal rate of return criterion

Table 2.1 also shows the importance of the rate of interest. As mentioned earlier, the higher *r* is, the lower is the NPV. When a rate of 48% is used to make the discounting, the tractor project's positive NPV all but disappears. The internal rate of return (IRR) criterion focuses on this last remark. It seeks to find that rate of interest (which will be labelled *R*) for which the NPV is exactly zero. That is, one solves for *R*, when *R* replaces *r* in equation (2.3), and the NPV is set equal to zero.

$$NPV = \sum_{t=0}^{t=T} S_t/(1 + R)^t = 0 \qquad (2.5)$$

It can be seen in (2.5) that the IRR is the solution to a polynomial equation (an equation that has the unknown raised to various powers: in terms of equation (2.5), *R* is the unknown and *t* is the power). The decision rule for the IRR is that one accepts projects that have an IRR greater than the interest rate. That is, a project passes the test if $R > r$. One can invest in the project, or one can use the funds elsewhere. If one invests in the project, one receives an average return of *R*. If one uses the funds elsewhere, one would have earned a return of *r*. Thus, if $R > r$, one is obtaining the highest return possible for those funds (assuming that *r* is the next best alternative return).

Unfortunately, it is not a simple matter to compute the solution to a polynomial. Some sort of trial and error procedure is necessary. One starts with a particular *R* figure, call it R_1, and uses this to calculate the NPV, just as in Table 2.1. If the NPV using R_1 is positive, then the next *R* figure one tries is higher than R_1. If the NPV using R_1 is negative, then the next *R* figure one tries is lower than R_1. The process continues until an *R* is found where *NPV* is exactly zero.

Gittinger (1984, p. 186) gives some useful advice on how to calculate the IRR. One should try *R* values that are 5 percentage points apart. When one does this, there will be an *R* (call it R_L, the lower limit for *R*) where *NPV* is positive, but closest to zero. Denote the NPV figure $NPV(R_L)$. There will also be an *R* (call it R_U, the upper limit for *R*) where *NPV* is negative but closest to zero. Denote this NPV figure $NPV(R_U)$. Clearly, *R* will lie between these two values. Gittinger supplies a rule for finding *R*. His 'interpolation rule' is as follows:

$$R = R_L + [R_U - R_L] \cdot [NPV(R_L)/NPV \\ (R_U) + NPV(R_L)] \qquad (2.6)$$

In adding the two NPVs on the denominator of the second term of (2.6), one has to ignore the negative sign attached to *NPV* (R_U).

We can return to the Moroccan tractor project to illustrate the calculation of the IRR. We see from Table 2.1 that at an interest rate of

Table 2.2 Calculating the IRR for tractors in the Morocco Fourth Agricultural Project

Year	Social net benefits (S)	Discount factor at 45%	Today's value at 45%	Discount factor at 50%	Today's value at 50%
1	−45,353	0.690	−31,295	0.667	−30,250
2	16,490	0.476	7,849	0.444	7,322
3	25,585	0.328	8,392	0.296	7,573
4	29,090	0.226	6,574	0.198	5,760
5	25,690	0.156	4,008	0.132	3,391
6	25,305	0.107	2,708	0.088	2,227
7	20,750	0.074	1,536	0.059	1,224
8	20,750	0.051	1,058	0.039	809
9	20,750	0.035	726	0.026	540
10	20,750	0.024	498	0.017	353
		NPV at 45% =	+2,054	*NPV* at 50% =	−1,051

48%, *NPV* is approximately zero. So *IRR* must be 48%. But suppose that we did not know this. We would then have to try various values for R. If we did this, at 5 percentage point intervals (starting, say, from 10%), one would eventually find the results given in Table 2.2.

To use Gittinger's rule, one sets $R_L = 45$, $R_U = 50$, $NPV(R_L) = 2,054$ and $NPV(R_U) = 1,051$. Substituting these values in (2.6) produces the following:

$$R = 45 + [50 - 45] \cdot [2,054/1,051 + 2,504]$$

or

$$R = 45 + [5] \cdot [0.662] = 48.31$$

Rounded to the nearest whole percentage point, R is 48% as confirmed by Table 2.1. Since 48% > 6%, the tractor project easily passes the IRR decision rule.

The benefit–cost ratio

It is often convenient to work with a modified version of (2.3). In the current period, $t = 0$, there are the initial capital costs K to be paid, but usually there are no benefits to consider (because the project has not yet been made operational). Thus, in the current period, $S = -K$. Now (2.3) can be split up into two amounts, the current year effect (which has a discount factor of 1) and the sum for all other years, starting from year 1. That is:

$$NPV = S_0 + \sum_{t=1}^{t=T} S_t/(1 + r)^t \tag{2.7}$$

So substituting for S_0 in (2.3), we obtain:

$$NPV = -K + \sum_{t=1}^{t=T} S_t/(1 + r)^t \qquad \text{(2.8)}$$

The (gross) benefit–cost ratio (B/K) criterion is based on the two components of (2.8). It combines the two by dividing rather than subtracting. That is, the second component is divided by the first to form a ratio of the two. The second component of (2.8) is obtained by adding K to both sides of this equation,

$$NPV + K = \sum_{t=1}^{t=T} S_t/(1 + r)^t \qquad \text{(2.9)}$$

So we can express the ratio as:

$$B/K = [NPV + K]/K \qquad \text{(2.10)}$$

The decision rule for the B/K criterion is that one passes projects where $B/K > 1$. The reason that the ratio must be greater than 1 is that K (the initial capital cost) is on the denominator; so one wants to ensure that one has gross benefits greater than this amount on the numerator of the ratio.

The benefit–cost ratio is simple to calculate once one has previously found the NPV. All one needs in addition is the value for K. This will usually be given in the first line of the table used to calculate the NPV. So, in Table 2.1, for the Moroccan tractor project we see that $K = 42,770$. This value, together with the NPV figure of 104,136, is inserted into equation (2.10) to obtain a value for B/K equal to 3.435. As the ratio is greater than unity, one again satisfies the decision rule being applied to the tractor project.

Gittinger clears up one item of ambiguity related to the B/K ratio. The K figure that was used to calculate the ratio for the Moroccan tractor project actually related to the first year, and not year zero, as equations (2.7) and (2.8) suggest. But this is not a problem as long as one remembers to apply the appropriate discount factor (using r) to the year that the capital costs are incurred. Gittinger's interpretation of the B/K ratio is that to obtain K, one sums the today values for all the years when the project does not give positive net benefits (1984, p. 187). So, in the tractor case, there was a zero value for the current period, and $-42,770$ in the first period, giving a total for non-positive net benefit years of 42,770.

With Gittinger's interpretation, the standard criticism of the B/K ratio does not apply. A problem is thought to arise over whether to classify an effect as a positive benefit or a negative cost. For example, when an airport is being constructed, landing fees of 50 units could be considered to offset the costs, or it could be considered as a benefit.

This problem does not affect the NPV which is increased by 50 under either classification. But if the fee is classified as a negative cost, it would reduce the denominator of the B/K ratio by 50 units (if it is just the pure capital costs on the denominator), whereas if it were treated as a positive benefit, it would increase the numerator by 50 units. In general, the ratio would be increased by different amounts in the two cases. However, as Gittinger has negative net benefits in the first year(s) on the denominator, and not just the pure capital cost K, only this is affected. The denominator would be reduced by 50 units no matter what classification.

2.2   Comparing the criteria

Now that the three main investment criteria have been explained, we shall make comparisons among them. Which criterion is best depends on whether one can consider an individual project independently from other projects.

2.2.1   Comparisons for independent projects

When one can consider projects independently, and there are no technical difficulties (explained below) with the IRR, the three criteria are equivalent (one rule implies the other two). One way of seeing this is to consider the case where the NPV rule is indifferent as to whether to accept or reject a project, i.e. $NPV = 0$. Then, by definition of the IRR, $R = r$. So the IRR rule would also be indifferent to the project. Finally, if one substitutes $NPV = 0$ into equation (2.10), B/K is equal to 1, which is exactly at its cut-off level.

There are two main technical difficulties with the IRR. The first is that the IRR may not exist. At the practical level this means that, as explained earlier, one starts by selecting a possible candidate for the IRR, say R_1. One then notes the NPV value. Say it is positive. This suggests that one has tried too low a value for R, and that one should try a higher figure. However, it may turn out that no matter how large (or how small) a figure one chooses, the NPV is still positive. Obviously, when R does not exist, there is nothing to compare with r to use the IRR decision rule.

The second difficulty is the opposite of the first, in that rather than having too few IRRs to use, one may have too many. Let us assume one follows the same procedure as before, starting with R_1, and continuing until one finds a value for R where $NPV = 0$. One might be tempted to stop there. However, there may be other values for R that also would have resulted in a zero value for the NPV. Which one of the Rs should one use to compare with the interest rate r? Unfortunately, there is no known answer to this question. When some of the Rs are negative, we can dismiss them as unreasonable, but not when they are positive. The IRR rule would then break down (assuming that there is an R both above and below r).

The likelihood of the second difficulty occurring is related to Descartes' 'rule of signs'. This states that the number of R that will appear depends on the number of times the net benefits change signs. For example, if net benefits change from negative to positive, and back to negative again, there have been two changes of signs. So there will be two Rs. Typically, as with the Moroccan tractor project we considered, projects start out negative (when the capital costs are being incurred) and then become positive. The project is usually terminated before negative effects are obtained. So there will be just the one change of sign, and therefore just the one R to consider.

While it is true that in most circumstances the three rules are equivalent, there is a strong preference among those involved with the practice of project appraisal to rely on the IRR. The concept is somewhat akin to the rate of profit notion understood by business executives. Moreover, as the IRR is expressed in percentage terms, it seems to be written in a universal language. A 48% rate of return on tractors in Morocco appears to indicate a good project, no matter what country one is in when one reads the appraisal. One does not even need to know the unit of currency used in Morocco! (This idiosyncratic preference for the IRR does not imply that there are any real advantages although, even today, there are some who still believe that there is an advantage with the IRR because one does not seem to need to know the rate of interest – see Dickey and Miller, 1984, p. 218. This is clearly wrong, since the IRR decision rule is to compare R with r.)

There is one final point of potential confusion to clear up. S & T (p. 38) claim that projects with a positive NPV should not necessarily be accepted. The opportunity costs of some inputs may have been underestimated (because their best alternative use may not have been identified). So, 'a high net present value may reflect an inadequate search for alternative projects rather than a potentially valuable project'.

The point that S & T make in relation to the underestimation of inputs is an important one. Say one is considering using some vacant land in the bush for an airport. Since there has not been, until now, any value placed on the land, the market price may be very small. This may mean that the airport would have very high net benefits, since the costs are so low. However, if the land were used as a safari park, it may produce even higher net benefits (again, because the costs are so low). Thus, there is no real presumption that one should build the airport (or any other project).

While the point is valid, it is a point that applies only in a world without constraints. In Chapter 1, it was recognised that some pre-screening of projects probably would have taken place. An appraisal would be made using social criteria only after political, and other, factors had determined which project is to be appraised. There was no guarantee that the best (in social terms) of all projects would be brought forward for appraisal.

In addition, S & T's point should not be directed solely at the NPV criterion. It applies to all the investment criteria. For example, if capital costs are underestimated, the IRR will be more likely to exceed r.

2.2.2 Comparisons for non-independent projects

The equivalence of the decision rules for the three investment criteria does not extend to the ranking of projects. It is possible that project 1 could have a higher NPV than project 2, but also have a lower IRR or B/K ratio. When projects are independent, these different rankings do not matter. As long as the NPV for project 1 is greater than zero, the project should be accepted. It is irrelevant that project 2 has a higher IRR and B/K ratio, but a lower NPV value. Project 2 should also be accepted. (The fact that it has a higher IRR and B/K ratio than project 1, which had a positive NPV, ensures that project 2 has an NPV greater than zero).

When projects are not independent, these differences in rankings become important. There are two main situations when projects are non-independent. The first is when projects are mutually exclusive, and the second is when there is a budget constraint.

When projects are mutually exclusive

To help see the issues involved, we can consider some of the other components in the Morocco Fourth Agricultural Project. For small farms (farms of six hectares) a well and pump project is to be tried. This allows the farmers to grow a different type of crop (potatoes instead of maize). For very large farms (farms of 120 hectares) an investment in a combine harvester can be added to make the use of the tractor (appropriate for sixty-hectare farms) more effective. The social outcomes in terms of the three investment criteria are summarised in Table 2.3

Table 2.3   The social outcomes for the components of the Morocco Fourth
Agricultural Project

	NPV	IRR	B/K	K
Tractor project	104,136	48%	3.435	42,770
Tractor and combine harvester	92,566	20%	1.612	151,163
Well and pump	12,115	53%	3.837	4,267

above. (This table is based on pp. 30, 38 and 40 of Cleaver, 1980. The
calculations are mine.)

Let us start the analysis by defining mutually exclusive projects. This
is when the adoption of one project automatically precludes the adoption of all others. This always comes about when one is considering
alternative scales for a particular project. For example, in the choice
between a one-, two- or three-lane highway to connect two end destina-
tions, only one of the alternative road designs can be adopted. Mutually
exclusive projects also arise when a scarce factor is being considered.
(Scarce capital is a special case of this, and leads to a particular method
of solution, i.e. using a budget constraint.) For example, if there is only
one plot of land to use for the airport or game park, then both projects
cannot go through. To make the issue of mutually exclusive projects
relevant to the Morocco Fourth Agricultural Project, we can assume
that there is only the one farm size, and the choice is between any one of
the three projects.

Judged by the NPV the tractor project is best (has the highest figure).
But, judged by the IRR and the B/K, the well and pump project is best.
Which criteria should one follow? It is clear that the NPV criterion
should be followed because if we adopt the tractor project, we have
the highest social net benefits available. The question to ask is why do
the IRR and B/K ratio give the wrong answers? The answer is entailed
in the different initial capital outlays required by various projects. In
Table 2.3, we see that the tractor project requires around ten times
more capital than the well and pump project. Its net benefits are not
quite ten times larger. So the IRR and B/K ratio both discriminate un-
necessarily against large-scale projects. This discrimination is seen even
more clearly when the tractor and combine harvester project is being
considered. The IRR and B/K ratios are less than half those for the well
and pump project. Note that it is not always the case that the larger the
project, the larger the net benefits. The tractor project has a larger NPV
than the tractor and combine harvester project, even though it involves
a lower capital outlay.

The conclusion is, then, that for mutually exclusive projects, the
NPV criterion should be used. However, the decision rule is not quite

the same as in the independent projects case. There, a project was accepted if it had an NPV greater than zero. Now, a project is accepted if it has the highest NPV of all the mutually exclusive projects being considered (provided that it also exceeds zero). If one still insists on using the IRR criterion, one can do so in an (unwieldy) modified form, as will now be explained.

In the 'incremental yield' approach, one can treat the difference in capital outlay between the tractor project and the well and pump project as a separate, incremental project. The procedure would be to first use the IRR for the well and pump project, to decide whether to spend the capital cost of 4,267. If this exceeds the rate of interest (as it does) one then proceeds to the question of whether to spend the extra capital (38,503) on the tractor project. The difference in the net benefits between the tractor and the well and pump project constitute the net benefits for the incremental project. The IRR on the incremental project must exceed r for the additional capital outlay to be warranted. If the extra outlay is warranted (and it is), one forgets about the well and pump project and spends the total sum (42,770) on the tractor project alone. (Of course, this approach is also subject to the two technical difficulties raised earlier against the IRR, that is, R on the incremental project may not exist, or may not be unique.)

When there is a budget constraint

The size of the initial capital costs was basically irrelevant in the previous context. The only issue was whether there were sufficient future net benefits to cover these costs. If there were sufficient net benefits, then the investment criteria should not discriminate against costly investments. Since the IRR and the B/K ratio did discriminate, and the NPV did not, the NPV criterion was best. However, the size of the capital costs is clearly not going to be irrelevant when there is a budget constraint. In these circumstances, and when the budget constraint applies only to year zero, the benefit–cost ratio is best (see Appendix 2.5.1 for a proof of this). The intuition for this result lies in the fact that the B/K ratio explicitly has capital costs (strictly, negative net benefits) on the denominator. So it tries to obtain the largest benefits per unit of the capital costs.

Table 2.3 can be used to illustrate the main points. Judged by the NPV, the tractor project would have the highest ranking, followed by the tractor and combine harvester and, finally, the well and pump. If the capital available was 50,000, then all three projects could not be passed. Judged by the NPV, one would accept the tractor project. There would not be sufficient funds to finance the tractor and combine harvester project, so this would have to be rejected. Guided by the NPV investment criterion, one could not accept the well and pump project, because it has a lower NPV than the rejected project. This would be a mistake. The well and pump project should clearly be accepted because, by doing so, net benefits would be greater by 12,115. So both the tractor and the well and pump projects should be accepted.

The benefit–cost ratio criterion would have passed exactly the two projects that we have just seen should have been accepted, for the decision rule, when a capital constraint is in operation, is to rank projects by their B/K ratios and work down the list by accepting projects until the funds have been exhausted. Thus, judged by the B/K ratio, the well and pump project is top of the list, followed by the tractor project. As there were sufficient funds, these two would be accepted. The tractor and combine harvester project is rejected. But this would be consistent with the benefit–cost ratio principle, seeing that this project has the lowest B/K ratio.

Irvin (1978, pp. 16–17) makes an interesting observation as to why the NPV criterion gives the wrong rankings when there is a budget constraint. If only 50,000 is available, then r could not have been 6% as assumed. Capital scarcity would imply a higher rate be used. If such a rate were used, and any rate above 20% and below 48% would do, then the NPV criterion would have given the right choice of projects. Only the tractor and the well and pump projects would have had positive NPVs using a rate above 20%. (The IRR on the tractor and combine harvester project was 20%, so any rate above this would make its NPV negative.)

As we shall see in Chapter 4, the interest rate is not set in order to exhaust the investment budget, nor should it be used for this purpose. But, if it were (and S & T sometimes assume this), one could conclude that for independent and non-independent projects the NPV criterion could always be relied upon to provide the appropriate decision rule.

We can summarise the whole analysis of investment criteria as follows. For all projects that one is evaluating, one should present both the NPV and the IRR. The NPV is vital to assess the desirability of the project. The IRR is a back-up statistic which, for some obscure reason, people connected with government projects wish to see. Following the rules strictly requires that when a budget constraint exists, one should provide just the B/K ratio. But this is only going to be in the context of a number of projects which are to be relatively evaluated. This takes place more at the national planning level than at the level of individual projects. For example, with the Morocco Fourth Agricultural Project, it was decided prior to the evaluation of the components how much of the overall budget would be assigned to each component. The largest amount (271,770 of 624,310 allocated) went to farms that would duplicate the tractor and combine harvester project, so benefit–cost ratios never appeared in the appraisals. (Nor did the NPVs!).

2.3 Problems

Let us return to the Pakistan tractor project presented in Chapter 1. The project led to many losing their jobs, but the economic net benefits were high. The issue was whether a social appraisal would make any difference. To show the possibilities, we analysed one extreme set of values considered by Tyler (1979). We also ignored the need for dis-counting. Under those circumstances, we found that a social appraisal could lead to a verdict opposite to that given by an economic appraisal. Let us see what the outcome will be when we introduce discounting and deal with a second set of possible outcomes considered by Tyler.

Background information

In the problems in Chapter 1, E was 1,530, C was $(-)$ 432, β was 0.67, and ω was 8.06. The net effect of the consumption was to lower E by 3,193. The social effect was therefore $-1,663$. (All monetary figures were in thousands of rupees.)

This time we consider a larger consumption reduction of 2,270. It will now be assumed that distribution is not as important as before, and the value to savings is very much more important. This means that ω (the relative importance of distribution to savings) is now much re-duced and equal to 0.65. As a result, the consumption effect is to raise E by 45, making S equal to 1,575. This social outcome occurred in each of years 1 to 7. In year zero, the capital cost was incurred, and this amounted to 5,231. Tyler used 7% as the interest rate. Table 2.4 sets out this information.

Questions

(a) Complete the information in Table 2.4 and, in the process, find the NPV.

(b) Use Table 2.4 to find the B/K ratio.

(c) Calculate the IRR. (Hint: try values for R equal to 20% and 25%, and then use Gittinger's interpolation rule.)

(d) Would the Pakistan tractor project, which made many thousands lose their jobs, be accepted by any of the three investment de-cision rules applied to the social net benefits?

Table 2.4 The flow of social net benefits for the Pakistan tractor project

Year	Social net benefits (S)	Discount factor at 7%	Today's value at 7%
0	−5,231		
1	1,575		
2	1,575		
3	1,575		
4	1,575		
5	1,575		
6	1,575		
7	1,575		
		NPV at 7% =	

2.4 Discussion

The aim of the discussion in this chapter is simply to broaden the analysis of investment criteria given so far. We will examine how UNIDO try to generalise the IRR approach. In the process we uncover how UNIDO are to calculate their discount rate.

2.4.1 Generalising the IRR approach

UNIDO (1972) have a general methodology for finding any parameter value, called the 'switching value' technique. The aim is to find that value for the parameter value for which the NPV turns from positive to negative. For that value, the project 'switches' from being acceptable to being unacceptable. One uses the switching value to help make minimum judgements as to where the true value for the parameter is likely to lie. UNIDO used this technique for finding their discount rate. As applied to the Moroccan tractor project, the explanation would be as follows.

The switching value for the tractor project is 48%. One may not know precisely the true value for r; but no theorist has ever suggested that it lies anywhere near as high as 48%. So, the argument goes, it is unlikely that by using a figure such as 6% one is accepting a project only because of the 'strange' interest rate used to evaluate the project. Any rate up to 48% would also have passed the project.

The technique works reasonably well for the tractor project considered in isolation. But, if one continually uses the technique, eventually one is bound to come up with a switching value that is not unreasonable. For instance, the tractor and combine harvester project has a switching value of 20%. Though on the high side (judged by the rates that have been used in practice) a rate of 20% may not be impossible to defend (especially if this is the rate charged on foreign loans). In these cases, one is forced to make an explicit judgement concerning r. The UNIDO general methodology then would not be of any help.

Of course, the switching value for r is just the IRR. It therefore has all the problems identified in this chapter related to R (its existence, uniqueness, etc.).

Appendices

Here we demonstrate a result that is stated in the text. The proof depends on an understanding of rudimentary calculus.

Why the B/K ratio is best with a single period capital constraint

In the chapter it was stated that when a single period capital constraint exists, the benefit–cost ratio can be proven to be best. We present a proof here adapted from Dasgupta and Pearce (1972).

Define S_j as the gross (inclusive of capital costs) benefits for project j and K_j as the initial capital costs. Assume that both S_j and K_j are functions of the scale of the project, represented by x_j. The problem is to maximise the total benefits for all projects, subject to the constraint that the amount spent on all the projects does not exceed the available capital, K^*. Forming the Lagrangian, H, and with L as the Lagrange multiplier, we get the following:

$$H = \sum_j S_j(x_j) + L\left[\sum_j K_j(x_j) - K^*\right] \tag{2.11}$$

Taking the partial derivative of H with respect to x_j and setting this equal to zero, one obtains

$$\left. \begin{array}{l} S_j - LK_j = 0 \\[2mm] \text{or} \\[2mm] \qquad L = S_j/K_j \end{array} \right\} \tag{2.12}$$

The interpretation of L is that it tells us the effect on the (maximised) value of the objective function of a small change in the value of the constraint. The objective is social benefits and the constraint is the capital costs. So equation (2.12) tells us that the impact on social benefits of the capital devoted to the jth project is indicated by its B/K ratio. Note that when the capital constraint is not just in year zero, a linear programming approach is required to obtain the best set of projects. See Baumol (1972, Chapter 19) for the details.

3
Distributional weights

3.1   Introduction

The issue of distributional weights is a simple one viewed from the
perspective of a private firm. The firm recognises 'dollar democracy',
whereby a dollar is given equal weight no matter which income group
is making the offer. When the distribution of income is equal, how
much people are willing to pay on the market for something reflects
their intensity of preference. However, when the distribution of income
is not equal, people do not have the same number of votes (i.e. dollars)
to offer. Even a perfectly competitive market is open to the criticism
(from the social perspective) that goods will be allocated to those with
the greatest ability to pay, rather than those with the most willingness
to pay.

We start our analysis of distributional weights from the social perspective by identifying the different types, and explaining the units in
which the weights are to be expressed.

3.1.1   Intragenerational and intergenerational weights

The previous chapter concentrated on interpreting the final outcome in
terms of whether to accept or reject the proposed project. This final
outcome is a weighted average of outcomes for particular groups occurring at different periods of time. In this chapter we examine the weighting procedure.

40

There are two dimensions to the income distribution issue. The first involves a comparison of the incomes of rich and poor groups at a point in time. This is the intragenerational dimension. On the other hand, one also needs to compare the income of a typical person today with that of a typical person in the future. The existence of economic growth means that people in the future will probably be richer. The inter-generational dimension therefore involves comparing the incomes of a relatively poor current generation with that of a relatively rich next generation.

To reflect the intragenerational dimension, S & T use the *d* para-meter which varies by income group. However, an intergenerational parameter is not applied to any particular income group; it is accom-modated by weighting the income source that is to lead to the economic growth and hence the future differences in income. It is implicitly assumed that investment is the main determinant of economic growth. Investment is therefore to be valued more highly than consumption. In a developing country the government is the main internal investing agency. Funds that are in the private sector are assumed to be devoted to consumption. This is the reason that S & T give a premium to funds from the project that are retained in the public sector. The premium to public funds relative to consumption is recorded by the parameter *v*, and it is this that represents the intergenerational income distributional dimension in the S & T framework.

3.1.2   The absolute and relative size of the weights

The main concern is with the relative size of the weights. It is only the relative size of the weights that determines the rankings of projects. But the absolute size of the weights will depend on the numeraire. i.e. the unit in which all calculations are to be expressed. The S & T numeraire is 'uncommitted public income measured in convertible currency' (S & T, p. 57). It is also called, throughout the book, 'public income', 'free foreign exchange', or values in 'border prices'. No explicit justification for its use is given in the book. As this numeraire was first used by L & M, we can use their justification: 'since social cost-benefit analysis is essentially addressed to governments, it seems natural [to help them solve problems of public investment in general and investment in par-ticular] to use as numeraire something in terms of which they must think and operate' (L & M, p. 146). The implications of using this numeraire are examined in Chapter 9, where a comparison is made between S & T's and the other main methods of project appraisal.

3.2   S & T's methods

Here we present the S & T methodology for weighting in basically the same terms as they do. The main difference is that we will be combining formulations that are spread out in S & T, and the ordering of the material is altered. For reference, S & T's equations are marked with an asterisk.

3.2.1   The overall framework for weighting

Assume that a project lasts one year, so there is no discounting involved. Its effect on the economy as a whole is denoted by E (to stand for economic efficiency). The E are the net benefits of the project and they will accrue either to the public sector or to the private sector. Let the private sector get C of these resources. (C stands for consumption because it is assumed that the private sector consumes all their share). The remainder, $E - C$, goes to the public sector. Clearly,

$$E = (E - C) + C \tag{3.1}$$

So the total equals the sum of the shares.

As E is in real resources and C is in domestic prices, there is a need to convert domestic prices into real resources in order to calculate the amount in brackets – the public share. Define β to be the consumption conversion factor, which converts the value of consumption in domestic prices to its real resource (border price) equivalent. Think of β as a number less than 1 because there are a lot of market imperfections (e.g. tariffs and monopolies) in the domestic economy. The public share will thus be $E - C\beta$.

The social value (S) of the two shares must be evaluated. One cannot simply add them, as the public share is taken to be investment, which is socially more valuable than the consumption that is the private share. If W_g is the social value of a unit of government resources, and W_c is the social value of a unit of private consumption, then the social net benefits of the project are given as

$$S = (E - C\beta)W_g + CW_c \tag{3.2}$$

A comparison of (3.1) and (3.2) illustrates the general proposition that an efficiency evaluation is simply an equally weighted version of a social evaluation. For, if $W_g = W_c = \beta = 1$ is substituted into (3.2), one returns to (3.1).

The numeraire has been defined to be real resources freely available to the public sector. Thus, one can set $(E - C\beta) = 1$ in (3.2). This involves dividing (3.2) by W_g to form

$$S = (E - C\beta) + C(W_c/W_g) \tag{3.3}$$

Strictly, the left-hand side of (3.3) should be S/W_g. But W_g can be regarded as a constant from an individual project point of view. So the ranking of projects according to S/W_g would be exactly the same as those given by S. Defining

$$\omega = W_c/W_g \tag{3.4*}$$

the social criterion then becomes

$$S = (E - C\beta) + C\omega \tag{3.5*}$$

Equation (3.5) tells us that consumption at domestic prices must be adjusted by ω to express it in terms of the numeraire. Collecting terms in C in (3.5) produces

$$S = E - C(\beta - \omega) \tag{3.6*}$$

The final expression shows clearly the relation between an efficiency and a social evaluation. One needs to deduct from E the social cost of the extra consumption by the private sector to obtain the social outcome. It also highlights the additive structure of a social evaluation. One first finds the outcome in terms of economic efficiency and subsequently one makes adjustments using the distribution weights and other parameters. A traditional cost–benefit analyst could see precisely how the outcome was affected by the adoption of the new social methodology. The additive structure was used by Irvin (1978) to organise his presentation of cost-benefit methods. But, while this is of historical interest, one should not lose sight of the fact that it is only the complete social outcome that will be used to make the rankings of projects. One needs the two-step procedure only if one fundamentally mistrusts the weighting part of the appraisal.

Finally, there is a concept that plays an important role in applied studies, though not strictly a part of the S & T methodology. If distribution were not important, then S would equal E in equation (3.6). Consequently, $\beta = \omega$. The income or consumption level for which the government judges that this equality applies, is called the 'critical consumption level', denoted by c^*, which is the level of consumption at which the government would be indifferent about letting the private sector consume the unit of foreign exchange rather than the government keeping it as public income.

3.2.2   Examination of particular parameters

Since distribution will be considered important, the need is to find estimates for β and ω.

Market imperfections are measured by β and its value depends on the types of goods consumed by the particular group who are consuming the output of the public project. As a first approximation one can assume that the goods are those that are entirely involved with foreign trade, i.e. exports (X) and imports (M) valued at border prices. In such circumstances, the main cause of deviations of market prices from their real resource values is the existence of government tariffs and export taxes. If t_m is the average rate of tax on imports, and t_x is the average rate of tax on exports, then β can be measured by

$$\beta = \frac{M + X}{M(1 + t_m) + X(1 - t_x)} \tag{3.7*}$$

The numerator is consumption at world prices (the numeraire) and the denominator is consumption at domestic prices. Thus β is the ratio (world prices/domestic prices). Multiplying any consumption item expressed in domestic prices by β means that the domestic price terms cancel out, leaving us with its world price (real resource) equivalent.

One may wonder why it is that in equation (3.7) one adds the import tax, while one subtracts the export tax. S & T must be implicitly assuming that the level of foreign trade in the country undertaking the project appraisal is small relative to the world economy. It therefore operates in a world of perfectly elastic demand for its exports. So firms cannot pass off any country-specific costs to the consumers. Any export taxes would, therefore, have to come out of domestic producers' profits, lowering the commodity's domestic price equivalent. The conventional wisdom (see De Wolf, 1975, but note that it was not observed empirically in Kenya by Brent, 1986b) is that indirect (consumption) taxes are fully shifted to consumers as higher prices. One can only assume that S & T are treating tariffs in this fashion in equation (3.7).

Equation (3.4) defined ω as: $\omega = W_c/W_g$. Define $W_{\bar{c}}$ to be a particular W_c; it is the marginal social value of one unit of consumption by a person in the group at the average level of consumption (the bar signifies average). Dividing the top and bottom of the ratio on the right-hand side of (3.4) leaves its magnitude unaltered. Equation (3.4) can therefore be written as

$$\omega = \frac{W_c/W_{\bar{c}}}{W_g/W_{\bar{c}}} \tag{3.8}$$

Both the numerator and the denominator of (3.8) have a clear interpretation. Define the numerator as

$$d = W_c/W_{\bar{c}} \tag{3.9*}$$

where d gives the social value of a unit of consumption to a particular consumption group relative to the social value of consumption at the average level of consumption. Thus d is the intragenerational (rich/poor) distribution parameter mentioned at the beginning of the chapter.

Define the denominator as

$$v = W_g/W_{\bar{c}} \qquad\qquad (3.10^*)$$

where v is the social value of a unit of free foreign exchange in the hands of the government relative to the social value of consumption (to a group consuming at the average level of consumption). It reflects the intergenerational (investment/consumption) distribution dimension mentioned earlier.

Thus ω can be expressed as

$$\omega = d/v \qquad\qquad (3.11^*)$$

Equation (3.11) helps us understand why S & T state in the introduction to their book that using distributional weights shows 'the trade-off between raising consumption levels of the poor and accelerating economic growth' (p. 7). This trade-off is d/v. To estimate ω, we therefore need to find values for d and v.

To find a value for d, one must specify a social valuation (utility) function. S & T make the following assumptions:

1. Everyone has the same utility function. Thus, one need know only the utility function for one individual to know the social utility function. Define U_c as the marginal utility with respect to personal consumption c. Hence, instead of (3.9) one has

$$d = U_c/U_{\bar{c}} \qquad\qquad (3.12)$$

2. Let the one (representative) individual's utility function exhibit diminishing marginal utility with respect to personal consumption (assumed to be the only aspect determining utility, there being no external utility effects from the consumption of others). S & T adopt the constant elasticity marginal utility function as it is one of the most analytically convenient functions that satisfies these assumptions. The S & T specification is then

$$U_c = c^{-n} \qquad\qquad (3.13^*)$$

where n is a positive constant that reflects society's aversion to inequality. Appendix 3.6.1 verifies that for equation (3.13) the elasticity equals $-n$ and that it does exhibit diminishing marginal utility.

The values for d are derived from (3.12) and (3.13):

$$d = U_c/U_{\bar{c}} = c^{-n}/\bar{c}^{-n} = (c/\bar{c})^{-n} = (\bar{c}/c)^n \qquad\qquad (3.14^*)$$

To find the weight to attach to a group's additional consumption, one must divide the average consumption level by that group's consumption level, and raise it to the power of n. Thus d is a function of two variables, n and $(\bar{c}/c)$. To appreciate what equation (3.14) implies for different values of these two variables, see Table 1 of S & T, which is reproduced below as Table 3.1. The average consumption level is assumed to be 100. First, note that the ratio $(\bar{c}/c)$ forms the base of the weight. The weight would be the same for two economies where everyone in the second economy had ten times the income of the first, e.g. 100/10 is the same as 1000/100. This is known as constant relative inequality aversion.

Second, we can see that a value of $n = 0$ implies that everybody receives an equal weight of unity. This is the 'dollar democracy' assumption of the traditional (efficiency only) school.

Third, let us chart the other values that S & T consider to be the most relevant: 'For most governments, n would probably center around 1. Values close to zero or 2, although possible, may be considered extreme' (p. 63). Consider somebody who is relatively very poor and who consumes one-tenth of the average. If $n = 1$, then $d = 10$. Their additional consumption is to have a social value ten times that of an average consumer, while, if $n = 2$, their additional consumption is valued at a hundred times that of an average consumer.

Finally, let us present S & T's recommended value, $n = 1$, in graphical terms (Figure 3.1). The d weight in this case is simply $(\bar{c}/c)$. Column five of Table 3.1 then tells us the weights for $n = 1$, so the relevant graph is the pairs given in columns one and five of Table 3.1. We draw the relation only for poor groups, i.e. those whose consumption levels are between 20% and 100% of the average consumption level (again assumed to be 100). It is clear to see that d is in this case a rectangular hyperbola (with an equation $dc = 100$). This confirms what was said earlier and is verified in Appendix 3.6.1. The assumed utility function

Table 3.1 Values of distribution weight d

At existing consumption level (c)	At relative consumption level $(\bar{c}/c)$	And when n equals				
		0	0.5	1.0	1.5	2.0
10	10.00	1	3.16	10.00	31.62	100.00
25	4.00	1	2.00	4.00	8.00	16.00
50	2.00	1	1.41	2.00	2.83	4.00
75	1.33	1	1.15	1.33	1.53	1.77
100	1.00	1	1.00	1.00	1.00	1.00
150	0.66	1	0.81	0.66	0.54	0.44
300	0.33	1	0.57	0.33	0.19	0.11
600	0.17	1	0.41	0.17	0.07	0.03
1,000	0.10	1	0.32	0.10	0.03	0.01

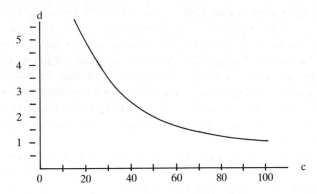

Figure 3.1 *S & T's marginal utility function for n = 1*

leads to weights that have a constant elasticity (equal to minus unity in this special case), and exhibits diminishing marginal utility of consumption (*d* has a declining slope). This completes the analysis of the numerator part of *ω* in equation (3.11). The determination of the denominator will now be explained.

To estimate the value of public income, one needs to know the uses to which public income has been put. Then *v* would be regarded as a weighted average of the values of different types of public expenditure, such as education, defence, consumption subsidies, etc. Because this requires a lot of information, S & T consider the case where government expenditures are optimally allocated. The social value of the last dollar spent on health would equal that of the last dollar spent on education. Thus, one need only estimate the value of one particular type of public expenditure to fix a value for *v*. Let *q* be the estimated marginal product per year on the particular public expenditure considered (measured in real resource terms). Assume that it is received by someone at the average level of consumption. At domestic prices, one can consume q/β. This needs to be discounted. Define *i* as the appropriate discount rate. Since *q* is the same amount each year, one can use the annuity formula (which is the common yearly value divided by the discount rate) to determine *v*:

$$v = (q/i)/\beta \tag{3.15*}$$

To summarise, in order to obtain distribution weights ($\omega = d/v$) in the S & T framework, one needs to estimate four parameters: β and *n* (to find *d*) and *q* and *i* (to find *v*).

3.3   Measurement practice

Although there are the four main parameters to estimate, β and n, and q and i, it is only the estimation of n that needs to be covered in this chapter; β will be seen as a special kind of shadow exchange rate formula, and this will be analysed in great detail in Chapter 8 (when we deal with the determination of shadow prices for minor non-traded goods). The determination of the discount rate involves a whole chapter of analysis, so discussion of the determination of i will be deferred till Chapter 4. However, analysis can proceed, largely due to the existence of a short-cut procedure suggested by L & M. This procedure basically allows one to avoid explicit mention of v, and consequently one need not know the precise values for q and i. The short-cut procedure will now be presented. Applications of distribution weights will be given, and problems will be set, in terms of the short-cut procedure.

3.3.1   The L & M short-cut procedure

S & T express ω in terms of the ratio

$$\omega = d/v \tag{3.16}$$

Both elements, d and v, need to be estimated separately. An alternative procedure suggested by L & M combines the two elements in one step. It avoids the need to estimate v explicitly. The procedure is based on the 'critical consumption level' c^* – the level of consumption at which the government would be indifferent between letting the private sector consume a unit of foreign exchange rather than the government keeping it as public income. Instead of using S & T's equation (3.14):

$$d = (\bar{c}/c)^n$$

L & M use the following for their weighting:

$$d^* = (c^*/c)^n \tag{3.17}$$

The relation between d^* and d/v is explained on pp. 62–3.

3.3.2   Estimation of parameters in practice: land resettlement in Kenya

A retrospective evaluation was made of the very large resettlement programme undertaken in the early 1960s as part of Kenyan independence. Arrangements were made for transferring land previously owned by immigrant farmers to African ownership. The programme was called the Million Acre Settlement Plan. Clearly, distributional issues were of paramount importance in this process.

Scott, MacArthur and Newberry (1976) based their estimation of distributional weights for Kenya on equation (3.17). The value parameters are n and c^*. The approach taken was, first, to read Kenyan development plans to uncover government intentions, and then to study actual policies to see the extent to which these intentions are to be taken seriously. From the development plans they concluded that the government did show some concern for inequality (n was positive) and the government valued public saving (c^* was below the average consumption level). For more precise values the following arguments were used.

While the government showed concern for inequality, there were signs that this concern was not acute, and hence n was not large. For evidence they cited the following points:

1. Income tax allowances were high relative to average incomes (i.e. people did not pay income tax until high levels of income relative to the United States or United Kingdom).
2. The Graduated Personal Tax then in existence (an income tax on the rural areas which was later replaced by a sales tax) was liable from those with low incomes, and had a rate structure which was barely progressive.
3. Primary (elementary) school fees were charged on the vast majority of children, rich and poor alike.

In sum, the authors' best guess was that $n = 1$. They argued that if the government were rational, c^* was to be located on the income scale at the level where consumption subsidies cease. When the government gives a subsidy it is valuing funds more highly in private hands than in their own. Thus, when the government ceases the subsidy, it must be indifferent. To help fix this level, an ILO mission's estimates of minimum income targets for Kenya were used. For 1978, income per adult should be K£16 in rural areas and K£27 in urban areas. (The actual averages were K£21 and K£39 respectively.) Because there were administrative costs involved in giving subsidies, and these costs were considered in the setting of the target levels, it was thought that the 'true' value for c^* would have been slightly below the ILO targets. Thus, they chose K£15 for c^* for rural areas and K£17 for urban areas (where the extra cost of living in urban areas was given no social significance).

The full set of weights for rural areas are given in Table 3.2 of Scott, MacArthur and Newberry (p. 62) and is reflected in Table 3.2 below.

Table 3.2 Weights given to marginal additions to African rural incomes at different income levels in Kenya

Percentage of households	Income per adult equiv. divided by critical income	Marginal value of additions to income as proportion of marginal value of additions to critical income, assuming		
	c/c^*	$n = 0.5$	$n = 1$	$n = 2$
(1)	(2)	(3)	(4)	(5)
41.5	1.73	0.760	0.578	0.334
20.9	1.87	0.731	0.535	0.286
14.4	2.13	0.686	0.470	0.221
8.0	2.27	0.664	0.441	0.194
5.8	2.80	0.598	0.357	0.127
5.1	3.53	0.532	0.283	0.080
4.3	6.00	0.409	0.167	0.028
100.0				

Sources: Columns (1) and (2) are from table 3.2 of Scott, MacArthur and Newberry. Columns (3), (4) and (5) are derived by taking the reciprocal of column (2) and raising it to the power n.

Note that they use e to stand for n, and column two contains (c/c^*) so must be reciprocated to obtain (c^*/c) which appears in our equation (3.3). It is column four that interests us most. This corresponds to equation (3.3) for the case (recommended by S & T) where $n = 1$. The average distribution weight for rural households in Kenya was determined to be 0.414 (using incomes to determine the average). In a project appraisal, a US dollar accruing to a person in the rural areas of Kenya is to be given a value equivalent to about forty-one cents. The obvious question to ask is why is this value less than one dollar? The answer is that this valuation, based on the L & M short-cut procedure, reflects both the premium on government income (v) as well as income distributional considerations (d). A person at the critical consumption level c^* would have a value equal to a dollar. The government would prefer to spend on investment any sums that accrue to persons with incomes above c^*. Thus, because people in the rural areas of Kenya were consuming at a level 2.4 times the critical level, their incomes were only 41% (the reciprocal of 2.4) as valuable as funds being devoted to public investment.

3.4 Problems

The following problems are based on the case study in MacArthur (1978) – an offshoot of the full study by Scott, MacArthur and Newberry (1976).

	Low density	High density
Alternative household income	68.25	45.5
Alternative income per adult equivalent	22.75	15.2
The critical consumption level was estimated to be 13.		
The (unweighted) net present value of benefits for the two groups were:	208,970	70,306

Figure 3.2 *Incomes and net benefits for low and high density settlements in Kenya*

Background information

The data are based on actual planning data for small-farmer settlement schemes in Kenya. A choice had to be made between two alternative means of using a given stretch of land in the early 1960s, namely a low- or high-density scheme. Farms in the high-density scheme would be relatively large and farmers would be expected to have previous experience of modern farming. Farms in the high-density scheme were designed for landless, unemployed people who need not necessarily have had previous agricultural experience.

There are 10,000 acres of land purchased for settlement. Each farm in the low-density scheme would be thirty-two acres, thus allowing for 285 farms to exist. The size of a high-density farm was twelve acres, so there could be 760 farms under this scheme. In the absence of a settlement scheme, the incomes of the two groups of farmers would have been as listed in Figure 3.2 (with all figures in Kenyan pounds).

Questions

(a) Find the distributional weights for the two groups of farmers for the three values of n equal to 0, 1 and 3.

(b) What were the weighted net benefits for the two schemes for the three sets of weights calculated in question (a)? (Hint: use $S = E \cdot d$ for each scheme, i.e. set $E = C$, $v = \beta = 1$ in equation 3.5.)

(c) What is the value of n that would make the high-density scheme have higher weighted net benefits than the low-density scheme? (This figure is known as the 'switching value' for the inequality aversion parameter n, as explained in Chapter 2.)

3.5   Discussion

With a clearer idea of the S & T methodology, one can deal with some of the fundamental issues involved with the construction and use of distributional weights. There are four main issues that will be discussed. Firstly, why use distribution weights in project appraisal? Secondly, will the political system allow one to use distributional weights? Thirdly, assuming one will be employing distributional weights and using the S & T framework, are there any difficulties in the particular way that distribution weights are to be derived? Finally, what alternative weighting procedures could be used?

3.5.1   The general rationale for using distribution weights

The analysis in section 3.2 made clear that the traditional efficiency-only school is merely a particular school of weighting that uses equal (unity) weights. As Brent (1984a) points out in a survey of schools on distributional weights: 'the set of schools of cost–benefit analysis that can avoid distributional weights is the null set'. It is not the case, therefore, that the traditional school is more scientific than those who recommend using unequal distributional weights. If using any weights is considered too difficult and subjective a task then one should stay outside the field of public policy. The traditional efficiency-only school is not outside the field of public policy. The only real difference between the S & T approach and traditional schools is that the former wishes to make the value judgements underlying its weights explicit, while the unity weights are implicit in the efficiency-only approach. There is no reason to think that being covert is being more objective.

It is somewhat ironic that at the precise moment that practitioners and academics working with project appraisal in developing countries had (according to Amin, 1978, p. 237) formed a 'strong consensus' that income distributional considerations have to be included, one of the leaders in the cost–benefit field should reaffirm the traditional position on the subject. In fact, some of the misgivings of Harberger (1978) were anticipated by the S & T text. Harberger was concerned that by using unequal weights one would be wasting resources (choosing projects that were not the most efficient). But, as S & T pointed out:

> The criterion for acceptability of a project is changed, but it is not more lenient. Some projects that otherwise would have been rejected will be acceptable because their distributional effects are given weight in the criterion; some otherwise acceptable projects will be rejected because of an adverse distributional impact. (p. 8)

There is no question of not putting the resources to their best use. The only difference is that in the modern approach social benefits are defined in terms of two objectives, not one.

That distributional weights be used 'consistently and systematically' in project appraisal procedure is almost an axiom of the S & T approach (p. 7). However, one main justification is presented in the text. It is the administrative costs argument for setting distributional objectives for projects (in addition to efficiency objectives) rather than using the tax system to redistribute incomes: 'All fiscal measures have an administrative cost and, at least in principle, a cost from an unfavorable effect on incentives' (p. 52). S & T do not develop the argument in their text. This argument was first formalised by Musgrave (1969). The latest restatement is by Ray (1984). Since he is also with the World Bank, it is useful to use his formulation. The full derivation (a complete version of Ray's proof) is included in the Appendices. Let the administrative costs be given by A, and the transfer of cash from the rich (group r) to the poor (group p) be equal to an amount T. Society's redistribution will be optimal when the weighted gain of any change in transfers is equal to the weighted loss:

$$W_p T = W_r(T + A) \qquad\qquad (3.18)$$

where W_p is the weight to the poor, T is the gain to the poor, W_r is the weight to the rich, and $T + A$ is the total loss borne by the rich (they pay for both the transfer and the administrative cost). As $(T + A)$ is greater than T, W_p must be greater than W_r. Unequal weights must be used.

Harberger's complaint with this argument is that the difference in weights given by a formula such as equation (3.14) may far exceed any administrative costs. A person with one-fourth of the average consumption level, when the inequality parameter is 3, would have a weight sixty-four times that of the average person. Surely, Harberger asks in his latest reflection on the subject (1983), one can devise redistributional schemes via means other than public expenditure that do not involve administrative costs sixty-four times the benefits that go to the poor? The basic issue here is whether the weights have in some sense been calculated 'correctly' (an issue which we will deal with in the next sub-section). Harberger is right in that the administrative costs argument cannot be pushed too far. But, one needs to be aware that there is a much more fundamental reason for including distributional weights, rather than using the tax system to redistribute incomes, which S & T have completely ignored.

The neglected reason is the redistribution in-kind argument, stemming from the work of Hochman and Rodgers (1971) and incorporated into cost–benefit analysis by Brent (1980 and 1984). A public expenditure project does not directly provide assistance to the poor in terms of money income although, if a person's earnings potential is increased, the assistance may ultimately be translated into a cash equivalent. Even in this latter case the needy are having to work to help themselves to the cash equivalent; it is not a simple 'hand-out'. Not only may society be concerned about how the poor are assisted, it may also be concerned about the particular goods consumed by the poor. Government expenditure is providing for a particular good or service, and it is the consumption/production of this that is increased. The rich may prefer the food or calorie intake of the poor to rise, but have no special interest in the poor's consumption of alcohol or cigarettes (items that can be purchased with cash assistance). In these circumstances, it can be shown that it is more efficient to provide the particular good (food) by way of public expenditure, rather than use the tax/transfer system that operates solely in terms of cash. The redistribution in-kind argument will be analysed further in Chapter 12, when the issue of how the S & T methodology can be made to relate to the basic needs approach to development is considered. Here the argument is invoked to justify using distributional weights in the first place.

If one accepts that a main justification for using distributional weights in project appraisal is the redistribution in-kind argument, one should, therefore, expect that different weights be given to benefits in-kind from benefits in cash. A simple way of doing this, which can easily be incorporated into the S & T methodology, is to keep the weighting formula (3.14) or (3.17) that applies to the total consumption of groups, but raise the shadow prices of outputs that give positive benefits to others (non-consumers) – see Chapter 12 on basic needs for the details of this method.

3.5.2   Distributional weighting and the political system

S & T briefly mention an argument for using distributional weights rather than using the fiscal system which requires detailed analysis. They make the point that there may be political constraints in using the fiscal system (p. 7), and elaborate a little: there is an 'inability to tax the rich sufficiently because of that group's political power' (p. 52). This argument raises a Pandora's box of points of objection that require response and clarification. The points of objection feed off from Stewart's fundamental question (1975): if the rich groups are strong enough politically to forestall income taxes, why would they not be powerful enough to block public expenditure decisions that aim at favouring low incomes via the use of distribution weights? Clearly, this question deserves a full answer.

Let us first deal with the three answers that Stewart puts forward to her own question. The first two argue that the government (trying to serve the interests of the rich) does not wish the impact of the project to be effective, while the third suggests that using distributional weights may actually be in the interests of the rich.

Stewart starts off by stating that cost–benefit analysis is applied only to a few projects and therefore the redistribution involved is limited. When it is no longer limited, the rich will make the effort to block it. Since project appraisal in any one country has not been used extensively, one cannot tell yet whether this prediction holds.

Next, Stewart makes the point that cost–benefit analysis is used only as a guide to decisions; there is no legal enforcement of the outcome recommended by the project appraisal. Unlike changes in the tax system, the rich could always see that the recommendation was not implemented. Again, time will tell whether this expectation is right.

Stewart's third and last answer focuses on the savings premium v. If savings has a premium, investment is being encouraged, and labour will be substituted by capital in the production process. Labour is, therefore, the group that has to give up its consumption rather than the rich capitalists. This view of using distributional weights cannot be correct. Stewart is only talking about the v parameter. She addresses intergenerational weights, but not intragenerational weights. The d parameter could counteract the v effect in the weight d/v; moreover, the ratio d/v is just one part of the formula that will be used to determine the shadow wage. Employment of labour is related to the shadow wage. When it is low, employment is encouraged. As we shall see in Chapter 5, there is a general presumption that the shadow wage will be low (relative to the market wage). This should counteract the general anti-employment bias posed by v.

Although the purported answers by Stewart may not be persuasive, the question raised is still a good one. Three further responses will now be considered.

(1) The finance for many public projects in developing countries comes from external sources. In these cases, the resources are not at the disposal of the indigenous elite. It may be that the choice facing the rich in developing countries is whether to allow the public investment (which is decided by outsiders using the S & T methods) or to block the expenditure. They may not have the option to use the funds for some other use, e.g. finance an income tax cut. Since it is likely that the rich

will obtain some gain from the externally financed project, even though not as much as the poor, it is hard to envisage them blocking the project.

(2) One can also use the 'redistribution with growth' rationale to explain why the rich may block a tax increase (which is to be transferred to the poor) and not block a public project which has the same outcome in favour of the poor. A tax increase means that the rich would actually have to give up resources, while the public project is generating additional income which may not be going to the rich. There is reason to think that the rich would feel the actual loss more than the forgone gain, and therefore try to oppose it. An actual loss may involve a change of current lifestyle that is not entailed with a forgone gain.

(3) Just as a particular government agency undertaking a project appraisal may have to assume that constraints (e.g. a tariff) imposed by other government agencies are to be taken as given in making its decisions, political power may also have limits on its 'areas of control'. In the United States, the agricultural lobby has been powerful enough to turn the terms of trade between rural and urban areas in their favour by raising agricultural prices via government price-support schemes. But this same lobby was not powerful enough to prevent the terms of trade being simultaneously lowered by the government issuing food stamps which lowered the effective price of food. Most countries have a budgetary process that divorces tax from public expenditure. In these circumstances, where often two different sets of individuals are involved with the decision-making, it is reasonable to expect that in many countries there are some government instruments which are in the control of the rich, yet others are outside their control.

3.5.3   *Finding the appropriate inequality aversion parameter*

(This sub-section and the next draw heavily on Brent, 1984a)

Here we shall assume that one is to use S & T's formula (3.14) for distributional weighting. This functional form has been criticised by Harberger (1978) as it has the property 'that the difference between the weights attaching to different individuals can be exceedingly large'. As already pointed out, if $n = 3$, the weight for a consumption group a quarter of the average is sixty-four. Harberger explains the implications of this in terms of redistributing ice cream from a rich oasis to a poorer one, when 'up to $\frac{63}{64}$ of the ice cream could melt away without causing the project to fail the test'.

The real issue here is not whether the weights are large, but whether they are in some sense the 'right' ones. If, in Harberger's example, the relative weights between the rich and the poor were correct (1 to 64) this would mean something specific. That is, the poor were in desperate need. In these circumstances, wasting $\frac{63}{64}$ of the ice cream would be justified, especially if it meant keeping the poor alive. There are two ways of approaching the issue of how to derive a correct value for n. They will be discussed in turn.

The a priori weighting school

The S & T methodology is an example of the determination of weights by a priori means. The project analyst must specify the weights in advance of the project appraisal. Certain limiting cases can be recommended to the project analyst on philosophical grounds. A value of $n = 0$ (the traditional approach) can be justified by assuming that this is the value that any individual would choose for society under conditions of uncertainty (see Harsanyi, 1955). A value of n equal to infinity corresponds to the objective of trying to maximise the position of the worst-off individual. (This is the difference principle of Rawls, 1971.) But if neither of the extreme positions is adopted, the a priori approach is not very helpful. Harberger is right in that, in the intermediate cases, fixing n would be somewhat arbitrary. Hence it would be 'all too easy for considerations of distribution to swamp those of efficiency altogether'.

The imputational school

An alternative approach is to seek the implicit value for n that lay behind past government policy decisions, and use this as a basis for setting values in the future. For example, Stern (1977) derived an estimate of n from the UK tax system. This turned out to be 1.97. The implicit value for n underlying the Norwegian indirect tax system was found to be 0.88 by Christiansen and Jansen (1978). What is the use of estimating the implicit value for n behind past public investment decisions? Musgrave (1969) has argued that there is no value in such estimates: 'If past investment decisions may be assumed to have been correct, why is cost–benefit analysis needed to validate future decisions?' Crucial in assessing this criticism is the extent to which the preferences of the decision-maker on distributional matters are complete. When these preferences are complete, Musgrave's statement implies a contradiction. When, as in my view, these preferences are incomplete and can only be made concrete by reference to a particular decision-making situation, there is no contradiction, for the implicit past values help to form the explicit future values of the weights. (See Brent, 1979, for a detailed defence of the imputational methodology.)

To understand this argument better, ask yourself what value for n you would choose for a particular developing country? My guess is that an answer would not be easily forthcoming. The problem is that one would not have any experience on which to base a value. But if you were told that in past development plans a value of n equal to 0.6 was actually implicit, an answer would be more apparent. For example, if you looked at the past history of development in the country and it was something that you approved, then a value of n equal to 0.6 would seem right. A precise value of 0.6 would have meaning; it would be a vote for the status quo. On the other hand, if you thought that poverty was not given enough attention in the past, you would opt for a higher value. Similarly, if you thought too much emphasis was given to schemes that were inefficient, you could choose a value less than 0.6. The point is that you would have some understanding of the implications of choosing one particular value rather than another.

The imputational approach is the implicit foundation of the rival UNIDO (1972) methodology to project appraisal. They call it 'bottom up' (from project analyst to public decision-maker) as opposed to the 'top down' (from public decision-maker to the project analyst) approach of the World Bank. The project analyst is supposed to consult the spokespersons for the government and ask them whether they would choose this or that parameter if the consequences were to take a particular direction. The 'switching value' approach recommended by UNIDO (finding the value of a particular parameter that would make the net present value of the project equal to zero) is in the imputational tradition. The switching value is lodged in experience; it tells what the critical value must be for the parameter given the inputs and outputs in the particular decision-maker situation. For example, in question (c) of the problems in this chapter (p. 51), one has to calculate the switching value for n in the context of choosing between a low-density scheme favouring the rich and the high-density scheme favouring the poor: this switching value is $n = 2.7$. One can now make a judgement on whether to choose the low-density scheme. The value 2.7 lies outside the 1 to 2 range recommended by S & T, so they would probably have opted for the low-density scheme. Clearly, one could still decide in favour of the high-density scheme. But one would be doing so in the realisation that one was putting a value on redistribution that was extreme in relation to both recommended S & T practice (if UNIDO cared about this!) and empirical experience (in the United Kingdom and Norway).

Let us summarise this discussion: S & T recommend a value of $n = 1$, and envisage a sort of confidence interval of between 0 and 2. The problem with these benchmarks is that their implications are not well understood. A value of $n = 1$ is in many ways a strong egalitarian position. Introspection would clearly require that a dollar be worth more to a poor person than to a rich person. But could we be sure that a poor person's dollar was worth ten times more (if the poor have one-tenth the consumption of the rich) or even 100 times more (if the poor have one-hundredth the rich's consumption)? Introspection would rule out the traditional value of $n = 0$, but it does not take us much further than this. A more useful approach would be to try to infer the value of n behind past policy decisions and use this figure as one point (perhaps the mid-point) in any sensitivity analysis one may make of the distributional weights. Its meaning would be the value that would hold if past policy practices were to continue into the future. Adjustments could then be made from this base, according to whether a more or less egalitarian stance should be adopted in the future.

3.5.4 *Alternative schools of distributional weighting*

So far it has been assumed that one is wedded to the S & T formulation given by equation (3.14). However, S & T themselves do not consider that this is the finished product for dealing with distributional weighting. They write:

> The most important issue, however, is not the technique for deriving the weights, which will undoubtedly be refined in due course; it is that, whatever weights are considered to reflect properly the relative value attached to benefits for various higher or lower groups and to additional investment, these weights be consistently and systematically applied when evaluating the socioeconomic merits of a project. (p. 6)

So let us consider some alternative approaches to weighting.

There are two properties of S & T's weighting function that are especially questionable. First, it is a function only of income. Second, it is a function as opposed to a constant parameter. We will deal with each of these points in turn.

Single index versus multiple indicator approaches

Low income/consumption by itself is not a sufficient index of social concern. College students consciously forgo current income to increase their future earnings potential. Usually social concern is a multiple dimensional characteristic. For example, it is low-income persons who are over the retirement age that most societies wish to protect. As a first step, then, one should consider broadening the weighting to bases other than income. Thus, if age as well as income were of social concern, equation (3.14) could be replaced by:

$$d = [d_c(\bar{c}/c) + d_a(a/\bar{a})]^n \tag{3.19}$$

where a denotes age, $\bar{a}$ denotes retirement age, and d_c and d_a represent the social importance of having low consumption and being old respectively.

Discrete versus continuous weighting approaches

Even equation (3.19) omits the second major objection with the S & T formula – that it is a continuous and smooth weighting function. As regards income, most people do not discriminate over the middle income ranges. It is not the case that one would want the person with the higher income, over the entire population, to have a lower weight. Also, it is only after an adult person becomes retired that age becomes an important issue. Thus, it is unrealistic to assume that society's preference function over income and age would be continuous and smooth. (It may not even be complete, in the sense that one may not have a preference either way about certain income or age levels.)

A way forward would be to return to the basics of the approach set out by Weisbrod (1968) in his pioneering contribution to obtaining distribution weights. (His particular estimation technique used to obtain the weights is not being advocated, though. For a discussion of the appropriate estimation technique to derive the weights, see Brent, 1990.) Weisbrod assumed that linear weights would be applied to the groups for which the decision-maker had particular concern. For illustration, Weisbrod distinguished four categories that were likely to be relevant: age, region and colour, as well as income. All the classification schemes used, including income, were conceived in discrete terms. For example, one was either white or non-white. The outcome was a set of numbers which were applied to various groups:

- − 1.3 for whites with incomes less than $3,000
- + 2.2 for whites with incomes above $3,000
- + 9.3 for non-whites with incomes less than $3,000
- − 2.0 for non-whites with incomes above $3,000

Let us see how the basics of Weisbrod's approach can be transferred to the project appraisal field. Given the absolute inequality specification of income classes by Weisbrod, a natural definition of the groups which justify special weights would be those at or below the poverty line. (This idea was employed in an axiomatic approach to poverty and measures of social welfare by Brent, 1986a.) Of course, there is an ongoing debate as to whether poverty should be viewed in absolute or relative terms. (For a summary by one of the chief protagonists on this topic, see Fields, 1982). As explained earlier, S & T's version uses the idea of relative income aversion. But the basic needs approach to development is worth trying; and this approach is based on absolute, not relative, needs.

If one wishes to be more traditional within the absolute inequality approach, one can follow the dual economy model emphasised in development economics. An urban/rural distinction would then be used to define the groups that are to be weighted. This, however, has a particular difficulty when dealing with the second aspect of Weisbrod's weighting methodology. Each group has its own numerical weight which is applied equally to all members of the group. A rich landlord would be weighted equally with a poor peasant farmer, and both would have a higher weight than a poor urban worker. Groups in poverty in developing countries are more homogeneous than groups living in rural areas. Thus, it would seem better to define groups in terms of poverty, for then one would be sure that one had identified a group in social need.

This chapter on distributional weights will conclude with two specific suggestions which follow the main points of the discussion. The first suggestion relates to the current S & T formula. The second suggestion assumes that the weights are linear, discrete and conceived in an imputational context.

(1) Given that ecomomic theory does not point to any particular value for S & T's inequality parameter n, one should be very careful about which value one chooses. A value of $n = 1$ is not in any way neutral, and probably overstates the desire for equality by those outside, as well as those inside, developing countries. Values for n within the unit interval (0 to 1) probably reflect the range that should be tried for both the best estimate and the values to be used in any sensitivity analyses. A value for $n = \frac{1}{2}$ is likely to be more appropriate than $n = 1$. (Incidentally, a value for $n = \frac{1}{2}$ was used by Loury, 1983, in his analysis of deregulation of natural gas in the United States.) Given the large variation in the relative consumption of groups in developing countries, a value of $n = \frac{1}{2}$ would lead to a range of weights which vary by up to a factor of 10. That is, the multiple by which the poor would be weighted relative to the rich could be 10, i.e. 3.2 for the poor and 0.32 for the rich (see Table 3.1). This should satisfy all but the most ardent egalitarian.

(2) Weights should be a part of any country's development plan. The weights should take the form of a particular number (say 5) for those in poverty and a value of unity for those above the poverty line. These

weights would then be used in the appraisal of projects which are to lead to the achievement of the plan. In a subsequent plan, these weights can be revised, either because the implications of the weights are not acceptable, or because the country has (on the fulfilment of the previous plan) reached a different stage of development.

Appendices

Here we derive a number of the technical aspects of distribution weights using rudimentary calculus.

Properties of S & T's marginal utility function

The particular marginal utility function used by S & T was given by

$$U_c = \mathrm{d}U/\mathrm{d}c = c^{-n} \tag{3.13}$$

If we take the derivative of this function with respect to an individual's consumption c, we get (using the power rule) the following:

$$\mathrm{d}U_c/\mathrm{d}c = -nc^{-n-1} \tag{3.20}$$

Assuming that n is non-negative, this derivative is negative. That is, marginal utility increases at a decreasing rate. In other words, equation (3.13) exhibits diminishing marginal utility with respect to consumption.

The elasticity of marginal utility with respect to consumption is defined as

$$\frac{\% \text{ change in marginal utility}}{\% \text{ change in consumption}} = \frac{\mathrm{d}U_c/U_c}{\mathrm{d}c/c} = \frac{\mathrm{d}U_c/\mathrm{d}c}{U_c/c}$$

The numerator has just been derived and given by equation (3.20), while the denominator has equation (3.13) in it. Substituting for these two expressions results in:

$$\textit{Elasticity of marginal utility} = \frac{-nc^{-n-1}}{c^{-n}/c} = \frac{-nc^{-n-1}}{c^{-n-1}} = -n$$

The elasticity of marginal utility is thus equal to minus n (the inequality aversion parameter).

The relation between the S & T and L & M formulae

The relation between the two weighting formulae was recognised by Irvin (1978) on pp. 143 and 144. Instead of the S and T formulation,

$$d = (\bar{c}/c)^n \tag{3.14}$$

L & M use the following:

$$d^* = (c^*/c)^n \tag{3.17}$$

To best see that d^* automatically allows for v, consider the special case where n and β are both equal to 1. This converts equations (3.14) and (3.17) into

$$d = (\bar{c}/c) \tag{3.21}$$

and

$$d^* = (c^*/c) \tag{3.22}$$

For the group that happens to be at the level c^*, their weight using (3.21) would be

$$d = (\bar{c}/c^*) \tag{3.23}$$

Because the definition of c^* implies $\beta = \omega$ (distribution is unimportant), and with $\beta = 1$, it means that $\omega = 1$. Since ω is given in equation (3.16) to be the ratio d/v, $\omega = 1$ implies that $1 = d/v$ or $d = v$. Inserting this value for d in (3.23) means

$$v = (\bar{c}/c^*) \text{ or } c^* = \bar{c}/v \tag{3.24}$$

Substituting for c^* from (3.24) into (3.22) results in

$$d^* = [(\bar{c}/v)]/c = [(\bar{c}/c)]/v \tag{3.25}$$

But the numerator of (3.25) is defined in (3.21) to be d. Thus

$$d^* = d/v \tag{3.26}$$

As alleged, L & M's formula d^* is S & T's formula divided by v.

The administrative cost argument for using unequal weights

Let p be the poor group and r the rich. Their utility functions, U_p and U_r, depend only on their own incomes, Y_p and Y_r. Now consider a transfer of T from r to p: p's income increases to $Y_p + T$, so $dY_p = T$. While r's income is reduced by the transfer T and any administrative costs A, which means $dY_r = -(T + A)$. The changes in utility that correspond to the changes in income are $dU_p = dU_p/dY_p \cdot dY_p$ and $dU_r/dY_r \cdot dY_r$. Substituting for dY_p and dY_r in these expressions produces

$$dU_p = dU_p/dY_p \cdot T \text{ and } dU_r = -dU_r/dY_r \cdot (T + A) \tag{3.27}$$

As social welfare, W, is a function of U_p and U_r, its total differential shows the changed social value which corresponds to the changes in utilities

$$\mathrm{d}W = \mathrm{d}W/\mathrm{d}U_p \cdot \mathrm{d}U_p + \mathrm{d}W/\mathrm{d}U_r \cdot \mathrm{d}U_r \tag{3.28}$$

Using the values for $\mathrm{d}U_p$ and $\mathrm{d}U_r$ from (3.27), equation (3.28) becomes

$$\mathrm{d}W = \mathrm{d}W/\mathrm{d}U_p \cdot \mathrm{d}U_p/\mathrm{d}Y_p \cdot T - \mathrm{d}W/\mathrm{d}U_r \cdot \mathrm{d}U_r/\mathrm{d}Y_r \cdot (T + A) \tag{3.29}$$

where $\mathrm{d}W/\mathrm{d}U_p \cdot \mathrm{d}U_p/\mathrm{d}Y_p$ is the social marginal utility of p's income, call this W_p, and $\mathrm{d}W/\mathrm{d}U_r \cdot \mathrm{d}U_r/\mathrm{d}Y_r$ is the social marginal utility of r's income, call this W_r. Equation (3.29) then turns into

$$\mathrm{d}W = W_p T - W_r(T + A) \tag{3.30}$$

At the social optimum, $\mathrm{d}W = 0$, which means that equation (3.30) implies

$$W_p T = W_r(T + A) \tag{3.31}$$

Equation (3.31) is equation (3.18) used in the text. Repeating the argument, as $(T + A)$ is greater than T, W_p must be greater than W_r. The existence of administrative costs requires that one use unequal weights when making a project appraisal.

4

The social discount rate

4.1   Introduction

This chapter continues the explanation of distributional weights begun in Chapter 3. We saw that there were two sets of distributional weights to consider, the intra- and intergenerational weights. For the intra-generation distribution, d was the key parameter. This was on the numerator of the ratio $\omega = d/v$ (equation 3.16). The role of v in this expression was to allow for the fact that the distributional gain by the poor receiving extra consumption, reflected in d, comes at the expense of investment. So the social value of investment, v, by appearing on the denominator of equation (3.16), enables the net effect of any extra consumption to be recorded (given by ω). Thus ω was the trade-off between intra- and intergenerational distribution weighting. We were able to isolate the intragenerational distribution aspect in Chapter 3, and focus solely on d, because of the L & M short-cut estimation procedure that we adopted. This estimated d in a way which implicitly allowed for v. In this chapter we deal explicitly with v. The analysis can be regarded as supplying the final (intergenerational) part of the distributional weights story. As v is the shadow price of (public) investment, and the shadow price of capital is determined by the appropriate interest rate, this chapter is basically concerned with the determination of the social discount rate. To isolate the intergenerational issue, we will ignore the intragenerational dimension by setting $d = 1$. The subject matter covers material in Chapters 7, 10 and the Appendix of S & T.

The literature on the social discount rate is anything but clear. (For the most complete statement and summary of the subject, see the book by Lind, 1982.) In part it is due to the inherent complexity of the subject. One is dealing with variables which change their values over time. The analysis has to be dynamic, which requires the use of specialised mathematical techniques. But it is also due to a basic exposition weakness. Many authors start their analyses with too many implicit assumptions. In the introduction section to this chapter we will assume very little. We will define terms and ask basic questions. From there it will be a relatively simple matter to deal with the specifics of the S & T methodology. Since there is no way of avoiding some of the technical/mathematical dimensions to the social discount rate issue, these will be covered in the Appendices.

Let us first consider how a private firm would set its discount rate. In a perfect capital market, the rate at which consumers are willing to substitute consumption today for consumption in the future (their time preference) would equal the rate at which it is technically possible to substitute consumption today for consumption in the future (the opportunity cost rate). These common rates would also equal the market rate of interest. The firm would therefore use the market rate of interest as its discount rate, which reflects its cost of capital.

Even in perfect capital markets, the market rate of interest would not be the social discount rate. Private savers would ignore the effects of investment on members of future generations that were not their heirs. The social time preference rate would differ from individual time preference rates. When there are capital market imperfections and capital taxes exist, there is a divergence between the time preference rate (private or social) and the opportunity cost rate. A choice needs to be made between these two types of rate. In the project appraisal literature, both rates play a role even though, as we shall see, only one will be the discount rate.

4.1.1 The need for both an interest rate and a shadow price

Consider a set of investment projects which are conceived in year 1, implemented in year 2, and have their pay-off in year 3. The time profile for the economy, in terms of consumption (C) and investment (I), using my notation, are presented in Table 4.1. There are two aggregation problems which this economy faces: what is the state of the economy in any particular year, and how does the state of the economy vary over time? These two problems will be analysed in turn.

The first problem is how to sum horizontally across rows of Table 4.1 to obtain an annual total. Different ways of solving this problem are given in Table 4.2. The national income accounting methodology simply sums C plus I. The aggregation is shown in the second column of Table

Table 4.1 The time profile of consumption and investment for an economy

Year	Consumption (C)	Investment (I)
1	150	150
2	130	170
3	180	150

Table 4.2 The aggregate state of the economy in any particular year

Year	National income method ($C + I$)	Consumption as the numeraire (price of I = 1.1)	Investment as the numeraire (price of C = 0.9)
1	150 + 150 = 300	150 + 165 = 315	135 + 150 = 285
2	130 + 170 = 300	130 + 187 = 317	117 + 170 = 287
3	180 + 150 = 330	180 + 165 = 345	162 + 150 = 312

4.2. The implicit weighting here is that a unit of consumption is equal to that of a unit of investment. In project appraisal this weighting is not accepted. A unit of investment is considered more important (from the social point of view). There are two ways to record the different importance of C and I. The first way is to calculate everything in terms of C (a unit of C is worth 1) and to give a premium to I. This premium is reflected in the shadow (social) price of I, i.e. the consumption equivalent of the unit of investment. If the premium to investment is 10%, the shadow price of I equals 1.1. Aggregation using C as the numeraire, and with the 10% investment premium, is shown in the third column of Table 4.2.

The other way to record I's relative importance is to calculate everything in terms of I (a unit of I is worth 1) and to give a penalty to C. This penalty is reflected in the shadow price of C, i.e. the investment equivalent of the unit of consumption. If the penalty is 10%, the shadow price of consumption is 0.9. The last column of Table 4.2 shows the effect of using investment as the numeraire.

The second aggregation problem involves how to move vertically down Table 4.2 to obtain the total over time. National income accounting would again use equal weights, but any cost–benefit methodology would not follow these weights. They would discount future values (assuming that one is in year 1, and one wants to view the total over time at this point in time). Let us set the interest rate for consumption at 6%, and the rate for investment at 10%. The discounted version of Table 4.2 appears as Table 4.3 below.

The aggregate for any method is the sum of the three years' outcomes. The outcomes for year 1 are the same as in Table 4.2, because discounting has not yet taken place. Since the national income method

Table 4.3   The discounted aggregate state of the economy in any particular
year, and the total for all years

Year	National income method $(C + I)$	Consumption as the numeraire (price of $I = 1.1$)	Investment as the numeraire (price of $C = 0.9$)
1	150 + 150 = 300	150 + 165 = 315	135 + 150 = 285
2	130 + 170 = 300	123 + 176 = 299	106 + 155 = 261
3	180 + 150 = 330	160 + 147 = 307	134 + 124 = 258
Total	460 + 470 = 930	433 + 488 = 921	375 + 429 = 804

never uses discounting, the outcomes for all years are the same as in
Table 4.2. Differences among the totals for the three methods do not
concern us here. What is important to understand is that for any method
there are two items one needs to know in order to obtain a total outcome. The first is the relevant shadow price, and the second is the
relevant interest rate.

4.1.2   Why there are two interest rates but only one social discount rate

An 'interest rate' is the rate of fall in the value of a variable over time.
Value falls because future values are worth less than current values. For
simplicity, it will be assumed that the value declines at a constant rate.
This makes it possible to talk about 'the' interest rate. If distribution
were not important, there would be just one interest rate. But, because
we are going to distinguish public income from consumption, there will
be two interest rates. Public income represents investment. The interest
rate that applies to this is called the 'accounting rate of interest' (ARI),
and is denoted by r. For consumption, the interest rate is called the
'consumption rate of interest' (CRI), and is denoted by i.

The 'social discount rate' is a particular interest rate. It is the rate of
fall in the value of the numeraire over time. As there is but one
numeraire, there will be but one discount rate. In S & T public income is
the numeraire, so the ARI is the social discount rate. When
consumption is the numeraire, as it is in the UNIDO approach, the CRI
is the discount rate.

4.1.3   The relation between the two interest rates

In the S & T methodology, v is the shadow price of capital. However, as
we saw in Chapter 3, the value of capital was expressed relatively to
the value of consumption (going to the group consuming at the average
level). Thus, we had from equation (3.10) the following:

$$v = W_g/W_{\bar{c}}$$

In the Appendices (pp. 90–1) we show that this expression for v can be used to state how the value of v falls over time. That is

The rate of fall of v over time = ARI – CRI **(4.1*)**

The notion underlying equation (4.1) is the expectation that investment will not always be more valuable than consumption. So, over time, the premium on capital would fall. Equation (4.1) tells us that this fall will be equal to the difference in value between the two interest rates.

On rearranging equation (4.1), we get the relation between the two interest rates

CRI = ARI – (The rate of fall of v over time). **(4.2)**

The relation given by equation (4.2) is not due simply to the way that S & T define v. Marglin (1976, Chapter 6) shows that there is an equivalent relation no matter what the numeraire. These relations follow from what Marglin calls the requirement for 'intertemporal consistency'. The value (return) of a unit of a resource used for current consumption must equal the return from investment plus any capital gain or else the consumption would not be worthwhile. So, if one is allocating resources optimally over time, the two conditions must be equal. That is, equation (4.2) must hold. In terms of equation (4.2), *CRI* is the return to consumption, *ARI* the return to investment, and (minus) the rate of fall of v is the capital gain.

4.2   S & T's methods

We start our exposition by explaining how S & T deal with the two aggregation problems outlined earlier. Then we present the formulae that are to be used for measuring the key parameters.

4.2.1   The overall framework

S & T's methods involve providing particular solutions to the horizontal and vertical aggregation problems identified in section 4.1.1. We deal first with the horizontal aggregation problem.

The important point to understand about how S & T deal with horizontal aggregation (across consumption and investment in a particular year) is that they supply two answers and not just one! To see this, return to Table 4.2. This shows that we had a choice of how to add consumption and investment. We could either work in consumption units and employ a shadow price of investment, or work in investment units and employ a shadow price of consumption. We know that, for S & T, an investment equivalent is their numeraire. So, clearly, they need a shadow price of consumption: β (the consumption conversion factor first defined in Chapter 1) is this shadow price. The horizontal sum is therefore $C\beta + I$. But to what does this aggregate correspond? For example, what is the meaning of the row number 285 for year 1? Although S & T never tell us this explicitly, one can deduce that the horizontal aggregate when investment is the numeraire is economic efficiency, E. That is,

$$E = C\beta + I \qquad (4.3)$$

One would think that there would now be no need for a shadow price of investment. This is not the case, for S & T employ the two-step procedure whereby additions or subtractions are made to E in order to find the social outcome, S. In terms of a horizontal addition of consumption and investment, S & T's social outcome can be deduced as the following:

$$S = C(1/v) + I \qquad (4.4)$$

Recall that v is the value of government income (in terms of consumption). When government income is judged to be equally valuable as investment, v acts like a shadow price of investment. However, the reciprocal of v is the value of consumption in terms of government income, so it can be attached to C in equation (4.4). This then explains why both a shadow price of consumption (β) and a shadow price of investment (v) are needed in the S & T framework. The former shadow price is needed to convert C into efficiency units, and the reciprocal of v is needed to convert C into units of the social outcome. (To check that we have deduced and interpreted correctly, subtract equation (4.3) from (4.4) to obtain $S - E = -C(\beta - 1/v)$, which is equation (1.4) when d is equal to unity.)

The vertical aggregation problem requires the use of an interest rate. We have already pointed out that with an investment equivalent as numeraire, the ARI is the social discount rate. The puzzling thing to understand is why one should bother to calculate the CRI (the interest rate when consumption is the numeraire). The answer is that, although i is not the social discount rate, it plays a role in the determination of v (the shadow price of public income/investment); v will be analysed in the next section. For now it is sufficient to reconsider a rearranged version of the simple formula given by equation (3.15). That is,

$$v = (q/\beta)/i \qquad (4.5^*)$$

The stream of constant returns to public investment, q, are in terms of the numeraire. Dividing q by β (the consumption conversion factor) expresses the return in units of domestic consumption. Finally, having i on the denominator of the formula converts this consumption equivalent into present value terms. (This is the perpetuity version of discounting. The relation between perpetuity discounting and that covered in Chapter 2 is shown in the Appendices, pp. 91–2.)

It is useful at this early stage to provide a summary. At the heart of project appraisal is the distinction between consumption and investment. To add the two in any one year, one can use the shadow price of consumption (β), or the shadow price of investment (v). S & T use both of these because they wish to supply both an economic outcome and a social outcome; β is needed for E, and $1/v$ is needed for S. To add outcomes over time, one needs an interest rate. To add consumption one needs a CRI, and to add investment one needs an ARI. S & T have an investment equivalent as the numeraire. This makes the ARI the social discount rate. One needs the CRI to be able to determine v. Consequently, although in general a project appraisal method would require only one interest rate and one shadow price (as Tables 4.1–4.3 illustrate), the particular S & T method uses two interest rates and two shadow prices.

4.2.2 Examination of particular parameters

There are four policy parameters to be estimated, the two interest rates (CRI and ARI) and the two shadow prices (β and v). The formula for β has already been given by equation (3.7). It will be derived in full in a later chapter. Attention will be directed now to presenting formulae for i, r and v.

The consumption rate of interest: i

The purpose of i is to reflect the government's preference concerning present and future consumption. This involves two considerations:

(1) The rate of pure time preference, ϱ. Society may not wish to consider future generations because there may not be any (!), or because the current generation are myopic (in Pigou's words, having a 'defective telescopic faculty') or irrational. A positive pure rate of time preference therefore puts a premium on the current generation's consumption; ϱ is, even more than n, a parameter which is outside traditional welfare economics. This is an example of the contention made in Chapter 1 that

project appraisal is less willing to rely solely on individualistic values. S & T (p. 109) recommend for ϱ 'fairly low values – say, 0 to 5 per cent – on the grounds that most governments recognize their obligation to future generations as well as to the present'.

(2) Distributional considerations. Future generations are likely to be richer than today's to the extent that economic growth will have taken place. They will have a higher income and this needs to be weighted lower (as would a rich person's income of the current generation). Distributional considerations therefore depend on g (the growth rate of per capita consumption) and n (the distributional parameter examined in Chapter 3).

These two considerations are combined in the following form

$$i = n \cdot g + \varrho \qquad\qquad (4.6^*)$$

Equation (4.6) is derived in the Appendices, p. 92.

The accounting rate of interest: r

The efficiency measure of the rate of interest (when investment is the numeraire) is given by the marginal product of capital, q. By using capital in the public project, one is forgoing its use in some other sector; q is this forgone output. Those in the social opportunity cost school of cost–benefit analysis usually assume that it is private sector investment that is being 'crowded out'. In project appraisal it is more often assumed that government output in some other part of the public sector is being forgone. In this chapter we have taken private and public investment to be equally valuable. So we can talk about 'the' marginal product of capital.

The next step is to adjust the efficiency measure for an allowance for distributional effects. The important effect in the current context is that between savings and consumption. Let s be the proportion of the forgone output that would have been saved. Then sq would be the total amount of savings forgone. This is automatically expressed in terms of the numeraire. The proportion consumed is $1 - s$, which makes $(1 - s)q$ the total amount of consumption forgone. S & T subject this consumption amount to a double conversion process which is not readily understandable. We need to be careful to explain just what is going on.

S & T require q to be measured in terms of the numeraire. So $(1 - s)q$ is consumption, but expressed in terms of the numeraire. We can consider this to be a special kind of consumption, say, the consumption of trucks. This is more valuable than other forms of consumption (such as TV sets which do not have an investment use). Dividing this special consumption by β, which is less than unity, expresses the trucks in terms of a larger amount of other forms of consumption. Dividing the resulting amount by v, as we did in equation (4.4), converts this consumption into terms of the numeraire. Hence, dividing $(1 - s)q$ by both β and v transforms the consumption use of trucks into the investment use of trucks.

The total (investment plus consumption) use of the forgone output is S & T's ARI. Thus:

$$ARI = sq + (1 - s)q/v\beta \qquad (4.7^*)$$

Shadow price of public income/investment: v

The simple formula presented in Chapter 3 gives v as

$$v = (q/i)/\beta \qquad (3.15^*)$$

The main omission in this formula is any reinvestment of the forgone output. Since S & T use (and acknowledge the use on p. 140) the UNIDO formulation for v, it is simplest to use the UNIDO derivation of v (p. 177–8). Their derivation fits in neatly with the explanation of the ARI just given.

The value of public income is due to its investment potential. The investment will realise a stream of output, part of which is saved, sq, and part of which is consumed $(1 - s)q$. The part that is investment is to be valued using the shadow price of investment, v. In each year, the value of public income will be $(sq)v + (1 - s)q$. As this is in consumption units, i can be used to discount the stream of outputs to find its present value. It is the present value of the stream of outputs, relative to consumption, which defines v. This means

$$v = [(sq)v + (1 - s)q]/i \qquad (4.8)$$

Solving equation (4.8) for v results in UNIDO's equation (14.8):

$$v = (q - sq)/(i - sq)$$

Because the S & T numeraire is public income, the UNIDO equation must be divided by β to obtain its S & T equivalent:

$$v = (q - sq)/(i - sq)\beta \qquad (4.9^*)$$

The relation between equation (4.9) and the simple version (3.15) is straightforward. If $s = 0$ is substituted into equation (4.9), one returns to the simple version ($s = 0$ means that there is no reinvestment of the forgone output).

4.3   Measurement practice

We will first indicate how i, r and v have been estimated using the formulae given in the previous section. The estimates are by Mashayekhi (1980) for Turkey. This was a study to derive measures of the parameters to be used in future project evaluations over the subsequent five-year period. Since these estimates were derived in advance of their application, political influence on these measures can be considered to be at a minimum. We can therefore be reasonably sure that they reflect S & T's intended methods. Turkey faced a severe foreign exchange constraint and the object was to see how this would impact on the parameters. Mashayekhi's assumptions will be related to the guidelines set by S & T. Next we will present some alternative methods which S & T suggest in order to estimate the ARI; then we will explain how in the S & T framework one can obtain consistency checks for parameters. Finally, we deal with the ARI estimate of Squire, Little and Durdag (1979) for Pakistan. This is of interest because we can see how one of the authors of the S & T text went about applying his own methodology.

4.3.1   Estimation of parameters using S & T's formulae

To simplify the exposition, most calculations will be made using Mashayekhi's 'best estimates' (given in his Table 1). He did consider other values, as we see in the coverage of the CRI. The first result to be explained is

$$CRI = n \cdot g + \varrho = 4.5\%$$

There are three components in the formula for the CRI. The growth rate, g, is a standard statistic which will be readily available for any project analyst. Over the period 1974–8, the average growth in real per capita income was 2.5%. Following recommended S & T practice, Mashayekhi used a value of $n = 1$ for the distribution inequality parameter. As an alternative, he also considered a lower value for n. The Fourth Development Plan was preoccupied with growth. A lower value for n would signify that preoccupation. A value of n equal to one-half was chosen. (Note that this was the recommended alternative value suggested in Chapter 3 of this book.) In the absence of the pure rate of time preference, Mashayekhi proposed values for i in the range 1.25% (0.5×2.5) to 2.5% (1×2.5).

The rate at which society wishes to discount net benefits that accrue to future generations (the rate of social time preference, ϱ) is thought by

S & T to be embodied in a country's development plan. A high preference for growth would imply using a low value for ϱ. This is because,
in order to have a fast rate of growth, LDCs need a high rate of (government) investment. A low CRI implies, in the S & T methodology, a high
value for v. For this reason, it was assumed that Turkey's priority given
to growth necessitates a low value for ϱ (in the range 0% to 2%). The
combined effect was that the CRI was thought to be in the range 1.25%
(1.25 plus 0) to 4.5% (2.5 plus 2). Mashayekhi chose the upper value as
his best estimate. The next result to be explained is

$$v = q/i \cdot \beta = 3.4$$

The 4.5% value for i will be inserted on the denominator of the simple
formula for v. The two other components are β and q: β was calculated
using equation (3.7) and found to be 0.79. This calculation will be
explained in a later chapter. Only the estimate for q need concern us
here.

Because the notion of forgone output at the margin is difficult to pin
down, S & T recommend that both macro and micro data be used to find
q. The macro approach involves finding the marginal product of capital
using a (Cobb-Douglas) aggregate production function. National output
is regressed on measures of the total labour supply and the capital stock.
The coefficient on the capital term indicates the marginal product of
capital. This appears to have been behind Mashayekhi's estimate of
12% for q. The micro approach would look at the rates of return of a
number of projects in the public sector. This indicates what sort of
return would have been forgone in the past, if the current project being
considered had taken place instead of these other projects. The World
Bank had estimated the economic returns for various public projects to
be in the range of 8–30%. The social returns (given all the import
substitution in Turkey) would be much lower. A value of q of 12%
would be consistent with the macro estimate.

With q equal to 12%, and $i \cdot \beta$ equal to 3.56% (4.5% × 0.79), a
unit of public income was valued at 3.4 (12% ÷ 3.56%) times that of
a unit of consumption (valued at the average level of consumption). The
final result to be explained is

$$ARI = sq + (1 - s)q/v\beta = 6.4\%$$

The estimate for s is the only outstanding component of the ARI formula. Mashayekhi's own estimates for the marginal propensity to save,
s, produced enormous annual variations. So he appealed to an independent estimate for s (by Devis and Robinson) of 0.25. Substituting
this value for s, and values for the other components just presented,
he obtained this value for r:

i.e. $ARI = (0.25)\,0.12 + (1 - 0.25)\,0.12/3.4\,(0.79)$
$$ARI = 0.03 + 0.034 = 6.4\%$$

4.3.2   *Alternative S & T approaches to estimation of the ARI*

S & T have misgivings about the usefulness of equation (4.7) to estimate the ARI. Presumably this is because there are a large number of separate estimates involved. S & T therefore suggest two alternative means for deriving a value for r. The idea is that one uses the approach that fits in best with the available data in the country whose project one is appraising. Should there be data available for all approaches to be used, one can use the alternative approaches to supply consistency checks on one's chosen ARI. This will be elaborated further in section 4.3.3.

Placing lower and upper bounds on the ARI

Rather than settling on a precise point estimate, S & T suggest that one forms lower and upper bounds within which the 'true' value must lie. The lower bound is implicit in the numeraire which S & T chose to adopt. The numeraire is free foreign exchange in the hands of the government. When the government borrows from abroad, the capital cost it pays for these funds is in terms of free foreign exchange. Suppose the debt service (interest plus capital) cost is 7%. This means that if the government actually borrowed at this rate, then it must have thought that it could have obtained higher returns than this from the government's own investment projects. This can be expressed in terms of the internal rate of return philosophy: that is, by discounting at a rate of 7%, government projects would be considered worthwhile. Hence, 7% is the minimum value for r in this example. S & T refer (p. 113) to an unpublished study by Lal which indicated that the historical, average rate on lending in international markets was 4%. Providing a country is borrowing from abroad, the ARI should always be at least 4%.

Mashayekhi derived an estimate of the lower bound for Turkey in the following way. In the 1970s the government was borrowing heavily on international capital markets. The Eurocurrency market was considered to reflect the marginal source of foreign funds for Turkey. A rate $1\frac{3}{4}$ percentage points above the LIBOR rate of 9–10% had been applied in the past. Since debts would have to be rescheduled, a risk premium was added to the past rate. This made the marginal rate equal to $11\frac{3}{4}\%$, in nominal terms. With an adjustment for the expected rate of inflation, the real cost of government foreign borrowing was set at 5%.

The maximum value for r is usually going to be q, the marginal product of capital. This conclusion is derived from an examination of the ARI formula given by equation (4.7). Obviously,

$$q = sq + (1 - s)q. \tag{4.10}$$

The *ARI* given by formula (4.7) differs from q only to the extent that the second term on the right-hand side of equation (4.10) is divided by $v\beta$. If this were equal to 1, then the two equations would be the same. If $v\beta$ is greater than 1, the ARI would be less than q. We shall now see that there is good reason for thinking that in general $v\beta$ will be greater than 1, making q the maximum value for the ARI.

In Chapter 3 we introduced the idea of the critical consumption level. This was defined as that level of consumption at which the government was indifferent about having funds at its disposal, or transferring these funds to the private sector. At this level of consumption, distribution is irrelevant. Consider again equation (3.6): $S = E - C(\beta - \omega)$. If distribution is to be irrelevant, S must equal E; $C(\beta - \omega)$ must be equal to zero, i.e $\beta = \omega$. Equation (3.11) defines ω as d/v. So, for distribution to be irrelevant, $\beta = d/v$, or $v\beta = d$. In this chapter intragenerational issues are ignored, by setting $d = 1$. The condition for distribution to be irrelevant thus reduces to $v\beta = 1$, the relation necessary for ARI to equal q.

Let us now summarise the argument: *ARI* would equal q if all the consumption that a project generates goes to a consumption group at the critical consumption level. Since, usually, groups above this level will receive the consumption, $v\beta > 1$, which makes $ARI < q$. The marginal product of capital is the upper bound for the *ARI*. For Turkey, we have already seen that q was estimated to be 12%. S & T's bounds for Turkey are that *ARI* must lie in the range of 5–12%.

Considering the ARI as a capital rationing device

We saw in Chapter 2 that r is to be used to help decide which projects to accept or reject. In a perfect capital market, and neglecting any distributional considerations, the rate of interest would act as a capital rationing device. If funds were left over after applying the relevant decision rule, then the discount rate used was too high. If projects were being passed for which funds were not available, then the discount rate used was too low. The rate that just exhausts the available funds would be the appropriate one. To find this rate, one has to look at the internal rate of return on the marginal project (the one which was the last to be accepted, assuming that projects were passed in order of their social contribution).

Rather than considering this approach as something completely different, it is useful to interpret it as a special case of the ARI formula given by equation (4.7). Since it ignores distribution, the method is basically returning to the efficiency approach which focuses solely on q, the marginal product of capital. In this context, the method should be viewed as one which emphasises that it is the marginal, rather than the average, product which should be used to find the forgone output. The implication of this is that, for example, when Mashayekhi found that the rates of return on World Bank projects were in the range of $8-30\%$, S & T would wish that one took the lowest value of this range, 8%, as the value for q, and hence r. (Since these were economic rather than social returns, a figure lower than 8% may be appropriate.)

4.3.3   *Consistency checks on estimates*

One of the virtues of the practice of project appraisal over the practice of cost–benefit analysis is that the former produces formulae for all the necessary parameters. These parameters would then appear in a number of different equations. This enables a consistency check to be obtained. This consistency check can take place in two different forms, as will now be explained.

Consistency checks for previously estimated parameters

There may be times when the 'best estimate' for a parameter, say r, may not appear to be a good estimate at all. In this case one can go back to estimates of other parameters in which one does have confidence, and deduce what must be the value for the first parameter (r). If the two estimates 'roughly' correspond, then one may not be too apprehensive at adopting the original estimate. If the two greatly diverge, then some other approach, or data source, may need to be explored.

A good example of how such a consistency check would be carried out is explained in Scott, MacArthur and Newberry (1976) for land resettlement in Kenya (referred to in Chapter 3). It was asserted by the authors (on p. 47), and is shown in Ray (1984, p. 91), that the growth rate in the critical consumption level (g^* in my notation) is related to the ARI in the following way:

$$ARI = g^*n + \varrho \tag{4.11}$$

Note that this has the same structure as the formula for the CRI given by equation (4.6).

Since measuring ϱ is always a controversial issue, the initial analysis ignored ϱ, by setting it equal to zero. Equation (4.11) reduces to

$g^* = ARI/n$. Accepted practice is to set n equal to unity, so $g^* = ARI$. Scott, MacArthur and Newberry had thought of using a 10% value for r: this would imply that g^* was 10%. The past growth rate of per capita consumption (g) in Kenya was 3%. It was considered unlikely that g^* would be able to grow at a rate so much higher than this. In addition, the ILO set future income targets for the poor which imply a g^* of 6%. So, on both counts, an inconsistency had to be faced. The authors considered reconciling the two estimates in a number of ways. For example, if either n or ϱ was higher than had been assumed, then the inconsistency would disappear. It turned out that none of the options that they considered satisfied the authors. They decided to stick to a value of 10% for ARI because lower values (6% or 7%) would not have altered their results by much.

The point of relating this is not to illustrate how the 'right' estimates were obtained. Rather, the objective is to show the rethinking process that the consistency checks encourage. Many times the checks will not uncover inconsistencies. We saw that using the S & T formula for r for Turkey produced an estimate of 6.4%. This was within the 5–12% range that was obtained by using an alternative approach. Some confidence can be placed by Mashayekhi on the 6.4% value.

An intertemporal consistency check

Equation (4.1), repeated below, plays an important role in the S & T methodology.

$$\textit{The rate of fall of v over time} = ARI - CRI \qquad (4.1)$$

This can be used, as in the manner just explained, to provide consistency checks for questionable parameter estimates. But it serves a much more basic kind of consistency check, for it shows the intertemporal relationships which must hold. If v is a constant, the rate of fall of v over time must be zero. If the rate of fall of v over time is zero, then the two interest rates must be the same ($CRI = ARI$). Note that all the formulae given in this chapter have v as a constant. For reasons explained below, S & T do not wish that r will always equal i. There is therefore a potential intertemporal inconsistency problem. S & T are aware of this and they recommend two solutions (p. 115). The first is to recognise that if v is falling over time, and a constant value formula is being used – say, equation (4.5) – then v is being overestimated. If, using this value for v, NPV is positive, one can be sure that the project is socially worthwhile. But, if NPV is negative, one may need to try lower (declining) values for v.

The second solution is to assume that the rate of decline for v is equal to one-half the difference between the initial difference between the ARI and CRI. The idea, developed by L & M, is that in some time in the future, year T, consumption and investment will be equally valuable (no investment premium will exist). In which case, $ARI = CRI$. In the meanwhile, the average divergence will decline at a constant rate. Formally, the relation is

$$v = 1/\beta[1 + 1/2 \, (ARI - CRI)]^T \qquad (4.12)$$

The problem with this formulation is that there is no clear guide to setting T. For Pakistan, using a modified version of equation (4.12). Squire, Little and Durdag (1979) arbitrarily choose values for T in the range of 15–20 years. Ray (1984, p. 96) reports a study by Lal which fixes T for India fifty years into the future. Apparently, the rationale was that by that date, India would (if development plans are achieved) reach a GNP level which would produce a savings ratio equal to that of today's Japan. By assumption, Japan is a country which does not have a savings shortage. This seems sensible to me. But Ray thinks that the choice of Japan is arbitrary. If the United States is taken as a benchmark, the result would be radically different. Nonetheless, the important point is that if one uses equation (4.12), there need be no intertemporal inconsistency.

4.3.4   Squire, Little and Durdag's estimate of the ARI

The main purpose of the paper by Squire, Little and Durdag (1979) was to show that the country-specific studies carried out by the World Bank would benefit greatly if they explicitly incorporated shadow prices into their analyses. My purpose is to uncover some of the later thinking by one of the authors of the S & T book (though clearly the paper is joint work). There is one aspect of the Pakistan study which is particularly noteworthy.

In the Appendix to their text (p. 142), S & T suggest that the main role of equation (4.1) is to provide an intertemporal consistency check. It was not thought to be useful for estimation purposes. However, for Pakistan, Squire *et al.* (p. 7) use equation (4.1) in a very novel way to estimate the ARI. The equation states:

The rate of fall of v over time = ARI − CRI

They calculate *CRI* in the standard way using formula (4.6). This produced a value of $CRI = 3\%$. Now comes the novel part. Because the rates of return on past government investment in Pakistan were so low, it was thought that the premium on investment would be getting larger, not smaller! With the rate of fall of v over time $= -1\%$ (a 1% rise), and $CRI = 3\%$, equation (4.1) places ARI at 2%. Not only is the method novel; so is the result. For the first time, an applied study comes up with an ARI lower than the CRI. There is nothing inherently wrong with this result. It does, however, contradict the usual a priori expectation that exists in the project appraisal literature.

4.4   Problems

The task that will be set is to reproduce, using equations (4.6), (4.7) and (4.9), the parameter estimates obtained by Ahmed (1983) for Thailand. Since he deals with a number of alternatives, we shall only focus on what he calls his 'central values'. Ahmed, like Mashayekhi, presents his estimates in advance of any particular study. They are expected to apply to all project appraisals carried out in Thailand.

The main lesson to be learned from these problems is an appreciation of the interdependence of estimations. Results obtained for one parameter are to be used to find other parameter values. Clearly, the sequence in which one makes the calculations is important. The problems below are deliberately out of order. The reader must look at the three equations for r, i and v together to decide which can be estimated first, given the background information. The sequence of estimation must be understood before one can tackle the practice project appraisal which will be given later.

Background information

The ARI, CRI and v depend on five parameters/variables, aside from their dependence on each other. These five parameters are s, q, β, g and ϱ. Their values for Thailand will now be presented.

The marginal propensity to save (s) was estimated to be 0.29. This was obtained by regressing total savings on national income (and real money balances). The slope of the savings function with respect to income is s, and this was 0.29.

Using a mixture of micro and macro techniques, the marginal product of capital (q) was found to lie in the range of 15–20%. The central value was 18%. As this was in domestic terms, and the S & T methodology requires this to be expressed in border price terms, the domestic value was scaled down to give a value for q equal to 16%.

A very disaggregated version of equation (3.7) was used to find the consumption conversion factor, β. A value very close to unity (0.94) was obtained, the reason being that, in Thailand, exports consisted largely of consumption goods. Consumption goods were therefore already mostly expressed in terms of free foreign exchange.

The growth rate in per capita consumption (g) over an 11-year period, 1970–80, was 4.25%.

The ϱ was estimated by reference to general S & T guidelines, and according to revealed investment behaviour in Thailand. A range of 0–5% is suggested by S & T. Ahmed reasoned that the lower limit was not appropriate for Thailand because Thais seem to place more of their wealth in the form of consumption goods (present consumption) rather than in insurance and financial assets (assets which lead to future consumption). This generation's strong preference for current over future consumption should be recognised, as well as the government's responsibility to future generations. A 3% value for ϱ seemed to be a good compromise position.

Questions

(a) Verify that *ARI* for Thailand was estimated to be 0.10.

(b) Calculate an estimate of v for Thailand. Why does this value not equal unity?

(c) Calculate an estimate of *CRI* for Thailand. By how much would this central value be reduced if one took the view that discounting a future generation's consumption was due to a 'defective telescopic faculty', and therefore socially unjustified?

4.5   Discussion

There has been almost endless discussion in the literature on cost–benefit analysis and project appraisal over whether the CRI or the ARI should be the social discount rate. Inevitably, by choosing the ARI as the discount rate, S & T are drawn into this general controversy. Separate from this general controversy, there has been a recent criticism by Berlage and Renard (1985) over the particulars of the S & T methodology as they relate to their choice of discount rate. Both the general and particular criticisms of S & T's social discount rate will be discussed in section 4.5.1. Section 4.5.2 will be devoted to extending S & T's CRI to allow for the 'numbers effect' outlined in Chapter 1.

4.5.1   S & T's choice of social discount rate

We will first deal with the general controversy, and then cover Berlage and Renard's criticisms.

The general controversy over the choice of social discount rate

Lind (1982) has recently provided two surveys on the social discount rate. I supply my own survey elsewhere (see Brent, 1987). There is therefore no need to give an elaborate account of the issues. The objective here is limited to one of (a) explaining the nature of the ARI/CRI controversy, and (b) identifying the circumstances under which the controversy can be ignored.

To the social time preference school (of which I am a member), the social discount rate is inherently concerned with the preference of consumption today relative to the preference for consumption in the future. The CRI is the appropriate rate for discounting purposes. The opportunity cost of the funds being used to finance government investment is not irrelevant. But it is of direct concern to the valuation of the shadow price of investment, not the discount rate. If we look at the details of S & T methodology, this view is accommodated, if not acknowledged. The *CRI* and *v* play a role, even though, as hinted in the introduction, one could avoid their use if one really wanted to do so. One interest rate, and one shadow price, would be sufficient to solve the two aggregation problems.

The fundamental question that now needs to be asked is this. How can it be possible that by merely changing the numeraire to investment rather than consumption, S & T (and L & M) can side-step the social time preference school and impose the ARI as the discount rate (based on the rival social opportunity cost school)? The answer is that, if a special version of the shadow price of investment is adopted, then the ARI acts 'as if' it were the social discount rate, even though the CRI is the 'true' discount rate. UNIDO (Chapter 14) were the first to provide this answer. But it was Gramlich (1981, p. 113, fn 23) who stated the answer in more general terms. The explanation below follows Gramlich's formulation.

The NPV rule, when the initial capital cost K was all that appeared in year zero, was given as the following:

$$NPV = -K + \sum_{t=1}^{t=T} S_t/(1 + r)^t \tag{2.8}$$

When rewritten using perpetuity discounting (T goes to infinity, and the social net benefits are the same in each year) the relation appears as

$$NPV = -K + S/r \tag{4.13}$$

Following the social time preference school, we need to make two changes to this relation. First, r must be replaced by i. Then the shadow price of investment, v, must be attached to K (to acknowledge the existence of a capital constraint). With these two changes, the NPV criterion becomes

$$NPV = -vK + S/i \qquad\qquad\qquad\qquad (4.14)$$

If the shadow price of capital can take this particular form:

$$v = r/i \qquad\qquad\qquad\qquad (4.15)$$

then equation (4.14) turns into

$$NPV = -r/iK + S/i \qquad\qquad\qquad\qquad (4.16)$$

Multiply both sides of equation (4.16) by i/r to get

$$(i/r)\, NPV = -K + S/r \qquad\qquad\qquad\qquad (4.17)$$

Note that multiplying NPV by i/r is tantamount to changing the numeraire. Since (i/r) is a constant, the ranking of projects would be the same as without (i/r) on the left-hand side. Therefore, (4.17) is effectively

$$NPV = -K + S/r \qquad\qquad\qquad\qquad (4.18)$$

The end result is that the social time preference formulation, when v takes the special form, is operationally identical to the social opportunity cost formulation. That is, equations (4.18) and (4.13) are identical. (UNIDO showed that this was so only in a two-period model, while we, following Gramlich, show that this result follows also in an infinite horizon model.)

Since the above argument only works for a particular kind of shadow price formula, one can still regard the social time preference school as the more generally sound approach, while continuing to adopt S & T's. This is the position that we shall take. But one needs to be aware that it is strictly only the simple v formula, equation (3.15), which permits the transformation. Moreover equation (3.15) has to be interpreted in a special way to correspond with the particular v formula given by equation (4.15). That is, r must equal q (the pure efficiency ARI formula must be used) and β must equal 1.

Berlage and Renard's criticisms

Berlage and Renard (B & R) consider that they have two substantive criticisms of S & T's work as it applies to this chapter. Both relate to the same issue. They focus on the intertemporal consistency condition, equation (4.1). If v is a constant, as it is in all the main formulae, then it does not fall in value over time. If v does not fall in value over time, then $ARI = CRI$. This is B & R's first point. Since B & R know that S & T are aware of this point, B & R go on to make their second point. When practitioners of L & M and S & T try to correct for the inconsistency, they typically use equation (4.12) – which is equation (19) in

B & R. B & R acknowledge (p. 695) that 'this approach is consistent' (p. 695). But they add, 'A highly unrealistic assumption is introduced ($s = 1$) which is never explicitly discussed or justified' (p. 696). If this is all that concerns B & R, then it is easily remedied. So there really is nothing in the analytics of B & R that is noteworthy, even though they are correct.

What is noteworthy is that they publicise the fact that L & M (who devised the investment equivalent numeraire) *consciously* chose the numeraire in order to increase the size of the discount rate! (Apparently, the World Bank have always wanted a rate around 10%, while economists have been more likely to recommend 4% or 5%.) This suggests that L & M would not want to remedy the overadjustment that $s = 1$ introduces in equation (4.12).

If L & M want to raise the value of the discount rate used in project appraisal, they should give a reason based in welfare theory for why this should be so. They should not try to do this artificially by changing the numeraire. In particular, as B & R show, one has to conveniently 'simplify' various formulae. It turns out, as will be explained in section 4.5.2, that if one adds the numbers effect to the *CRI* one gets a higher figure. However, this was not my intention when I began the analysis.

As I know nothing about S & T intentions, I will not speculate. I will merely point out that when Squire (of S & T) and Little (of L & M) got together with Durdag, they produced an estimate for the discount rate which was only 2%! Not only was this much less than 10%; it was also less than the CRI – the rate which L & M would have chosen if they had not changed their numeraire!

A final comment on the ARI and its size is in order. If L & M, and others involved with project appraisal, wish to recognise that LDCs have a severe funds constraint, then the best way to achieve this is via higher values on v rather than the discount rate. L & M, S & T and Irvin (mentioned in Chapter 2) all consider the ARI as a capital-rationing device. It is clear that this is not project appraisal practice. But, in addition, I wish to argue that this should not be the appropriate procedure even if it were common practice. The drawback with the idea of the interest rate as a rationing device is that it treats the problem as one where a fixed sum of capital is to be allocated to projects. Funds available should be considered to be variable. It all depends on how participants in the project appraisal process view the potential net benefits of a project (exclusive of the capital costs). A clearly worthwhile project will receive financial backing. In any case, varying v according to the general financial circumstances of the public sector is the way to treat the funds constraint.

To deal with the fact that external funds are available for certain projects and not for others, I wish to introduce project area-specific *vs.* For instance, the belief in Kenya was that outside funds were freely available to fund population control programmes, when such programmes were unpopular with the Kenyan government. Since these funds were not transferable for other uses, rather than adjust the global value for *v* (lowering *v* by the weighted average of population control projects in the public budget), one could use a much lower value of *v* just for population projects. (Of course, if the politics in Kenya are such that no population control project will be contemplated domestically, such projects will not appear in the policy set, so there will be no need to use an adjusted *v*. But the general point concerning the desirability of using an area-specific *v* remains valid.)

4.5.2 Including the numbers effect in the CRI

(This section is based on Brent, 1987.)

The numbers effect will be introduced into the CRI in two stages. Firstly, the S & T formula will be extended to allow for the number of people who are at the average per capita level. Then the intra- rather than the intergenerational 'numbers effect' will be incorporated.

The generalised S & T formula

The S & T formula for the CRI was given by the following:

$$i = n \cdot g + \varrho \tag{4.6}$$

To aid exposition, we will discuss equation (4.6) without the pure rate of time preference, ϱ, that is,

$$i = n \cdot g \tag{4.19}$$

S & T's formulation ignores the size of the population (P) that exists in any time period. It is the second of two cases given by Layard (1972). The first case, which includes the rate of growth in population (p) as a separate element, is given by

$$i = n \cdot g + p \tag{4.20}$$

The effect of p, for a given g, is to raise the CRI. Any gains from growth have to be spread over a larger population. If future gains are being reduced in this way, there is a greater premium on gains which occur today, when the population is not as large. By definition, the social time preference rate (the rate at which society discounts gains in the future relative to today) will be higher. Paradoxically, if S & T wanted a higher *i*, this could easily have been achieved by their adopting the first Layard case, rather than the second.

Before proceeding, we need to clarify a fundamental philosophical issue concerning the CRI. Whose time preference is one trying to record? The two cases considered by Layard assume that either (a) individuals have the same consumption level and, as they have the same utility function which depends solely on *c*, any individual's preferences can be used; or (b) it is the person at the average per capita consumption level whose preferences are to count. In either case there will be only one individual who represents the generation, no matter what the size of the population.

As an alternative, it would seem sensible to find out how many persons are in the position of the average, P_c. When we multiply the time preference of a person at the average consumption level by the number at that level, the CRI becomes

$$i = n \cdot \dot{g} + p - p_{\bar{c}} \qquad (4.21)$$

where $p_{\bar{c}}$ is the growth rate in the number of people who are at the average consumption level. When $p_{\bar{c}}$ equals *p*, we return to the S & T formula. What this implies is that the consumption of the group at the average level will rise in line with the growth of per capita consumption, *g*. Only the magnitude of *g* will be important, not any population growth dimension. When the two population growth rates are unequal, we can regard equation (4.21) as the generalised S & T CRI formula. The greater the gap between the national and the average group's growth rates, the less will be the future gains to the group at the average level (who are determining *i*), so the higher will be the CRI.

The CRI and the numbers effect

In the previous discussion, it was the population between generations with which the literature was concerned. Now we are going to deal with the possibility that different populations (groups) from the same generation may be affected differently. In this context, we will not focus on whether the various sub-populations are rich or poor (for the inclusion of distribution weights allows for this). The issue will be whether they gain or lose from the public project.

As explained in Chapter 1, the welfare economic base behind cost–benefit analysis and project appraisal rests on the concept of Pareto optimality. When the sum of the net benefits is positive, the gainers can compensate the losers and everyone can be made better off. Nonetheless, in practice, such compensation rarely takes place, in which case there will be some uncompensated losers. Given this, it seems advisable to consider the numbers of these losers as well as the size of the net benefits. For the original S & T CRI formula, the social marginal utility of consumption, W_c, was equal to the individual's marginal utility of consumption, U_c. The latter was defined as

$$U_c = c^{-n} \tag{3.13}$$

To accommodate the numbers effect, W_c will be defined by

$$W_c = -P_1/P + U_c \tag{4.22}$$

The additive structure in equation (4.22) was suggested by the empirical relation which was found in the railway closure study (Brent, 1984). The role of P on the denominator of the ratio is as a weight. It signifies the weight on departures from unanimity. If there were no uncompensated losers, there would be unanimity over the value of the project. All of the population P would be in favour. Any one individual causing a departure from unanimity would be represented by $1/P$; P_1/P is the total effect of departures from unanimity. Equation (4.22) states that the larger the proportion of losers relative to the total population, the lower will be the social marginal utility of consumption. Using this specification of W_c, the CRI transforms into

$$i = (p_1 + n \cdot g \, c^{-n})/(-P_1/P + c^{-n}) \tag{4.23}$$

where p_1 is the growth rate in the number of uncompensated losers. This version is considered in full in Brent (1987). It is useful here to concentrate on a special case.

A standard argument for ignoring distributional effects in project appraisal was that over time the full set of development projects would cause adverse effects to be neutralised by positive effects. Although the empirical validity of this line of reasoning is lacking in LDCs (and elsewhere), this can be thought of as an objective of the central planning authority. We can therefore consider the 'steady state' CRI, found by setting $p_1 = 0$ in equation (4.23). The CRI would then be

$$i = (n \cdot g)c^{-n}/(-P_1/P + c^{-n}) \tag{4.24}$$

The larger the proportion of uncompensated losers, the lower will be the denominator, and hence the larger will be the CRI. This is the result referred to earlier.

Equation (4.24) has an interesting property. The denominator could actually be negative. This occurs when the negative numbers effect dominates the marginal utility effect. This means that any positive improvement in the future would make the project socially worthwhile. Note that a negative CRI could also occur under the original S & T approach, if the growth rate in consumption (g) was negative.

Table 4.4 Values for the CRI based on equation (4.24)

	$n \cdot g$	c^{-n}	$(n \cdot g) \, c^{-n}$	$-P_l/P$	$-P_l/P + c^{-n}$	CRI
$c = 0.5$	0.01	2.0	0.020	−0.2	1.8	0.011
	0.01	2.0	0.020	−0.8	1.2	0.017
$c = 1.0$	0.01	1.0	0.010	−0.2	0.8	0.013
	0.01	1.0	0.010	−0.8	0.2	0.050
$c = 2.0$	0.01	0.5	0.005	−0.2	0.3	0.017
	0.01	0.5	0.005	−0.8	−0.3	−0.017

To help provide some insights into how i can be calculated using equation (4.24), Table 4.4 shows how the CRI varies with the main parameters. We follow S & T by considering the value for n equal to 1. The growth rate in consumption (g) will be assumed to be 1%. S & T's value for i would therefore be 1% ($n \cdot g$) for all values that we consider. The important point to be aware of in making equation (4.24) operational is the need to standardise the consumption term. The consumption levels, c, relate to some base figure, which for convenience is fixed at $c = 1$. There will then be three levels considered in the table: $c = 0.5$ is the low level, $c = 1$ the base level, and $c = 2$ the high level. P_l/P will take the values 0.2 and 0.8. Apart from the anomalous negative case, *CRI*s are larger with the numbers effect. The highest value would be 5%. When we consider the full version given by equation (4.23), where the numbers of losers can rise or fall at a rate of 2% over time, the highest value becomes 13% – see Table 1 of Brent (1987).

Both the full version – equation (4.23) – and the special case – equation (4.24) – were constructed on the assumption that ($-$) P_l/P and U_c were additive components of W_c. It is important to ask the question, what precisely does the additive property of the numbers effect introduce to the CRI? An additive specification of W_c introduces a regard for utility levels and not just rates of growth. Thus the levels of P_l/P and c (which has to be set by the social planner) are to augment the rates of p_1 and g. Sen (1982, sections 5 and 6) has argued that the main drawback of the utilitarian social welfare function – given by equation (A.2) in S & T – is that it concentrates on interpersonal utility differences and ignores level comparability. His solution is to *add* a shift parameter to the utility function. Additivity and a regard for utility levels seem to be inextricably linked. But the conceptual framework differs from Sen's. He wishes to appeal to notions of subsistence and basic needs, while I wish to go back to the very heart of the welfare economic base to project appraisal, i.e. Pareto optimality. A three-objective welfare function wishes to record, and make allowance for, the fact that most expenditure decisions involve some deviation from unanimous approval. There will be uncompensated losers to consider in addition to the size of aggregate net benefits.

As a postscript, if one wishes to avoid the additivity property, one can always return to the generalised S & T version and replace the number at the average consumption level by the number of uncompensated losers. Equation (4.21) would become

$$i = n \cdot g + p - p_1 \tag{4.25}$$

Provided that the growth in the number of uncompensated losers (p_1) is expected to rise at a lower rate than the rate of population growth, p, this formulation raises the value of i relative to the original S & T formulation (if this is the object of the exercise!). The higher i does not depend on the additive property introduced above.

Appendices

Many of the derivations in this Appendix are in S & T. Our purpose is to give fuller derivations, so that the technical aspects will not appear so forbidding. The most appropriate mathematical tools for this subject are those of optimal control. Marglin presents these techniques in addition to the usual static formulations. S & T, unlike Marglin, do not use an explicit model of economic development, and this is why optimal control theory was not needed in this chapter.

How the value of v falls over time

The definition of v was given as

$$v = W_g / W_{\bar{c}} \tag{3.10}$$

Take logs of both sides:

$$\log v = \log W_g - \log W_{\bar{c}} \tag{4.26}$$

Take the derivative of both sides with respect to time (using the log rule of differentiation):

$$\frac{dv/dt}{v} = \frac{dW_g/dt}{W_g} - \frac{dW_{\bar{c}}/dt}{W_{\bar{c}}}$$

or, by multiplying everything by -1:

$$-\frac{dv/dt}{v} = -\frac{dW_g/dt}{W_g} - \left\{ -\frac{dW_{\bar{c}}/dt}{W_{\bar{c}}} \right\} \tag{4.27}$$

All the terms in equation (4.27) are rates of fall in the value of variables over time. The left-hand side is the rate of fall in the value of v. The *ARI* is the rate of fall in the value of public income and this is the first term on the right-hand side. The second term is the rate of fall in the value of consumption, which is the definition of *CRI*. So, (4.27) corresponds to equation (4.1) in the text; that is,

$$\text{The rate of fall of } v \text{ over time} = ARI - CRI \qquad (4.1^*)$$

Perpetuity discounting

Consider the present value (*PV*) of a stream of social benefits over time, starting from year 1 (the year when net benefits become positive). This can be expressed using Chapter 2 notation as

$$PV = \sum_{t=1}^{t=T} S_t/(1 + r)^t \qquad (4.28)$$

When *S* is the same in each year (it is an annuity) we can take *S* outside of the summation sign:

$$PV = S \sum_{t=1}^{t=T} 1/(1 + r)^t \qquad (4.29)$$

The object is to show that, when *T* is infinitely large, the sum equals $1/r$. Let us call the sum *H*. Then,

$$H = \sum_{t=1}^{t=T} 1/(1 + r)^t$$

or

$$H = 1/(1 + r) + 1/(1 + r)^2 + \ldots + 1/(1 + r)^T$$

$$\qquad (4.30)$$

Multiply both sides of (4.30) by $1/(1 + r)$ to get the following:

$$(1/(1 + r))H = 1/(1 + r)^2 + \ldots + 1/(1 + r)^T + 1/(1 + r)^{T+1} \qquad (4.31)$$

Now subtract equation (4.31) from equation (4.30):

$$[1 - (1/(1 + r))]H = 1/(1 + r) - 1/(1 + r)^{T+1} \qquad (4.32)$$

Note that $1/(1 + r)$ is a fraction. The larger the power to which it is raised, the lower its value becomes. When $T + 1$ is infinitely large, its value approaches zero. Equation (4.32) then simplifies to

$$[1 - 1/(1 + r)]H = 1/(1 + r)$$

or

$$[r/(1 + r)]H = 1/(1 + r)$$

$$\qquad (4.33)$$

and, finally,

$$H = 1/r$$

Hence the present value formula (4.29) using perpetuity discounting can be written as

$$PV = S/r \tag{4.34}$$

This process is what is involved with the transformation of (2.8) into (4.13) in the text of this chapter.

Derivation of the CRI formula

The social value of consumption, for one at the average consumption level, was given in Chapter 3 by $\bar{c}^{-n}$. This depends on the time period considered. The present value, using continuous time discounting (as opposed to discrete discounting which was used in this chapter), can be represented by

$$W_{\bar{c}} = \bar{c}_t^{-n} \, e^{-\varrho t} \tag{4.35}$$

where ϱ is again the pure rate of time preference. The definition of *CRI* was given in the Appendices (pp. 90–1)

$$CRI = -\frac{dW_{\bar{c}}/dt}{W_{\bar{c}}} \tag{4.36}$$

The numerator of equation (4.36) is the derivative of equation (4.35) with respect to time. This can be found using the product rule

$$-dW_{\bar{c}}/dt = \varrho \bar{c}_t^{-n} \, e^{-\varrho t} + n\bar{c}_t^{-n-1} \, e^{-\varrho t} \, d\bar{c}_t/dt$$

or
$$-dW_{\bar{c}}/dt = \bar{c}_t^{-n} \, e^{-\varrho t} \, [\varrho + n\bar{c}_t^{-1} \, d\bar{c}_t/dt] \tag{4.37}$$

The denominator of equation (4.36) is given by equation (4.35). Inserting equations (4.35) and (4.37) into (4.36) produces

$$CRI = \bar{c}_t^{-n} \, e^{-\varrho t} \, [\varrho + n\bar{c}_t^{-1} \, d\bar{c}_t/dt]/\bar{c}_t^{-n} \, e^{-\varrho t}$$

or
$$CRI = \varrho + n\bar{c}_t^{-1} \, d\bar{c}_t/dt = \varrho + ng \tag{4.38}$$

where

$$g = (d\bar{c}_t/dt)/\bar{c}_t \text{ [the growth rate of per capita consumption]}$$

Equation (4.38) is formula (4.6) in the text.

5

The shadow wage rate

5.1   Introduction

We have completed the analysis of the main social parameters. S & T label all of these factors 'distribution weights', because none of them would be needed if one were not concerned with inter- and intragenerational distribution. The other parameters needed can be called shadow (or accounting) prices. This chapter is devoted to an analysis of the shadow wage rate (SWR). It is the first of four that deals with shadow prices. The SWR is in many ways a hybrid, since it mixes shadow price issues with a presentation of the remainder of the social parameters. This is the main reason for starting our coverage of shadow prices with the shadow price of labour. The other reason is that the methodology is very similar to that carried out in dealing with shadow prices in cost–benefit analysis, and so may be somewhat more familiar. The starting point is market prices (wage rates) and adjustments are made from this to arrive at the social prices.

A private firm hires labour up to the point where the marginal revenue product (its demand for labour) equals the marginal wage. In competitive labour markets, the marginal wage equals the average wage. This means that when the firm uses the (average) wage to decide how many to hire, it is basing its decision on what labour could produce in its next best alternative occupation. Social decisions in LDCs are not usually based on market wages. This is not only because actual wages (both urban and rural) are more likely to be set by institutional rather than market forces. It is also because the government has different objectives in mind when deciding how much labour to use.

S & T's analysis of the SWR is by far the clearest section of their text.

They present the material in self-contained chapters (8 and 11), and devote some space to explaining the rationale and implications of what they are discussing. Their main omission is the standard one, that they do not present any applications. (In the discussion section we deal with their other omission: that they do not explicitly allow for employment as a separate objective.) After the SWR concept is defined, we explain how it fits in with the overall S & T methodology.

5.1.1   Defining the SWR

A shadow price shows the effect of a (small) change in the quantity of an input or an output on social welfare. The shadow price of labour thus records by how much welfare will be altered when an extra unit of labour (say a working-hour) is made available for (or is used up in) the public project.The value of a shadow price is specific to the set of social objectives that defines social welfare, and the constraints that are imposed. Both these aspects warrant some discussion now, and will be covered in much greater detail in the next chapter.

Whether a change in availability of a quantity is an advantage or a disadvantage depends on what society is trying to achieve. More labour is a plus if one wishes to fight a war, but may be a minus if one wishes to maximise output per head. S & T basically use the objective function outlined in Chapter 1; that is, considerations of economic efficiency and distribution were to be important. For the SWR this means that the market wage rate may need to be adjusted for labour market imperfections, and additions to consumption (which affect savings and consumption inequality). However, S & T do introduce some other social objectives in an informal way. In particular, S & T make an allowance for the possibility that an LDC government may wish to increase output (or growth) irrespective of the extra effort by individuals which is entailed. As is almost universal in the project appraisal literature, specific objectives are accommodated as special cases of more general formulations. So one can choose just those assumptions with which one is most comfortable – recall that one can use the S & T framework even if one does not want to allow at all for distribution, by picking the appropriate parameter values ($\beta = d/v$).

The other aspect which makes a shadow price specific is the choice of constraint. Although labour does not directly enter the objective function, it does affect the efficiency and distribution objectives via the production constraint. It is only by assuming that society is trying to maximise something which depends on labour availability, that one can define the shadow price of labour at all. In the project appraisal literature this optimisation process is often made explicit. For example, Ray (1984, Appendix) defines the SWR as the change in the social value of national income (wages plus profits) which a change in availability of labour generates. The constraint here is that output is a function of capital and labour. So using the extra labour leads to more output and more profits, as well as a higher wage bill. The point to be emphasised is that if one sets the constraint up differently, then the shadow price will be different.

The optimisation process underlying S & T's shadow price of labour is entirely implicit. If a firm is trying to maximise profits in a competitive market, subject to a production constraint, then the market wage would be the SWR. (This is the 'wage equals the value of the marginal product' principle of elementary micro-economic theory.) The adjustments which are going to take place to this market wage rate, to record the social wage, are informal ways of solving optimisation problems with alternative objectives and constraints.

5.1.2   How the SWR fits in with the overall S & T methodology

At one level the S & T SWR is just another shadow price. On a different level, it is an alternative mechanism by which distributional issues can be introduced into project appraisal. Recall the S & T method of integrating efficiency and distribution given by equations (1.4) and (3.6):

$$S = E - C\,(\beta - \omega)$$

This focuses on the output side of the public project. The income associated with the output gets distributed to the inputs by way of the factor prices that they receive. An alternative way of allowing for distribution is to structure the social factor prices accordingly. This is what will be happening in this chapter. The social factor price equivalent of equations (1.4) and (3.6) is

$$Social\ price = Efficiency\ price + C\,(\beta - \omega) \tag{5.1}$$

An input can be regarded as a negative output. This explains the change in sign accompanying the distribution term – i.e. $C\,(\beta - \omega)$, the 'net social cost of increased private sector consumption'.

The only practical consideration to keep in mind is that one should not allow for distribution on both the output and input sides in the same project evaluation, for this would be double-counting. Notice that an SWR was not included in the tractor project appraisal in Pakistan. All

of the domestic effects of the projects were concentrated on the incomes of farmers. One could just as well have labelled these incomes 'wages' (or profits) and applied the same set of adjustments as will be included for the SWR.

5.2   S & T's methods

S & T present their SWR formula for unskilled labour in full and then consider special cases. Since the formula has many ingredients, it may appear forbidding at an initial glance. We shall, therefore, reverse the order and present the.components first. Then we can combine these components to form the full equation. Subsequently we deal with the special cases. As we shall see, it is useful to consider the SWR for skilled labour as just another special case.

5.2.1   The three components of the SWR for unskilled labour

The many ingredients in the SWR formula for unskilled labour can be grouped under three headings, or components. The components are the three kinds of costs which are associated with the transference of unskilled labour from the rural to the urban area, where the project is assumed to take place. The three kinds of costs are forgone output, extra consumption, and disutility of work effort. They will be discussed in turn.

Forgone output

When labour is transferred out from the rural area, there is some loss of output from that sector. This forgone output defines the marginal product of labour (m). In an introductory course in economics one is taught that in equilibrium, the wage rate will be set (by the employer aiming to maximise profits) equal to the marginal product of labour. As a starting point, we can use the rural wage (if it is determined in a competitive labour market) to measure the forgone output.

There are two main issues to resolve concerning the use of the rural wage to measure m; both issues involve distinguishing the individual from the total family output effects:

(1) It used to be thought that labour in rural areas of LDCs was typically unemployed, in which case the forgone output would be zero

rather than equal to m. Alternatively, if labour were not unemployed, the rest of the family may work harder and make up the slack. This would lead to the same result, i.e. total family output was left unchanged. Very few now believe that rural labour is unemployed at all times (seasons) of the year, and in all years in which the project is likely to last. Moreover, Sen (1966) has shown that only in the extreme case where the extra disutility is constant due to the other family members having to work harder, will they fully replace the migrant worker's output. In general, we can conclude (in terms of this first issue) that m will be equal to the rural wage.

(2) On the other hand, for every person who is employed by the project in the urban area, there is usually more than one person in an LDC who migrates. With more than one migrant, there will be more than one person's forgone output to consider. The total forgone output would then be equal to the number of migrants times m. Even if m is less than the rural wage, m times the number of migrants may still be greater than the rural wage. To help predict the number of migrants, one can use (as we shall see in the applications section) the Todaro (1969) migration model.

The forgone output (m) just estimated will be in terms of domestic prices. This needs to be converted into terms of the numeraire. Let α be this output conversion factor. It plays a role similar to the consumption conversion factor β. The difference lies in the size of market price imperfections involved with (domestic) production rather than with (imported) consumption. S & T (p. 83) define $m \cdot \alpha$ as

Labour's forgone marginal product at accounting prices $= m \cdot \alpha$ **(5.2)**

Extra consumption

A crucial point to understand is that the worker is not paid the social wage, but the (urban) market wage. If all of this is consumed, then we need to consider this as an additional cost of hiring the labour even if the marginal product of labour were zero. The extra consumption in this case is given by the extra income earned by being employed on the public project, that is, it is given by the difference between the urban and rural wage rates. Defining w as the urban wage, and m as the rural wage, we obtain $(w - m)$ as the extra consumption.

   (L & M (Chapter 14) tell the following story. Let a be the average product of labour in the rural area. For social reasons a is the rural wage, even though it is greater than the profit maximising wage rate m. The migrant will receive, and consume, the extra wage earned in the urban area, i.e. $(w - a)$. Those left behind can consume the difference between what the migrant was paid, (a), and what was contributed to output, (m), before the migrant moved out, i.e. $(a - m)$. Since $(w - a) + (a - m)$ equals $(w - m)$, the sum of the two groups' extra consumption is the same as with S & T.

Having determined the amount of the extra consumption, we need to know its social cost. This was already discussed on the output side, when we translated any additional consumption from income generated by the public project into social terms by multiplying by $(\beta - \mathrm{d}/v)$. The social loss, therefore, of paying the market wage and not the social wage, is the product of the amount of the additional consumption times its social cost; that is,

Net social cost of increased consumption $= (w - m)\,(\beta - \mathrm{d}/v)$ **(5.3)**

Disutility of effort

The migrant worker may have to work harder in the new urban job. In competitive markets the disutility of working is reflected in the wage given. In developed countries, one would measure the extra disutility of having to work harder in the new job by the difference in wage rates, i.e. $(w - m)$. However, in LDCs, wages are less likely to be competitive ones. An adjustment needs to be made to signify the migrant worker's own evaluation of the wage difference. Define by e the proportion of the wage rate differential that reflects the worker's evaluation of the extra effort involved in the new job; $e = 1$ reflects the fact that in the migrant's view, all of the wage differential is needed to compensate for having to work harder; $e = 0$ denotes the case where no extra effort is anticipated by the migrant worker. The individual's disutility of having to work harder in the new job would then be measured by $(w - m)e$.

An individual's evaluation is reflected by $(w - m)e$. What we are concerned with is a social evaluation. In much of cost–benefit analysis, individual evaluations are all that matters. However, as seen at a number of points in the analysis of the social discount rate, project appraisal is willing to go 'beyond' individual evaluations. In practical terms this means that objectives, no matter how they were determined, set out in development plans are considered important. It could be that even though individuals do actually experience the disutility of having to work harder in the new job, society (the development planners) may wish to disregard this disutility. A country's development plan may request that everyone work hard for development (and not be compensated for this). Even in an individualistic country such as the United States, the protestant work ethic is so strong that it is often socially unacceptable to say that one is not willing to take a new job because one would have to work harder. To allow for such non-individualistic sentiments, one can define by F the proportion of an individual's evaluation that will be valid from the social point of view. The consumer sovereignty assumption of cost–benefit analysis is measured by $F = 1$ and $F = 0$ is the protestant work ethic assumption; $(w - m) F \cdot e$ is the social effect of the loss of leisure from having to work harder.

S & T consider the reduced leisure just defined to be like any other domestically produced good. It has a distributional effect, so it must be multiplied by d. As it is a 'good' produced domestically, it needs to be expressed in terms of the numeraire by dividing this by v. So the social evaluation of having to work harder is the previous effect multiplied by d/v, i.e.:

$$Social\ cost\ of\ reduced\ leisure = (w - m)\ F \cdot e\ d/v \qquad (5.4)$$

5.2.2 S & T's SWR formula

The SWR for S & T is found by summing the three components (equations 5.2–4) to obtain

$$SWR = m \cdot \alpha + (w - m)(\beta - d/v) + (w - m)\ F \cdot e\ d/v \qquad (5.5^*)$$

This should be compared, component by component, to equation (5.1) which defined a social factor price. The $m \cdot \alpha$ correspond to the efficiency price. Since all of the wage differential is assumed to be consumed, $(w - m) = C$. So $(w - m)(\beta - d/v)$ corresponds to the distribution term. There is nothing in equation (5.1) to correspond with the 'disutility of effort' component of equation (5.5). In principle this could be added to both equation (5.1) or the output version covered in previous chapters. We can presume that S & T do not consider that the third component is of general applicability. This is certainly mirrored in the applications, where it is usually assigned a zero value. Lal (1973) presents a number of reasons that a zero value is generally appropriate in LDCs.

5.2.3 Special cases of the SWR formula

Because the general formula looks to be so complicated, S & T consider a number of special cases. We shall only cover the two which supply the lower and upper bounds for the SWR. To understand why they are the limiting cases, one needs to be aware that in most LDCs there is an enormous gap between what labour is paid in the urban areas, and what it earns in the rural areas. The former is measured by w, and m approximates the latter. The more one advocates an SWR closer to w, rather than to m, the higher the resulting value will be. (Since additional consumption is more likely to affect foreign trade – and hence free foreign exchange – than domestic output, generally it will also be the case that β is greater than α.)

In the first case, the government is assumed to be indifferent about distribution, and it disregards any individual perceptions of having to work harder on the government project. These assumptions require $d/v = \beta$, and $F = 0$ respectively. The second and third components of the SWR formula drop out. One is left with this lower bound:

$$SWR = m \cdot \alpha \tag{5.6}$$

In the second case, the government wishes to maximise growth (an assumption that cropped up a number of times in the applications in Chapter 4). With v approaching infinity, d/v would approach zero. Substituting this value for d/v produces the following:

$$SWR = m \cdot \alpha + (w - m)\beta = m(\alpha - \beta) + w \cdot \beta \tag{5.7}$$

If there is not much of a difference between the two conversion factors, i.e. $\alpha = \beta$ in equation (5.7), the upper bound becomes

$$SWR = w \cdot \beta \tag{5.8}$$

What happens if the analyst does not like either of the two sets of assumptions (or those in the other cases discussed in S & T)? There is always the option of using the traditional approach, which sets *SWR* equal to m. But, as we saw in Chapter 3, the traditional efficiency approach cannot avoid making 'arbitrary' assumptions; it merely avoids making the assumptions explicit. S & T show that the implicit assumptions behind the traditional approach are formidable indeed. The full set of assumptions are as follows:

$$F = 0; \ d = 1; \ v = 1/\beta; \ \alpha = 1 \text{ and } Total \ forgone \ output = m.$$

With these assumptions, equation (5.5) yields $SWR = m$.

5.2.4 The SWR for skilled labour

Although the general SWR formula was devised with unskilled labour in mind, it can also be used to obtain estimates of the shadow wage for skilled labour. This is achieved by treating skilled labour as just another special case. Any skilled labour employed by the public project will not have an opportunity cost equal to the rural wage. Skilled labour can be assumed to be currently employed in the urban sector. Its forgone output will have a value equal to the urban wage, w. With $m = w$, or $w - m = 0$, in equation (5.5), SWR is equal to $m \cdot A$. In this case, this implies

$$SWR = w \cdot A \tag{5.9}$$

This is similar to the second of the special cases given earlier ($SWR = w \cdot \beta$). A high social wage is obtained because the public project is drawing labour away from highly valued urban employment.

5.3   Measurement practice

The applications deal with the full S & T version, as well as with particular cases. Because the migration effect warrants further coverage (which will be presented in the discussion section), we will also highlight a study which explained, and attempted to quantify, the Todaro model of migration.

5.3.1   An application based on the full S & T SWR formula

The Turkish labour market was very segmented with much government intervention in terms of wage controls. The Mashayekhi (1980) analysis of shadow prices for Turkey contained a detailed account of shadow wages for three types of labour: rural, urban formal and urban informal. We will concentrate on labour in the urban informal sector (where wages are not controlled by the government). This sector requires a transfer of labour from the rural areas. It therefore fits in with the underlying philosophy behind the S & T formulation. To mirror the exposition in section 5.2, we will present the estimation of each of the three components separately, and then combine them at the end. All financial figures are in units of Turkish liras.

Forgone output: $m \cdot \alpha = 35$

This corresponds to the efficiency estimate of the SWR, and is the minimum value. Mashayekhi recognised that the forgone output of labour that comes from the rural area depends on the time of year. During the peak season, when even family farms may have to hire labour, m was estimated (by the Northern Forestry Report) to be 110, while during the slack season, m was estimated to be 40. Mashayekhi took the weighted average of these two amounts to arrive at a value for m equal to 60. The output conversion factor A was replaced by an average conversion factor for the economy as a whole, which was placed at 0.59. This multiplied by m produced the efficiency estimate of 35.

Extra consumption: $(w - m)(\beta - d/v) = 25$

The market wage in the urban (informal) sector was taken to be 110. This made the extra consumption $(w - m)$ caused by labour moving to the towns equal to 50 $(110 - 60)$.

Whether this extra consumption was a net benefit depends on the size of β relative to d/v. In the previous chapter we showed that β was 0.79 and v was 3.4. Mashayekhi seemed to take a value for d equal to 1. This made the net contribution of a unit of consumption equal to 0.79 − 0.29 (i.e. 1/3.4) = 0.5. The total consumption loss (the saving loss was larger than the distribution gain) was 50 × 0.5, i.e. 25.

Disutility of effort: $(w - m) F \cdot e \, d/v = 8$

Mashayekhi does not tell us explicitly what his assumptions were concerning the individual (e) and social (F) evaluations of the disutility of effort. However, he does inform us of the overall magnitude of the third component, equal to 8. We can therefore deduce what the joint effect of $F \cdot e$ was assumed to be, using the previously estimated values of the other parameters in the expression. We know $(w - m) = 50$, and $d/v = 0.29$. Inserting these values in the disutility of effort expression shows that $(50) F \cdot e (0.29) = 8$. Thus $F \cdot e$ can therefore be deduced as 0.55. While we do not know the individual contributions of e and F to this estimate, this result should be contrasted with most other applications which implicitly put $F \cdot e = 0$.

The best estimate of SWR for labour in the informal urban sector of Turkey was thought to be the sum of the first two components, 35 + 25 = 60. The third (disutility) component was excluded by Mashayekhi 'on the grounds of practicality and not any other criteria' (p. 55).

5.3.2 Applications as special cases of the SWR formula

Only rarely do applied studies use the full S & T formula:

$$SWR = m \cdot a + (w - m)(\beta - d/v) + (w - m) F \cdot e \, d/v \qquad (5.5)$$

However, equation (5.5) is used as the point of departure from which special cases arise. We illustrate with two such cases (which come from previously mentioned studies).

The SWR in Thailand

In Ahmed's (1983) study of the SWR for Thailand, it was argued that the labour market worked reasonably efficiently, in spite of the existence of government minimum wage legislation. Since the effective urban wage was not high (relative to the rural wage), there was little migration and urban unemployment was low (relative to most LDCs). A job created in the urban sector would have to be filled by someone already working in the towns. This meant that Ahmed could set $m = w$ in equation (5.5) (as we did in the skilled labour case). As a result, the second and third components of the SWR formula disappear (with the added virtue that there is no need to specify the disutility of labour parameters, F and e). The special case for Thailand was that the social wage was the efficiency wage, $w \cdot a$ (equal to $m \cdot a$). As with Mashayekhi's study, A was measured by the average conversion factor, equal to 0.92 in Thailand. The SWR was therefore 0.92 of whatever was the urban market wage (we are not told the actual wage figures).

The SWR in Morocco

The Morocco Fourth Agricultural Project focused on agricultural investments that were to be carried out by the farm owners themselves. Their 'wages' were the profits from the farms. This meant that all the considerations that are usually contained in the SWR were analysed in terms of the output of the project – there being no explicit SWR for the farm owners. However, they did hire labour, and this was where an SWR was required. Cleaver's (1980) study estimated the SWR for labour hired and used in rural areas; no rural–urban migration was involved. He used S & T's formula. But, in this application, we need to be aware of the different definitions of m and w.

Farmers in the Morocco Fourth Agricultural Project had very low incomes. Cleaver assigned them to the critical consumption group, c^*. By definition, for this group, $\beta = d/v$. The second component of the SWR formula disappears. Cleaver did not refer at all to the third component. Either F or e (or both) was implicitly placed at zero. Again we obtain the efficiency wage, $m \cdot a$, as for Turkey. But the implication is entirely different because, this time, m is not equal to w. In fact, m is not even the rural wage. Since the public projects are to take place in the rural areas, w is the rural market wage and m is the forgone output, which was thought to be 50% of the rural wage paid.

It is interesting to consider the main role played by the SWR in the Moroccan study. With the capital-intensive projects in the scheme (especially the combine harvester project), labour was being displaced.

The SWR reflects the resource savings that resulted. A low SWR therefore does not treat this displacement as much of a benefit. The consumption implications of the labour displacement, the social loss involved, was included in the output side of the appraisal (the evaluation of the distributional effects of changes in consumption, $\beta - d/v$).

5.3.3   Estimation of the migration effect in the SWR

Scott, MacArthur and Newberry (1976, pp. 93–4), in their appraisal of land resettlement in Kenya, used the Todaro model (as well as their own) to estimate how many people will leave the rural area when a job is created by a project in the urban area. In fact, Todaro developed his model with Kenya in mind. The urban unskilled labour wage was around five times the rural wage, which provided a very large incentive for migration. It is central to the Todaro model that these wage differentials do not disappear over time (as they would in a competitive labour market); w and m are to be regarded as fixed. According to Todaro's theory of migration, workers migrate up to the point where the expected gain equals the expected loss. The gain is the urban wage to be earned on the public project, w, and the loss is the rural wage forgone, m. Expectations are given by the probabilities associated with the gain or loss. The probability that the migrant was employed in the rural area is assumed to be equal to 1. This is not unreasonable, because migrants tend to be the more enterprising, and better educated, members of an LDC's rural workforce. However, the probability ($Prob$) of obtaining a job in the urban area is not certain. The 'expected gain equals expected loss' relation can therefore be expressed as

$$Prob\ w = m \tag{5.10}$$

The probability of finding a job in the urban area is to be measured by the urban employment rate. Thus, with N as the numbers employed in the urban area, U the numbers unemployed, and $N + U = L$ (L is the size of the urban labour force), the probability is to be given by

$$Prob = N/[N + U] \tag{5.11}$$

Let the project cause an increase of DN in employment in the urban area (where D denotes a change in the magnitude of a variable, in this case employment). If wages in the LDC economy are set by institutional rather than market forces, there will be no bidding up of wages in the urban area, and wages in the rural area will be unaffected. With w and m constant in equation (5.10), the probability must also be constant. For this to happen in equation (5.11), the numbers unemployed (migrants who cannot find a job) must increase in the same proportion as those employed, i.e.

$$DU/U = DN/N$$

or,

$$DU = DN [U/N]$$

(5.12)

The total number of migrants (M, using Lal's notation – 1973) is the sum of those who are employed on the public project (DN) and those who come to the towns and are unsuccessful in finding a job (DU). So

$$M = DN + DU$$

(5.13)

Substituting equation (5.12) into (5.13) produces

$$M = DN + DN [U/N] = DN [1 + (U/N)]$$

or,

$$M = DN [(N + U) / N] = DN [L/N]$$

(5.14)

The relevant magnitudes in Kenya were: $U = 30,000$ and $N = 180,000$, which made $L = 210,000$. Substituting these values of L and N into equation (5.14) produces the following estimate of the number of migrants:

$$M = DN [210,000/180,000] = DN [7/6]$$

For every six extra jobs provided by a Kenyan public project in the urban area, seven persons migrate (six fill the job vacancies and one swells the ranks of the urban unemployed).

The significance of all this for the estimation of the SWR is as follows. The S & T formula contains m, the marginal product forgone in the rural area by withdrawing one person and transferring that person to urban employment. If, in addition, other migrants are attracted who seek employment unsuccessfully, we need to multiply m by M, the total number of migrants attracted (per job created in the urban area). For Kenya, forgone output in the rural area was $7/6$ m.

5.4   Problems

Most applications derive their SWRs as special cases of the general S & T formula. In light of this, the first problem requires particular values to be inserted to provide an estimate of the SWR for skilled labour in Kenya. This problem also shows that there is more than one way of justifying a particular outcome for the SWR. Because most of the literature on the SWR since 1970 has been devoted to an analysis of the role of migration, the second problem focuses on this aspect.

Background information for the SWR for skilled labour

Scott, MacArthur and Newberry (1976) developed an interesting approach to finding the SWR for skilled labour. They thought that such labour could be regarded as being highly paid, i.e. high income. This implies that the distribution weight, d, given to this type of labour can be very low. As a limiting case, the distribution weight would be zero. Since they did not mention the disutility of effort component of the SWR, it can be assumed that F was also set equal to zero.

Question

(a) Put a value of d (and F) equal to zero in the general S & T SWR formula, and thereby derive the shadow wage that would correspond to the case where skilled labour is considered to be very wealthy. S & T's approach (section 5.2.4) involved assuming that m was equal to w for such labour. What was the SWR when $m = w$? Thus, what is the difference between taking Scott, MacArthur and Newberry's approach and using S & T's assumptions?

Background information for the migration effect

Mashayekhi's (1980) study of the SWR for Turkey contained the most complete use of the S & T formula. Not only did he produce an estimate which included the disutility of effort component, he also presented an allowance for the effect of migration. Mashayekhi did not report his detailed calculations, but he does tell us the migration model he used. So, from his final outcome and the parameter values he did report, we can deduce the missing information.

Mashayekhi refers to a paper by Mazumdar (1975) for his migration model. The estimate for M was given by L/N. Note that this is identical to the prediction using the Todaro model – see equation (5.14). We are not told the figures for L & N. But we are told that the unemployment rate, u, was around 22% ('in the range of 15% to 25%'). It is shown in the Appendix that $L/N = 1/(1 - u)$. So it is possible to estimate M from the unemployment rate. The only other consideration to be aware of is that when migration is involved, the forgone output would be M times as large as without the migration effect: that is,

$$Forgone\ output = M \cdot m \cdot a \tag{5.15}$$

It seems that Mashayekhi includes the migration effect only in the forgone output component. For the purpose of the question below, make the same assumption. The more general case (where other components are affected) is considered in the discussion.

Question

(b) Calculate the forgone output component of the SWR for Turkey. Does the allowance for migration raise or lower the estimate of the SWR? What then is the total value of the SWR?

5.5   Discussion

S & T mention the migration effect, but do not explicitly include it in their general formula. The first part of the discussion inserts M into their formula and examines the implications of using this in conjunction with the Todaro model. The second part considers the case for dealing with employment as a separate objective for project appraisal.

5.5.1   Alternative formulations of the SWR

Lal (1973) has analysed the effect of using the Todaro model in the L & M SWR. We can use this analysis once we have explained the relation between the S & T and the L & M formulae.

The general S & T SWR formula was given as

$$SWR = m \cdot a + (w - m)(\beta - d/v) + (w - m) \, F \cdot e \, d/v \qquad \textbf{(5.5)}$$

This SWR is constructed from two concepts in the SWR literature. One is the disutility of effort idea developed by Lal. S & T have formulated their own version of this concept. This is the third component of equation (5.5). For our purposes, we shall consider S & T's formula throughout this discussion section without this component. The two-component version is

$$SWR = m \cdot a + (w - m)(\beta - d/v) \qquad \textbf{(5.16)}$$

Equation (5.16) expresses the second concept behind the S & T formula, i.e. the L & M SWR formula. L & M's formula (equation (1), p. 270) can be written as

$$SWR = w - (w - m)(1/s) \qquad \textbf{(5.17)}$$

where s is the premium on savings relative to consumption. (Strictly, the first w on the right-hand side of equation (5.17) should include the extra costs of living in towns as well as the consumption out of wage income.) The relation between equations (5.16) and (5.17) is easy to show. First, remove the brackets from equation (5.17) to obtain

$$SWR = w - w/s + m/s \qquad\qquad (5.18)$$

Next, add and subtract m to the right-hand side of equation (5.18) and rearrange terms:

$$SWR = w - w/s + m/s + m - m$$

or

$$SWR = m + (w - m)(1 - 1/s)$$

$$(5.19)$$

The L & M version of the SWR, as given in equation (5.19), corresponds to S & T's equation (5.16) provided that

$$1 - 1/s = \beta - d/v \text{ and } \alpha = 1 \qquad\qquad (5.19)$$

Apart from setting both α and β equal to 1, the L & M version ignores intergenerational distribution (by implicitly using $d = 1$). Once these differences have been allowed for, one can identify L & M's s with S & T's v.

Now let us – following Lal, equation (3) – extend the L & M SWR formula for the migration effect, M. This involves replacing m by $M \cdot m$ to produce

$$SWR = w + (w - M \cdot m)(1/s) \qquad\qquad (5.20)$$

Lal argues that the Todaro model implies that $M = 1/Prob$, which, as we can see in equation (5.10), implies that $M = w/m$. Substituting this value for M in (5.20) results in

$$SWR = w \qquad\qquad (5.21)$$

The Todaro migration model therefore implies another special case. This time it is the SWR formula recommended by Harberger (1971). That is, the SWR should equal the urban wage (which Harberger takes to be the one ruling in the informal urban sector). This way of allowing for migration has the same effect as if one were considering the project worker to be skilled labour. As the S & T version is based on the L & M SWR formula, the above implication of the Todaro model basically applies also to S & T. The only difference is that for S & T the SWR would be $w \cdot A$, somewhat lower than the urban wage w.

Lal thought that the Todaro model had two major omissions which he sought to remedy. Lal added to the basic migration model the additional costs of living in urban areas ('migration costs'), and the existence of the informal urban sector offering a wage w_i (lower than w). The Lal SWR was a function of migration costs and w_i, as well as of m, w and s. In general, the Harberger result would not hold in Lal's model (even ignoring the disutility of effort component which he was to introduce). Heady (1981), on the other hand, returned to the Harberger result, when he included an allowance for the agricultural workers having a preference to live (remain) in the rural area.

What then is the relevance of this discussion of the migration models for the S & T SWR formula? There are three points that need to be made.

(1) S & T (Chapter 11, p. 119) subscribe to a model (attributed to Mazumdar) that predicts M by the ratio of L/N. We have already noted that this is the identical prediction given by the Todaro model – see equation (5.14). The reason the two predictions coincide is contained in the assumption (which Heady also adopts) of a constant unemployment rate, u, before and after migration. The rate of migration that follows from this assumption is given by $1/(1 - u)$. We show in the Appendix that $1/(1 - u) = L/N$, the Todaro prediction for M. (Recall that we also used this relation to extract the migration prediction from the Mashayekhi study.) Consequently, S & T seem to be recommending something like the Harberger special case for the SWR.

(2) Even if the Todaro equivalent migration model is what S & T have in mind, they would not quite be recommending the pure Harberger result, seeing that (as we stated above) the S & T version would be less than w (i.e. $SWR = w \cdot \alpha$).

(3) Neither Lal nor Heady (nor L & M) allow for distributional considerations. As long as there is some difference between w and m (strictly, a difference between w and $M \cdot m$) distributional considerations will play a role in the determination of the SWR according to S & T. Moreover, distributional factors will lower the SWR, provided that workers come from a group consuming at a level below the critical consumption level, c^*; for then $\beta < d/v$, and this would make negative the second components of equations (5.5) and (5.16). Consequently, Heady is wrong to state that the only reason for adopting an SWR lower than w is due to the possibility that migration may lower the post-migration unemployment rate. Distributional considerations could also lead to an SWR lower than w.

5.5.2 *Allowing for employment as a separate social objective*

The standard view of employment in the context of development has been stated by Lal, while he was working at the World Bank:

> I believe there is some sort of professional consensus amongst economists that employment as such cannot be considered to be a sensible objective, but is rather a means of providing output and incomes. (1978, p. 234)

This belief is endorsed by S & T who argue that the setting of the SWR reflects the trade-off between growth and distribution – 'The growth objective may require an upward adjustment' while 'the income distribution objective may require a downward adjustment in whatever level of the shadow wage rate would otherwise have been appropriate' (p. 30).

Such a 'consensus amongst economists' is unfortunate if it does not reflect what policy-makers actually think about the matter. Most development plans give separate statements about employment objectives. It is difficult to accept that such statements are merely concerned with employment as a means to an end (social welfare based solely on efficiency and distribution). I think economists are implicitly aware of this, and this awareness is reflected in the practice (as we shall see below) if not the theory of project appraisal.

If employment is to reflect something other than growth and distribution, what can this be? If one accepts the arguments given in Chapters 1 and 4 of this text concerning the numbers effect as a third social objective, we have a natural vehicle for accommodating employment considerations, for jobs created by public projects can be expressed immediately in terms of numbers affected. To obtain an exact parallel with the numbers effect as we have defined it, it is necessary to focus on the converse of employment, i.e. unemployment.

The numbers effect was expressed as the number of uncompensated losers of a public project. Clearly those unemployed can be considered losers from the development process. Since unemployment insurance/compensation is very limited in LDCs, the unemployed will usually be uncompensated losers. In the context of the SWR, the unemployment is generated by the migration mechanism. Below we explain how unemployment can be introduced explicitly into the determination of the SWR via the migration term, M. But first we need to give an account of how current project appraisal practice deals with the employment/unemployment issue.

Allowing for the employment objective in practice

The message here is that not only does current practice (a) recognise employment as a third social objective, it also (b) sometimes gives employment greater priority than either efficiency or distribution. Part (a) of the proposition is supported whenever a project is chosen for appraisal because of its employment-generating effects. Once chosen on these grounds, the evaluation is to establish whether it is socially worthwhile (using a two-objective, social welfare function). Part (b) follows because, even were such a project judged socially beneficial, the process is not like adopting a three-objective welfare function. It ignores any trade-off among objectives: that is, there may exist an alternative project which does not contribute as much to the employment objective, but furthers efficiency and distribution to a much greater extent. The following two applications illustrate the proposition and its implications.

A good example of a project chosen for appraisal on employment grounds was the Morocco Fourth Agricultural Credit Project (previously discussed). One of the main objectives was to create 115,000 working-years of rural employment. Since the project was shown to exhibit a high social rate of return, Cleaver (1980) could ignore further mention of the employment objective. But should the appraisal have had a negative outcome (on the basis of the two objectives), there would have been no guideline on whether to proceed with the project.

For the extension of smallholder tea production in Kenya, the political process had already decided that tea projects were worth pursuing, so the extension had actually taken place. Stern (1972), as with the tractor project in Pakistan, carried out an *ex post* evaluation of the tea extension. He stressed that one of the major advantages of tea cultivation is that it is a labour-intensive crop (extensive hand pruning and picking is required). For example, tea involves 2,000 hours per acre per year, as compared with 300 hours for maize. Presumably, the political process was aware of tea's employment contribution when it classed the project 'worthwhile'. Stern also found a positive social outcome based on efficiency and distribution. If he had not, we would have had to infer that employment was more important than the other two objectives.

One way of looking at the use of employment as a method of screening which projects to appraise, is in terms of the two-step procedure outlined in Chapter 1. There we argued that 'political' forces may decide which projects are feasible, and then a formal social appraisal decides among the feasible set. It could be that employment is one of the 'political' factors involved. Given the consensus among economists to ignore employment as a 'sensible' objective in its own right, perhaps using employment as a criterion for inclusion in the feasible set was thought the only way for policy-makers to incorporate employment in project appraisal. But, as will now be explained, employment can be brought explicitly into the evaluation process via its inclusion in the SWR formula. The advantage of including employment as a third objective is that one can allow for a trade-off among objectives.

Introducing a separate concern for employment in the SWR

(This section is based on Brent, 1989.)

To an economist, the most obvious way of influencing employment is via the price that is being charged. It is true that we are discussing the social price of labour and not the market price, but the same principle applies: the lower the price, the more employment there will be. A low accounting price means that public projects which use relatively more labour than capital will show larger social net benefits than a project which is more capital-intensive (all other things held constant).

Apart from those who considered labour employment the sole criterion for judging the social value of a project, the project appraisal literature in the 1960s was not too concerned about incorporating an employment objective explicitly. The labour surplus theories which then abounded put the SWR at close to zero. Employment would then almost automatically be encouraged. But with the disappearance of the belief in surplus labour in the 1970s, and the theories of migration which were introduced into the discussion, much more support was given to the idea that the SWR should equal the (urban) wage rate. In this context, employment is not given any more consideration than it would be in a private investment decision. This seems out of line with policy-makers' preferences on this matter. We shall introduce employment into the SWR in such a way that there is a separate influence working towards reducing its size. (Actually, we adopt the reverse strategy: an unemployment term is introduced that raises the SWR.) Since we wish to add to (rather than replace) the S & T analysis, we shall present the preference for employment as a fourth component in the general S & T SWR formula. We start by defining the employment/unemployment measure, and then establish the weight that is to be attached to it.

The migration term, M, can be used as a basis for the measure of the effect on employment and unemployment; M appears in the extended SWR formula (of the previous sub-section) per unit of job created by the public project. A value of 1 for M means that the only migration that takes place is to fill the vacancy provided by the public project. No (urban) unemployment would be generated by the public project. Any number greater than this would imply that unemployment would increase. For example, if $M = 2$, two people come for every job generated by the project. One would be employed on the project and one would join the ranks of the urban job-seekers. Unemployment would therefore increase by one. So $(M - 1)$ can be used as the unemployment index – the per job number of uncompensated losers. If one is considering a project which provides employment directly to the rural area, $M = 0$, and -1 (a one-job reduction in unemployment) would be the index.

Once one has the index, one needs to attach a social value to it. Let a^* be the social value of a reduction in unemployment. In keeping with the rest of S & T's general SWR formula, we shall express this value parameter relative to a wage rate (a job is more valuable the higher the wage rate). The job that is being lost is assumed to be in the rural area, so m would be the appropriate wage. This specification of 'a job equals the wage' has a natural interpretation in terms of our definition of the numbers effect as uncompensated losers. The amount m can be considered the amount necessary to compensate a person for the lost job. The parameter a^* is to be expressed as a percentage of the lost job/wage; a^* is the percentage of the lost job that society feels is not worth giving up, and $a^* = 1$ means that society regrets all the wage that is not being earned; while $a^* = 0$ is the consensus position – that a job is just a means to an end and not an end in itself. (As always in the S & T framework, the appraiser is being given the option not to adopt a particular consideration in the final outcome.)

Up to this point, the value of the lost job can be expressed by the term $a^* \cdot m (M - 1)$. To enable one to trade off the concern over unemployment against the efficiency and distributional considerations (the other objectives in the three-objective welfare function), it is consistent with the overall S & T methodology to treat a lost job like any other 'good' and multiply it by d/v. The social value of a lost job would be greater the lower the income of the migrant, and would be lower the higher the premium put on growth. The fourth component of the SWR can now be fully specified as

$$\text{Social cost of unemployment} = a^* \cdot m (M - 1) \, d/v \qquad (5.21)$$

This should be added to equation (5.5) to represent a three-objective SWR. It should be added to the SWR because the higher the social cost of unemployment, the more employment in the urban areas (which attracts 'over-migration') should be discouraged. Using the figures in Mashayekhi's study ($m = 60$, $d = 1$, $v = 3.4$ and $M = 1.28$), the maximum correction ($a^* = 1$) the fourth component would make to the SWR for Turkey would be to raise it by 9% of the rural wage, i.e. 5.4 Turkish lira.

To conclude this chapter: with perfect markets (and with no constraints on government policy instruments) the shadow price of labour would be given by the market wage in the urban sector, w. If the forgone output is the rural marginal product, m, then a lower value would be taken. If the number of migrants from the rural area (M) is greater than the number of jobs created, then the total forgone output would be $M \times m$. The SWR would once again be close to the urban wage. While the fact that the job seeker was from a low-income group would lower the SWR, a high premium on growth would tend to raise the SWR, to penalise any extra consumption that the new urban workers may make. So additional consumption by workers has a theoretically ambiguous effect on the SWR. The disutility of having to work in the new job would raise the SWR. Finally, accepting employment as an objective in its own right means that any unemployment caused by excess rural migration would, of itself, raise the SWR.

Appendix

The object is to show that if one can predict the number of migrants per job created using L/N, one can use also $1/(1 - u)$, as they are numerically equivalent under specified circumstances.

The relation between L/N and 1/(1 − u).

The urban labour force is the sum of those employed and those unemployed:

$$L = N + U \tag{5.22}$$

and the urban unemployment rate is given by

$$u = U/L \tag{5.23}$$

For u to remain unchanged, du must equal 0. Using the quotient rule for differentials to find du, and substituting for dL from the differential of equation (5.22), we obtain the following:

$$
\left.
\begin{aligned}
0 = \mathrm{d}u &= L\,\mathrm{d}U - U\,\mathrm{d}L = L\,\mathrm{d}U - U\,(\mathrm{d}N + \mathrm{d}U) \\
&= (L - U)\,\mathrm{d}U - U\,\mathrm{d}N = N\,\mathrm{d}U - U\,\mathrm{d}N \\[4pt]
\mathrm{d}U &= (U/N)\,\mathrm{d}N
\end{aligned}
\right\} \tag{5.24}
$$

or

The number of migrants is given by the sum of the change in urban employed, dN, and the change in urban unemployed, dU:

$$M = dN + dU \tag{5.25}$$

Substitute dU from equation (5.24) into equation (5.25):

$$M = dN + (U/N)\ dN = dN\ (1 + U/N)$$

or

$$M = dN\ [(N + U)/N] = dN \cdot L/N$$

(5.26)

This tells us that per job created (for dN), the number of migrants is L/N when u is constant. Note that this is the same result as was derived in the text under the assumption that the probability of migration would be unchanged. Since $N = L - U$, we can substitute for N into equation (5.26) to obtain

$$M = dN \cdot L/(L - U) \tag{5.27}$$

Now divide top and bottom of the right-hand side of equation (5.27) by L to result in

$$M = dN \cdot 1/(1 - u) \tag{5.28}$$

A comparison of equations (5.26) and (5.28) shows that under the assumption of a constant u,

$$L/N = 1/(1 - u) \tag{5.29}$$

6
Shadow prices for traded goods

6.1 Introduction

This chapter deals with shadow prices, a concept at the heart of project appraisal and therefore also of S & T's methods. The aim of the literature was to find a simple replacement for using market prices to value the physical inputs and outputs generated by the public project. The recommended alternative was to use world prices as the shadow prices. The objective of this chapter is to examine the main kinds of justifications for using world prices, and to identify the circumstances under which they may, or may not, be appropriate. We cover parts of Chapters 6, 9, 12 and the Appendix of S & T.

A private firm in perfect competition knows precisely what it has to give up to obtain any particular good or service. It is reflected in the market price that it has to pay. This principle applies regardless of whether there is a tax in existence. If the firm gets its inputs from overseas, and there is a tax (tariff) on them, the tax-inclusive market price still represents what has to be forgone in order to import the good. This will not be the case when we view matters from the social point of view. As we shall see, the tax is not a real (production) cost. Ways will be found to eliminate the tax from the social reckoning. This is, in effect, a primary purpose of using world prices in project appraisal.

6.1.1 Four categories of commodities

The first persons to propose using world prices were L & M. Their original proposal came under widespread attack (see for example Joshi,

1972, and all the other contributors to the volume). All kinds of situations were suggested where world prices would not be appropriate. The S & T response to this debate can be viewed as recognising from the start that there are four different categories of commodities, and that world prices would be most appropriate for the first of these. The four categories of commodities (including services) that need to be distinguished are:

1. Traded goods for which the elasticities of world demand and supply are infinite.
2. Traded goods for which elasticities are less than infinite.
3. Non-traded goods, which are not currently traded, and ought not to be traded if optimal trade policies were employed.
4. Potentially traded goods, which are not currently traded, but ought to be traded if optimal trade policies were employed.

Since world prices are recommended only for traded goods whose prices are fixed in international markets, this chapter will concentrate on category (1). The other categories will be analysed in the next two chapters.

6.1.2 Definitions and basic rationale for using world prices

A shadow price was defined in Chapter 5 as the effect on social welfare of a small change in quantity of an input or output. Its value depends on the welfare function being used and the constraints imposed. The welfare function will be the S & T one based on efficiency and distribution. The numbers effect fits in best with shadow prices in the context of basic needs. The third social objective will therefore be integrated into shadow prices in Chapter 12. There are no new constraints imposed in the S & T justification for using world prices as shadow prices. But in alternative derivations, additional constraints are introduced. They will be identified and highlighted in the discussion.

A traded good is one whose price and quantity is determined on an international market – 'traded' thus refers to it being internationally traded. When world demand and supply elasticities are perfectly elastic, adjustments in the availability or use of a traded good do not affect its price. With domestic prices unaffected, domestic production and consumption will remain unchanged. Recall that it is through changes in consumption that the distributional objectives are affected. When there is no distributional effect, the sole impact of changing the resource will be given by the world price which is paid or received. Exportables involve using the 'free on board' (fob) border price, while importables involve using the 'cost, insurance and freight' (cif) border price. There are a number of domestic services (distribution, transport and marketing) which are involved in making an export or an import; so these domestic margins (valued at their shadow prices) will be subtracted from the fob price for exportables, and added to the cif price for importables, to obtain the net price of the tradable resource. The problem set in section 6.4 takes one through such an adjustment process.

The fact that tradables have their impact recorded in terms of foreign exchange means that they are immediately expressed in terms of the numeraire. This is a major reason that S & T (following L & M) chose free foreign exchange as the numeraire in the first place. However, one must not be misled by the fact that the shadow prices (and the social outcomes) will be presented in terms of the local currency. The world prices are converted to local currencies at the official exchange rate. This is done only to assist understanding of outcomes by officials in the country undertaking the project. It is still with reference to the government's ability to command foreign goods and services with that local currency amount against which the tradable's contribution (or use) is being gauged.

The basic rationale for using world prices just explained is more convincing when one considers the world prices in a general equilibrium setting. The commodity itself does not have to be traded in the particular project being considered. The assumption is that ultimately the commodity will have to be imported (or not exported). LDCs have a limited ability to substitute domestic for foreign production. If the project attracts a key resource from a domestic user, then that user will have to enter the foreign trade market to replace it. And, if not the current user, there will be some other domestic user who will have to do the importing.

6.2   S & T's methods

We start by explaining the role of shadow prices in S & T's methodology, and then proceed to show that the shadow price for a tradable is given by its world price.

6.2.1   How shadow prices fit into the overall S & T methodology

Up to this point in the exposition of this text we have outlined how efficiency and distribution are to be integrated into project appraisal and covered in detail the distribution objective. On the other hand, the analysis of shadow prices is primarily concerned with the efficiency objective. This is not to say that distributional aspects will be ignored for, as we shall see in the next chapter, distribution plays an important role in the determination of shadow prices for non-tradables. The point is that for tradables, where world prices are the shadow prices, we can supply a simple definition of E which is separable from the distribution objective. This makes operational the $S = E - C(\beta - \omega)$ formulation central to the S & T approach.

The quantity Q of any resource output or input j will be represented by Q_j. Let us define by p^* the world price of a traded good (and its domestic price by p). (S & T use p to stand for both the world price and the domestic price – see p. 143, fn 13 – which confuses matters; especially as the glossary on p. 149 defines p as the domestic price, and the object of the exercise is to analyse shadow prices.) The contribution of that resource to economic efficiency can now be defined as

$$E_j = p_j^* \cdot Q_j \qquad (6.1)$$

So E is just the sum of the E_j, the total contribution of all resources to economic efficiency, i.e.

$$E = \sum p_j^* \cdot Q_j \qquad (6.2)$$

Note that in equation (6.2) the outputs enter positively, and the inputs enter with a negative sign; only tradables are being considered.

6.2.2 Deriving the shadow prices for traded goods

In S & T's Appendix they outline a general formula for shadow prices which can apply to any of the commodity categories; each category is a kind of special case. This formula has particular relevance for non-tradables – and category 4 – and will be presented in the next chapter. However, S & T (pp. 135–6) also detail a framework for considering shadow prices which complements their treatment for the integration of efficiency and equity described many times in this text. So, to enhance continuity, emphasis will be given to this framework in this chapter.

From the outset it will be assumed that the shadow prices do not change over time and this will simplify matters considerably (particularly the notation). The shadow price for Q_j can be represented by W_j and defined as

$$W_j = DW/DQ_j \qquad (6.3^*)$$

where D is, as before, the symbol for a change in the magnitude of a variable. Equation (6.3) defines the shadow price as the effect on social welfare of a change in availability (or use) of a resource j by the public project. Since this definition is general, we can also apply it to free foreign exchange, the numeraire commodity, which can be represented as the quantity of government income, or Q_g:

$$W_g = DW/DQ_g \tag{6.4}$$

Equations (6.3) and (6.4) enable us to represent shadow prices in relative terms. The shadow price for Q_j in terms of the shadow price for Q_g is represented by λ_j and can be stated as

$$\lambda_j = W_j/W_g = [DW/DQ_j]/W_g \tag{6.5*}$$

The resulting change in welfare by altering the resource, DW, can be decomposed into the welfare effects in the public and private sectors. With $W_g \cdot DQ_g$ as the welfare effect in the public sector (the social value of the change in public income) and H as the welfare effect in the private sector, the resulting change in welfare can be given by

$$DW = W_g \cdot DQ_g + H \tag{6.6}$$

When we substitute for this change in welfare into the definition of the shadow price, equation (6.5), we obtain

$$\lambda_j = [(W_g \cdot DQ_g + H)/DQ_j]/W_g \tag{6.7}$$

If we set our units for the change in the resource such that $DQ_j = 1$ (for example, we define a 10,000-acre agricultural project as constituting an increase in agricultural production by 'one farm'), equation (6.7) simplifies to

$$\lambda_j = DQ_g + H/W_g \tag{6.8*}$$

This states that the shadow price for commodity j (in terms of the numeraire) is equal to the change in the numeraire itself plus the change in welfare in the private sector (relative to the numeraire). This equation needs to be compared with the definition of a shadow price given by equation (5.1):

$$Social\ price\ =\ Efficiency\ price\ +\ c(\beta - \omega) \tag{5.1}$$

or,

$$Social\ price\ =\ [Efficiency\ price\ +\ c\beta] - c\omega \tag{6.9}$$

Matching the right-hand sides of equations (6.8) and (6.9) produces these equivalencies:

$$DQ_g\ =\ Efficiency\ price\ +\ c\beta \tag{6.10}$$

and

$$- c\omega = H/W_g \qquad (6.11)$$

See S & T, fn 5, p. 135, but note that equation (A8) of S & T excludes the c term included in equation (6.11).

In general, the social price is the sum of the two components contained in equations (6.10) and (6.11). But, for the special case where a traded good is involved and the world elasticities of demand and supply are infinite, there is no effect on domestic prices of the change in availability of the commodity. As a consequence, there is no effect on consumption per person, and so there is only one component in the social price definition; that is,

$$\text{Social price of traded goods} = \text{Efficiency price} = DQ_g \quad (6.12)$$

The magnitude of the change in free foreign exchange (DQ_g), per unit of the commodity, is exactly given by the world price of the traded commodity. In which case we have the result that we are seeking:

$$\text{Social price of traded goods} = \text{World price} = p^* \qquad (6.13)$$

6.3   Measurement practice

One may think that presenting an application of the S & T methodology of shadow prices for tradables is a trivial task, in that one just needs to look up the relevant world price in the international trade statistics. But this is not the case, for two reasons. First, as we shall see in this section, there may be more than one statistical candidate to represent the world price. The causes, and consequences, of this non-uniqueness were analysed by Guisinger and Papageorgiou (1976) in their study of textile pricing in Nigeria. Second, as we shall see in the problems in the next section, the world price for tradables needs to be adjusted (to allow for various domestic margins) to obtain the net outcome in terms of the numeraire.

Once one has an idea of the complexities of calculating a unique, and net, world price, one needs to have an appreciation of the implications for development policy generally of evaluating project resources by their world prices. Stern's account (1970 and 1972) of the small-holder tea project in Kenya is included to provide such an appreciation.

6.3.1   Textile prices in Nigeria

Guisinger and Papageorgiou's study of shadow pricing in Nigeria can be interpreted as a study to evaluate the textile industry as a whole, rather

Table 6.1   White shirting prices in Nigeria (US cents per linear yard)

Source	Description	1968–9	1971–2
Ex-factory selling price of Nigerian manufacturer	White shirting	27.4	35.2
Nigerian trade statistics	Bleached cotton	51.4	40.7
Nigerian manufacturer	White shirting	18.0	37.5
Textile consultants	Cotton bleached shirting	not stated	83.0
IBRD reports	Bleached cloth	13.0	not stated
Indian textile exporter council	Bleached shirting	14.7	17.5
Purchasing agent (a) High	White shirting	20.5	22.0
(b) Low	White shirting	19.5	21.0

than an appraisal of a particular textile project, which is the usual role of project appraisal. Its focus was very narrow as it did not consider any of the elements of project appraisal other than the choice of which price to use for evaluating outputs.

Guisinger and Papageorgiou sought to estimate the world prices for a number of products. We report in Table 6.1 above the findings for just one of these products, white shirting (see Table 1 of Guisinger and Papageorgiou), which was typical of the full study.

Guisinger and Papageorgiou found that there were no less than six different sources of world prices for white shirting in Nigeria (and there were variations even within the same source). The sources were domestic manufacturers, Nigerian trade statistics, textile consultants, previous World Bank (IBRD) reports, textile exporters and Crown agents (agents of the British government in Commonwealth countries whose role is to facilitate international trade between the United Kingdom and the host country). The existence of different sources would not be a problem if they all indicated approximately the same values. But, as Table 6.1 shows, the prices were widely different. For instance, for 1968–9, prices ranged from 13 to 51.4 cents per yard.

The two aspects that require an explanation are why different prices exist, and why such differences lead not only to contrary outcomes, but also 'wrong' outcomes (in a sense to be defined).

Causes of price variation

L & M suggested that one select the lowest of the available price alternatives. Guisinger and Papageorgiou, however, argued that this was not a generally valid procedure. There may be many reasons for the differences, and not all of these would simply reflect inefficiencies.

The three main causes of price variation identified by Guisinger and Papageorgiou were:

1. A price is a mix of payments for the product and payments for product services, e.g. suppliers' credit, or technical advice. However, it is often impossible to disentangle the various parts.
2. Quality differences may exist.
3. What is observed is not free trade prices, but a mixture of market imperfections and government intervention. For example, multinationals often use 'transfer pricing' (setting prices in such a way that profits appear least in high-tax countries), and governments impose foreign exchange constraints.

While it is only the third reason that reflects inefficiencies, any one or more of the three reasons may be hidden in any of the data sources.

Consequences of price variation

Since we will not usually be able to identify the particular cause which has led to the price variation, one has to live with the consequences, which may be to undermine the whole basis of the project evaluation. The size of the efficiency net benefits – see equation (6.2) – and hence the efficiency rate of return, depends on the world price chosen. The higher the price figure, the higher the rate of return. For a simple average of the price sources indicated, the efficiency rate of return for Nigerian textiles was estimated by Guisinger and Papageorgiou to be 11.1%. If a price figure 10% higher than this average were taken, the rate of return would be 17.4%, and if a figure 10% lower were taken, the rate would fall to 4.2%. Thus a 10% variation in price produces a 60% variation in the economic rate of return. This 'elasticity' means that a 10% variation in prices converts an acceptable project into an unacceptable one (assuming a cost of capital figure in excess of 4%). This result poses a very serious problem because it makes no economic sense (presumably, according to the theory of comparative advantage) for textile production to be classed as 'unacceptable'. LDCs should be profitable in textiles if they are to be profitable in anything. To conclude, as Guisinger and Papageorgiou see it, in a rational world some of the world prices in Table 6.1 must be wrong.

6.3.2 *Small-holder tea in Kenya*

This was the project with the labour intensive characteristic referred to in Chapter 5. It was in operation in advance of a complete social

evaluation. The main objective of Stern was to identify the major implications of using world prices as shadow prices. Because it is only for
tradables faced by perfectly elastic world demands and supplies which
should be valued at world prices, the first part of this account of the
tea appraisal will examine the nature of the world trade market for tea;
then a brief description will be given of the organisational features of
Kenyan tea production. This will be referred to later on in the discussion section. Finally, the main elements which determined the appraisal
outcome will be explained. On the basis of this, it is a simple matter to
understand the main implications of using world prices in the context
of the Kenyan tea project.

The world market for tea

The project under examination was the Third Plan of the KTDA (Kenya
Tea Development Authority) involving the planting of 35,000 acres of
tea from 1968–9 to 1972–3. The issue is whether the price for Kenyan
tea would remain constant after the expansion of production. Stern had
three reasons for thinking that the world price would remain constant:

1. Kenya's tea exports were only 5% of the world market. Even with
    the Third Plan plantings, the share would not exceed 7%.
2. Kenyan tea prices in the past have been maintained, while others
    (especially the two largest exporters, Ceylon and India) had very
    large price reductions.
3. Tea buyers in London were of the opinion that the willingness to
    pay (demand) for Kenyan tea would be maintained into the future
    because of the desire to use Kenyan tea for blending purposes.

   Having established that the world price for Kenyan tea would remain
constant, it must then be decided at what level the fixed price is to be
set. Following the devaluation of sterling in 1967, which had an adverse
effect on the market for tea, a FAO (Food and Agricultural Organisation) committee was set up in 1970 to establish quotas. This managed
to stabilise the 1968 price. Stern took this 1968 world price (3 Kenyan
shillings per pound) as the relevant fixed price. He assumed that the
quota restrictions would continue to hold, and that Kenya's increased
output (which was acknowledged in principle by the FAO quotas)
would be accommodated in practice.

The organisation of the tea production

Many countries experienced organisational difficulties involved with
small-holder tea production. The KTDA was set up to circumvent these

problems. The functions of the KTDA were supplying planting material and fertilisers to the farmers on credit terms; supervising cultivation; arranging for the inspection, collection and transporting of green leaf; and arranging for processing and marketing. For these services the KTDA would receive a sum deducted from the payments made to the farmers. The farmers would receive payment in two stages. The KTDA would give them first a fixed sum per ton, and then, after deducting its expenses, a second payment. The point here is that by acting as a marketing board, the KTDA could be used as an implicit commodity tax mechanism. That is, the difference between the market price and the farmers' receipts was somewhat in the control of the KTDA.

The social outcome

Reduced to its essential ingredients, the tea project can be viewed as consisting of the use of a domestic input (labour) to produce an output for export. The predicted output from the Third Plan was 41 million pounds of tea per year. Using 3 Kenyan shillings as the world price, the gross benefits per year – the counterpart of equation (6.1) – were

$$E_{\text{tea}} = 3 \cdot 41 \text{ million shillings} = \text{Kenyan £6.15 million} \quad \textbf{(6.13)}$$

Note that there are 20 shillings in a Kenyan pound (£).

The key element on the input side was the value for the SWR. Stern used the market wage for unskilled labour for the SWR. This was because the labour market was considered to be fairly free due to the following factors:

1. There were many buyers and sellers of labour.
2. Farmers in one of the main districts (Nyeri) claimed that they had difficulty in obtaining labour.
3. Most hired workers interviewed claimed that they had immediate alternative work (e.g. with a relative).

The total labour cost of tea per year was Kenyan £7.67 million. Since the labour cost is in domestic prices, it needs to be scaled down to obtain its value in terms of the numeraire. Just like the SWR estimates for Thailand and Turkey presented in the last chapter, Stern applied an average conversion factor to the domestic cost. The average conversion factor chosen was equal to 0.75. This made the labour costs in terms of public income equal to Kenyan £5.75 million. In rough terms then, there was a net benefit of Kenyan £0.40 million per year in terms of the two main ingredients. When all elements were included, the NPV was Kenyan £12.59 million at shadow prices, and Kenyan £8.02 million

at market prices (the respective internal rates of return were 38.8%
and 22.0%).

The main implication of using world prices

By concentrating on the two essential ingredients in the tea project, we
can see precisely why there was a difference between using world prices
and using market prices to value the resource flows from the project.
The main input, tea labour, was scaled down by $\frac{3}{4}$ while the main output,
being traded, was not marked down.

The policy significance of this result (drawn by Stern) is that using
world prices would channel more resources into producing exports than
would be the case using market prices, in countries employing protectionist policies. Tariffs would raise the market price over the world
price. An import substitution project which used the L & M pricing
methodology would scale down both domestic inputs and outputs while,
as we have just seen, if the project was export promotion, only the
inputs would be scaled down. So the net benefits would appear larger.
Using market prices would leave alone input and output prices. There
would be no relative difference between the two kinds of project (export
promotion or import substitution).

6.4 Problems

The world price for a tradable is expressed in terms of foreign exchange,
and has associated with it a domestic margin for transport and marketing.
The problems require this world price to be converted into the local
currency and adjusted for the domestic margin. For the data, we return
to Cleaver's (1980) study of the Moroccan Fourth Agricultural Project.

Background information

The Moroccan project was designed to extend domestic farm production
to satisfy domestic consumption and save/earn foreign exchange. The
smaller farms were expected to engage in meat and dairy products.
Here we single out the computation of the shadow price for imported
beef cattle.

Beef imported into Morocco would cost about US $1.50 per kg.
This is the cif price of beef at Casablanca. The official exchange rate
converts 4.3 units of the domestic currency (dirham) into a US dollar.
Domestic transport and handling charges are 0.2 dirham per kg (measured in shadow price terms). This charge takes the meat from the port
(Casablanca) to the edge of a typical small farm on the project, i.e. the
'farm gate'. The domestic price of beef was 6.1 dirham per kg.

Questions

(a) Calculate the price of beef at Casablanca in terms of dirham.

(b) Obtain the (net) shadow price of beef at the farm gate.

(c) Which price is cheaper, the (net) shadow price or the domestic price of beef? If the objective is to trade efficiently, should beef be imported? How much foreign exchange (measured in dirham) is saved by not importing?

6.5   Discussion

The whole of this discussion section will be devoted to an assessment of the validity and usefulness of using world prices as shadow prices. The S & T rationale for using world prices was presented in section 6.2. The literature has proposed two other kinds of justification, one theoretical and one pragmatic. The theoretical justifications are based on the notion of being efficient and this is examined in section 6.5.1. The pragmatic justifications are introduced in section 6.5.2, when all three kinds of argument for using world prices will be reviewed. Finally section 6.5.3 covers the summary and conclusions.

6.5.1   Justifying the use of world prices on efficiency grounds

Equation (6.12) stated that the social price of a tradable is equal to its efficiency price. The word 'efficiency' has been interpreted in two different ways in the literature, so we now outline two efficiency arguments for using world prices.

Trade efficiency and world prices

We have already provided in section 1.5.1 a statement of how world prices fit in with the argument for free trade. We concluded there that although using world prices can lead to gains for trade, world prices could still be desirable even if trade barriers persist. Here we develop the arguments in detail.

Irvin (1978, pp. 69–71) outlined the 'gains from trade' argument for using world prices as shadow prices. To simplify the exposition, assume that there are only two traded goods, x and y. When an LDC has a small open economy, the producers would face a set of prices (i.e. the world prices p_x^* and p_y^*) which are determined independently of the domestic distribution of income. If the government allows private producers to be guided by these world prices (they try to maximise profits at these prices), and it uses the same set of prices to determine its own investment projects, it would be producing output levels x^* and y^*; x^* and y^* would be the amounts of x and y that maximise the total value of output at the world prices (i.e. $p_x^* \cdot x + p_y^* \cdot y$), and would also be the productively efficient levels of output. That is, the economy would be on its production possibilities curve which means that the economy would be producing the maximum amount of good x for given inputs, and for given amounts of good y (or vice versa).

The consumption options are determined by what the optimal production amounts can be exchanged for on the international trade market. It can be shown that there will be more of good x available for domestic consumption (and no less of y) by producing at the optimal production levels, and trading with other countries for more of good x, than if the country tried to produce all of x itself. (The same would be true for good y.) The actual consumption levels of x and y – call them x_c and y_c – are what the country chooses from the increased consumption options provided by the trading policy. If the economy is capitalistic, it would choose x_c and y_c to correspond with domestic market prices, p_x and p_y. However, the LDC could just as well be socialist, in which case the consumption levels would correspond with planners' prices of x and y, whatever they may be.

It is important to understand that what makes the 'gains from trade' argument work is the ability of the country to separate production decisions from consumption decisions. One can produce what one is most efficient at, and consume a different (but larger) bundle of commodities. However, the more general advocacy of world prices as shadow prices (explained below) is valid even if no trade takes place. But it also relies on the separation of consumption decisions from production decisions. The world prices which determine the production decisions are determined exogenously. Any changes in the scale of public production will not change the prices of other domestic goods, nor the domestic distribution of income. The value of the public output can therefore be determined separately. This is relevant when non-free trade exists.

Productive efficiency and world prices

Irvin's account of the 'gains from trade' argument for using world prices is a good first step in understanding the theoretical literature. But, by concentrating on international trade, it provides too narrow a focus on what the modern literature is trying to achieve. The real issue is how one finds social prices in a mixed economy. We know how to set prices in the extreme cases. In a completely privately owned economy, market prices are the appropriate social prices; while in a completely publicly owned economy, planners' prices are the correct social prices. But all economies today have a mix of private and public ownership. The problem, then, is to set prices when the two kinds of ownership coexist.

The pioneering attempt to determine shadow prices in a mixed economy was by Diamond and Mirrlees (1969). All economies face a production constraint. Ignoring the options of going into debt or engaging in trade one can consume only from what it is technologically possible to produce given the resources available. The public sector first deducts the resources it needs to produce the goods that it wishes to supply (defence, health, etc.). The remaining resources are available for production by the private sector. Since the privately produced output is to be allocated by market forces, consumers will choose combinations which best satisfy their preferences, given their incomes and the market prices. The additional constraint, then, that any mixed economy faces is that consumers must be in market equilibrium. In the Diamond–Mirrlees framework, the government is unable to alter consumer incomes directly (via 'lump sum' taxation); but it can alter consumer real incomes by changing the prices that consumers face by using commodity taxation. The additional constraint becomes that consumers must be on their 'price-offer curve' (the locus of points of tangency of indifference curves and all alternative price lines).

The formal problem is to maximise welfare, subject to the two constraints, production and the consumer market equilibrium. The main result, the Diamond–Mirrlees theorem, involved the requirement that the economy be productively efficient. Just as with trade efficiency, the economy would be producing on its production possibilities curve. Production would not necessarily be at the same point (x^*, y^*) as with trade efficiency because of the need to satisfy the consumer constraint also. Call the output levels that the firms wish to produce x_f and y_f, and the producer prices that they face P_x and P_y; x_f and y_f maximise the total value of output at the producer prices, i.e. maximise $Px \cdot x_f + P_y \cdot y_f$.

With the trade efficiency situation, the consumption and production levels differ. Firms produce x^* and y^*, while consumers receive x_c and y_c. Consumer prices can therefore differ from producer prices. In the Diamond and Mirrlees case, however, consumption and production are to take place at the same point on its production possibilities curve, i.e. at x_f and y_f. The problem is that in general consumers will not choose to buy those particular output levels if they face the producer prices P_x and P_y as market prices. To ensure that consumers do choose to purchase the output levels x_f and y_f, the government has to introduce a set of taxes on x and y (called 'optimal commodity taxes', t_x and t_y) which alter relative prices by the requisite amount. The optimal commodity taxes are given by the difference between the (desired) domestic market prices and the producer prices: that is,

$$t_x = p_x - P_x, \text{ and } t_y = p_y - P_y \tag{6.14}$$

The argument so far is that if a country adopts an optimal set of commodity taxes, then firms should be productively efficient. L & M (p. 371) make this result relevant to LDCs, and the issue of shadow pricing, in the following way. A public project (in a world where there are only tradables) can be thought of as transforming imported inputs into exported outputs. If any firm should be productively efficient, then so should the government when it gets involved with production when undertaking the public investment. This means that it should also be using producer prices to maximise the total value of output, i.e. $P_x \cdot x + P_y \cdot y$. The question is, what are the producer prices for firms engaged in tradables? Clearly, the prices P_x and P_y would be the world prices p_x^* and p_y^*. The complete argument is therefore that if public projects should use producer prices, and the producer prices are the world prices, then world prices should be the appropriate shadow prices for public project evaluations.

6.5.2 Arguments for the use of world prices

Stern (1972) has identified three main arguments for using world prices as the shadow prices for tradables. The first is the S & T argument covered in section 6.2. The second is the efficiency argument just outlined. The third is a pragmatic argument, which was implicit in the two case studies presented in section 6.3, and needs to be made explicit. The three arguments will now be discussed in turn. We follow Stern by using case studies to help specify the conditions under which each of the arguments are most likely to hold. (Note that we will be using both the shirting and the tea studies – and those cited in previous chapters – while Stern only referred to his tea study; and we will present alternative versions of the second and third arguments for using world prices.)

World prices as the actual prices of project inputs and outputs

The first, and simplest, argument for using world prices as shadow prices is the one presented by S & T. The actual prices attached to project resources are world prices, and they are already expressed in terms of free foreign exchange, which is the S & T numeraire. The world prices are not affected by altering the scale of public activities, therefore there need be no price-induced consumption effects to trigger off distributional concern. The only effect is the efficiency effect measured by the world price.

It is a relatively simple matter to check whether this argument is valid or not for a particular project evaluation. If there is no domestic production of a certain input, then we know for sure that ultimately it will have to be imported if the public project uses it. However, very few projects will involve tradables on both the input and output sides. The tea project had an exportable output, but a domestic input. This also applies for import substitution policies, since local resources are being substituted for foreign inputs. The Pakistan tractor project was a good example of where the argument would be applicable, as the tractors were imported and the wheat output was for export. But not all tractor projects would be in this same position. For the Moroccan tractor project, the agricultural output was largely for domestic consumption.

World prices as the efficiency set of prices

We start off our assessment of the second argument for using world prices by examining Irvin's 'gains from trade' efficiency argument. Then we cover the Diamond and Mirrlees theorem and its extensions.

Trade efficiency Irvin's argument was that if a country wished to realise the gains from trade, then it would need to use world prices as its shadow prices. The argument is like the classic one in support of free trade and, as such, can be criticised for all the standard reasons stated in international trade theory (see for example Joshi, 1970; Irvin, 1978, pp. 71–4; and Guisinger and Papageorgiou, 1976, pp. 80–3). Overall, the trade efficiency argument does not seem to be a particularly strong one from the point of view of LDCs. But the issue of the role of trade in the development process is a controversial one and basically outside the scope of a discussion of S & T's text.

Productive efficiency Unlike the trade efficiency argument, L & M's argument is a lot more robust. It can hold despite the existence of extensive domestic and foreign market imperfections, and despite there being a number of constraints on government behaviour. We start with a discussion of the original Diamond and Mirrlees result, then deal with an extension, and end up with a qualification to the result.

The major problem with the Diamond and Mirrlees result is that productive efficiency is desirable only if an optimal set of commodity taxes are imposed. This condition is as equally unsatisfactory as the traditional approach to cost–benefit analysis, which concentrated only on efficiency because it was assumed that the distribution objective could be satisfied by an optimal income tax. As explained in Chapter

1, the position taken in this book is that the project appraisal sector operates on the assumption that other branches of government do not operate optimally. There can be no general presumption that optimal commodity taxation exists in LDCs. In particular cases, however, the assumption of optimal commodity taxation may be tenable. Stern argues that 'there is a fairly wide range of purchase taxation and control of prices via market boards in Kenya so the tools needed for public sector efficiency are probably there' (1972, p. 121). To provide additional support for Stern's contention, we should note the point stressed in the account of the Kenyan tea project. The KTDA could operate its pricing policy just like a commodity tax. It does not violate the general presumption that taxes will not be set optimally if the setting of taxes is itself a part of the public project 'control area'. If the KTDA are to administer the project, then clearly they could also administer the necessary withholding of revenues from the tea planters, and thereby tax them.

What, then, of the general case, where optimal commodity taxes cannot be presumed to exist? Dasgupta and Stiglitz (1974) extended the Diamond and Mirrlees analysis for the case of non-optimal taxation. They concluded that the shadow price of a tradable was still its world price, with four exceptions:

1.   When there is a government budget constraint, the shadow price is greater than the world price, but less than the domestic price.
2.   When there is a foreign exchange constraint, relative shadow prices are given by relative world prices.
3.   When there is a quota on the commodity, the shadow price is less than the world price.
4.   When the level of net imports of that commodity influences its tariff level (or some other instrument in the government's control), the shadow price is above or below the world price according to whether the tariff change causes consumption of that commodity to fall or rise.

It is important to realise that the four exceptions were derived on the assumption that the government is simultaneously determining shadow prices for projects, taxes for commodities, and tariffs on imports. In the more limited context of the government trying to find the shadow prices with taxes and tariffs fixed, shadow prices are again equal to their world prices (see Dasgupta and Stiglitz, 1974, section 5.1). This result follows basically because if taxes and tariffs do not alter when the public project uses more resources, there will be no effects on consumption. All effects are concentrated on the foreign exchange consequences as determined by the world prices.

Note that although we have termed this last case the 'more limited context', it is the one that we argued in Chapter 1 was the most appropriate for project appraisal. The project evaluation sector makes the appraisal on the assumption of given policies in other areas. We return to the presumption that world prices are the appropriate shadow prices. However, we need to consider one qualification arising out of some recent work by Blitzer, Dasgupta and Stiglitz (1981) (and mirrored in Bell and Devarajan, 1983).

Blitzer, Dasgupta and Stiglitz agree that it may be unrealistic to assume that the project evaluation sector is trying to optimise not only with respect to its investment decisions but also with respect to the determination of commodity taxes and tariffs. However, the project sector must still behave *systematically* with respect to the other aspects of government policy. Specifically, if the particular project being evaluated requires an increase in imports, then the government will need to adjust some other policy to restore the balance of payments. Different adjustment mechanisms will lead to different shadow prices. The intuition behind their results will be explained now, while deferring a fuller statement of their analysis to the Appendix. Blitzer, Dasgupta and Stiglitz's analysis involves first showing that a distortion in domestic prices will lead to a 'foreign exchange constraint', and then examining the implications of different methods of adjusting to this constraint.

There is going to be a balance of payments problem if domestic prices are different from world prices. Consider x and y again, and let x be the export good while y is the import good. Assume that the relative price of x to y is higher using domestic rather than world prices. Local firms will therefore produce more of x and less of y. People will be willing to pay more in domestic prices for the import good than can be earned for the export at world prices. There will thus be a foreign exchange constraint caused by local consumers being faced by domestic and not world prices. The correct shadow prices will depend on how the government intends to adjust to the foreign exchange constraint.

Assume that the government is trying to act 'systematically'. The government is aware of the foreign exchange constraint and undertakes a particular strategy to satisfy it. The analysis involves examining the implications of the various government strategies for the choice of shadow prices. We shall focus on two of the strategies. In the first the government uses an income tax to choke off local demand for all goods. In this case, both goods are scaled down in proportion to their world prices and therefore the ratio of the shadow prices is still given by their world prices. However, if the government uses an alternative strategy, imposing a tariff on the imported good, relative prices are affected non-proportionally. There is, then, no necessary correspondence between shadow and world prices.

A pragmatic justification for using world prices

The third reason for using world prices is that one obtains more 'sensible' projects (from the development point of view) using these prices than an alternative set of prices. The main alternative to using world prices would be market prices. Stern argues that by looking at case studies where world prices have been used, we can obtain an appreciation of what difference was made to the outcome of the appraisal by using these prices. If one approves of the difference in outcome, one could then endorse the use of world prices.

To illustrate how the process works, refer back to the account of the Kenyan tea project. We can see that the main difference following the use of world prices was that it favoured export promotion projects relative to those involving import substitution. If one adheres to the export promotion school of development, then one can advocate the use of world prices as the appropriate set of shadow prices.

The Nigerian shirting study presented a variant of this kind of reasoning. It argued that the use of certain sources of data on world prices must be wrong (non-sensible from the development point of view). This follows from Guisinger and Papageorgiou's judgement that of all the types of project undertaken by LDCs, textile projects should be socially profitable. If a data source suggests otherwise, then that data source must be wrong.

My only complaint with this type of reasoning is that it is somewhat circular. One should use project appraisal to decide whether projects are sensible or not. One should not turn this logic around to decide whether to adopt a particular project appraisal method because it leads to sensible projects. The difficulty is in understanding how one can adopt a development strategy independent of carrying out project appraisal. For example, how can one look at a project and decide that because it is labelled 'export promotion', then it must be accepted, while if it is labelled 'import substitution', the project should be rejected? Surely a project appraisal needs to be carried out before one can decide whether it is socially worthwhile? It is true that I am in the *ex post* school for determining distributional weights. But I am in this position because there is no clear way of deciding a priori what the distributional parameter n should be. This contrasts sharply with the determination of shadow prices, where there are precise theoretical arguments to help decide what set of shadow prices should be used.

6.5.3   Summary and conclusions

The issue of shadow pricing is central to any project appraisal methodology. The main objective is to find a system of pricing that does not suffer from the multiplicity of imperfections associated with market prices. Unlike cost–benefit analysis, which has developed particular shadow price formulae (see, for example, Boadway, 1975 and 1976), the project appraisal literature has concentrated on finding a single alternative to using market prices that is easy to quantify. The general rule (first suggested by L & M) is that the world price of a commodity will be the alternative to market prices. This explains why Stern contrasted the implications of using world prices as against using market prices. These two extreme cases are, on the whole, all that is really being considered. Put this way, with only these two alternatives, the general case for using world prices as shadow prices is relatively unobjectionable. However, we did also consider more detailed defences for using world prices.

Stern's approach, which asked the analyst to choose between market and world prices on the basis of which system produced the most sensible type of development project, was just one of three reasons justifying the use of shadow prices. The S & T justification depended on the fact that firms would be actually using world prices when making production decisions. Unfortunately, very few projects would satisfy the necessary preconditions for this argument to hold. So greater space was devoted to the more advanced, theoretical justifications.

The main theoretical case for using world prices was based on a theorem by Diamond and Mirrlees. This implied productive efficiency and, if the government followed this path when undertaking projects, it would be using world prices. This result depended on the existence of optimal commodity taxes. Without these taxes, exceptions to the rule of using world prices would appear. However, these exceptions disappeared in the context of project evaluation decisions being determined independently from tax and tariff decisions. Since we have claimed throughout that this independence was the appropriate context for dealing with project appraisal, we tended to endorse the world price rule. The only qualification was that we had to recognise that the adoption of a project would set in motion a demand for foreign exchange. We then had to note how the government in the country undertaking the appraisal was likely to adjust to this demand. If the government was likely to use (because it had done so in the past) a non-distortionary type of adjustment mechanism (like an income tax), then we could go ahead and use world prices. But if the government was more likely to use tariffs which caused changes in relative prices, then the simple L & M rule did not apply. We would then need to follow the type of analysis developed by Dasgupta and Stiglitz. As pointed out by Ray (1984, p. 46), in this case one also needs to consider the premium on public income, v.

Parallel with the main theoretical case was a subsidiary line of argument. This justified the use of world prices on the grounds that these prices would be necessary to guide production in order to achieve the gains from trade. Because this kind of justification was developed outside the main body of the literature of project appraisal, we did not really attempt to assess its general validity.

The biggest criticism of using world prices was practical rather than theoretical. A study for shirting in Nigeria showed that 'the' world price was not a unique figure, and dependent upon the source consulted. Even if one does not share Guisinger and Papageorgiou's conviction that some sources must be wrong if they render unprofitable a textile project in an LDC, one must accept that the degree of variation in the prices was too great to be overlooked. They are right to suggest that researchers should devote much more time and effort to this issue.

Recall that a shadow price varies with the type of constraint as well as the form of the objective function. So, underlying the analysis in this chapter was the theme of what constraints one should consider appropriate in the context of maximising welfare in a mixed economy. We have just seen that one of the issues was how much control one should assume those undertaking project appraisal have over those responsible for government policy dealing with taxes and tariffs. In the Diamond and Mirrlees model, the government could not use income taxes to correct any inequities in the distribution of income. The government was constrained to use commodity taxation only. (This starting point, although conceived in the context of developed countries, would actually be more appropriate for LDCs, where income taxes apply only to a small number of households.) In the context of LDCs, the main constraint assumed is that tariffs have been employed. This is one of the chief reasons that market prices are imperfect. Although there are these two different constraints assumed in the literature, they need not lead to any inconsistencies for shadow pricing. This is because, in their extension to the Diamond and Mirrlees theorem, Dasgupta and Stiglitz built their analysis on the presumption that for some unspecified reason, the relative price of the export good to the import good is higher using domestic rather than world prices. We are free to fill in the reason, whether it is because of commodity taxation or because of tariffs.

At the practical level, one should appreciate that the main significance of using world prices as shadow prices is that one is systematically referring to the effect of the project on foreign exchange. Traditionally, the effect on foreign exchange was considered only for certain types of project (e.g. building a hotel for tourists). Now all projects would be considered from this viewpoint, and at all stages. One would not just record the final consumption effects in terms of foreign exchange, for one would also be including the production effects as well.

Appendix

We present here a condensed version of the work of Blitzer, Dasgupta and Stiglitz (1981). This serves two purposes. Firstly, it provides the reason for the qualification to using world prices, stated in section 6.5.2. Secondly, it gives a simple example of how, technically, shadow prices are determined. In particular, we can see that shadow prices are derivatives of the welfare function with respect to changes in a resource. Note also how the 'total value of output' plays a role in the derivation. The notation is a mix of what has been used in this chapter, and that used by Blitzer, Dasgupta and Stiglitz.

Shadow prices and adjustment to external imbalance

Assume that the public project sets in motion a demand for foreign exchange. (As explained in the text, this is because domestic prices are different from world prices.) In the first strategy the government imposes an income tax to satisfy the foreign exchange constraint. This income tax is levied on income measured in domestic prices, Y_d. To satisfy the foreign exchange constraint, this must be scaled down to equal income measured in world prices, Y_w. The scaling down is to take place at the consumption mix that people would choose if domestic prices were allowed to rule. As dY_d is the change in income at domestic prices, and dY_w is the change at world prices, the scaling down requires setting:

$$dY_d = \beta \, dY_w \tag{6.15}$$

where β is the scaling parameter.

Clearly, β would equal $1 - t$, where t is the income tax rate. Let x be the export good and y be the import good. Then Y_w is the sum of expenditures on the two goods at world prices, p_x^* and p_y^* respectively:

$$Y_w = p_x^* \cdot x + p_y^* \cdot y \tag{6.16}$$

One can define Y_d in a similar fashion using domestic prices p_x and p_y:

$$Y_d = p_x \cdot x + p_y \cdot y \tag{6.17}$$

Social welfare, W, depends on Y_d. Thus changes in W are related to changes in Y_d by:

$$dW = M \, dY_d \tag{6.18}$$

where M is the social marginal utility of income (similar to the S & T d coefficient). Substitute equations (6.15) and (6.16) into (6.18) to obtain

$$dW = M \beta \, dY_w = M \beta (p_x^* \cdot dx + p_y^* \cdot dy) \tag{6.19}$$

The definition of a shadow price, S, is the change in welfare that corresponds to a small increment in the use of a particular commodity. Thus:

$$S_x = dW/dx \text{ and } S_y = dW/dy \tag{6.20}$$

The particular values for the shadow prices can be obtained from equation (6.19):

$$S_x = M \beta p_x^* \text{ and } S_y = M \beta p_y^* \tag{6.21}$$

The ratio of the shadow prices is thus given by the ratio of world prices:

$$S_x/S_y = p_x^*/p_y^* \tag{6.22}$$

This happy result does not necessarily follow if tariffs are used as the adjustment mechanism. Here the price increase for x will be different than for y. Let p_x rise by the rate $(1 + f) p_x^*$ and p_y by the rate $(1 + g) p_y^*$. Instead of equation (6.17) we now have:

$$Y_d = (1 + f) p_x^* \cdot x + (1 + g) p_y^* \cdot y \tag{6.23}$$

Substitution in equation (6.18) results in:

$$W = M[(1 + f) p_x^* + (1 + g) p_y^*] \tag{6.24}$$

The ratio of shadow prices becomes:

$$S_x/S_y = (1 + f) p_x^*/(1 + g) p_y^* \tag{6.25}$$

The world prices now do not alone define the shadow prices.

7
Shadow prices for non-traded goods

7.1 Introduction

In the last chapter we identified four different categories of commodity for shadow pricing purposes, and we concentrated on the first of these, traded goods. In this chapter, we deal with the three other categories, giving special emphasis to non-traded goods. We cover material in Chapters 9, 12 and the Appendix of S & T.

The main method that we will be discussing for making social evaluations of non-traded goods is a decomposition procedure. To introduce the idea, let us consider a similar problem faced by a private firm. The most straightforward way of finding the value of a firm's output is to use the price of the product sold, on the market. But say the firm does not know this price. How can the firm find the appropriate value? If the firm operates under perfect competition (with constant returns to scale) there is a simple answer. The firm knows that the value of its output is completely accounted for by the payments that it makes to all its factors of production (its inputs). So, if it knows its factor usage and the factor prices, the firm can aggregate forward to derive the value of output. Dividing this by the physical quantity of output produces the appropriate price. The social method will follow an analagous process, which depends on disaggregating the inputs, applying their shadow prices, and combining them to form the value of the final output.

7.1.1 Accounting ratios

Although S & T never explicitly tell us this, their discussion of shadow price formulae for commodities is almost entirely in terms of accounting ratios. An accounting ratio is defined as the shadow price expressed relative to the market price:

Accounting ratio = Shadow price/Domestic market price **(7.1)**

The general advantage of using accounting ratios is that once they have been calculated, they can be applied to domestic currency valuations in all years, irrespective of the rate of inflation. For example, if the accounting ratio for rice is 1.2, one can multiply the local price by this factor, no matter what the year of the data. The other advantage of adopting accounting ratios is that by expressing shadow prices in terms unrelated to any country's currency, they facilitate cross-country comparisons. They can thereby be more easily 'transplanted' should they be unavailable in the particular country in which one is making an appraisal.

The concept of an accounting ratio is not a new one for us. It was introduced in earlier chapters under the disguise of a 'conversion factor'; so β and α are really just special kinds of accounting ratios. In this chapter we see that the basic method for valuing non-traded goods is to develop commodity-specific conversion factors. This is in contrast with the aggregate conversion factors β and α which we have used so far.

7.1.2 Definition of a non-traded good

The definition of a non-tradable follows from the idea of an optimal trading policy. If the domestic cost is cheaper than the export price, then one should export the good. If the domestic cost is greater than the import price, then one should import the good. But if the domestic cost is less than the import price and greater than the export price, then the good should not be traded. Thus a non-traded good is a commodity whose domestic cost lies between the export and import price. Good examples of non-tradables are transportation, electricity and domestic margins for dealing with traded goods.

As explained in the last chapter, the category of a non-tradable grew out of the recognition that world prices would not be applicable to all types of goods. Clearly, a good which is a non-tradable does not have a border price. Some other way of valuation needs to be considered.

7.2 S & T's methods

In this section we focus on S & T's general accounting ratio formula. It has five components. After outlining these components, we combine them to form the general formula. We are then in a position to apply the formula to each of the four categories of commodity.

Unavoidably, we face some serious notational problems in this section. They arise from two main sources:

1. S & T state (p. 143 fn 14) that the border price and the domestic price can be assumed to be the same. They use p to stand for both of these prices, which is very confusing. However, to keep the exposition as close as possible to that of S & T, we will not resort to using p and p^* for these two prices, as we did in the last chapter. One does though have to keep in mind that the domestic prices may have a whole set of taxes and subsidies in them.

2. S & T use the letter 'd' to perform three separate tasks: d stands for a distribution weight, as in chapter 3; d is a subscript which stands for the word 'domestic' when applied to a particular elasticity; and, finally, d is the mathematical symbol for an infinitely small change (a 'differential') as used in calculus. We will adopt the first two uses of the letter 'd', but introduce a different letter for the mathematical symbol. As in previous chapter, we use D to represent a change in a variable, without specifying its magnitude. This enables us to keep the mathematics as simple as possible, i.e. as close to arithmetic as we can.

7.2.1   The five components of the shadow pricing formula

Consider the case where the public project utilises a commodity that would have otherwise been exported, say rice. As a consequence the demand for rice increases. In the last chapter, we assumed that world demand and supplies were perfectly elastic. So the increased demand for rice did not affect its price, and hence there were no domestic repercussions to analyse. This time we will take it that world demand is less than perfectly elastic. Any reduction in rice availability on the world market (caused by the increased public sector use) would lead to a rise in the border price by Dp. There are five effects of this price rise, one main effect and four others. These five effects will be identified and explained separately. Then they will be combined to obtain the aggregate effect.

The main effect: changes in consumer and producer surpluses

The domestic production of rice, Q, can be devoted either to exports, X, or be used for domestic consumption, C. That is,

$$Q = X + C \text{ or } X = Q - C \tag{7.2}$$

The effect on the private sector of the price change can be approximated by the size of the price change multiplied by the amount of exports, $X \cdot Dp$. Using equation (7.2), the private sector effect can also be written as follows:

$$\text{Private sector effect} = (Q - C)Dp = Q \cdot Dp - C \cdot Dp \tag{7.3}$$

The rise in 'producer surplus' $Q \cdot Dp$. This means that since producers were willing previously to accept a price p in order to put a particular level of Q on the market, the higher price is an amount over and above that necessary to encourage production; it is a surplus. Similarly, $-C \cdot Dp$ is the loss of 'consumer surplus'. Consumers now pay a higher price for consuming the same amount of rice as before.

The effect on social welfare of the private sector effect depends on the weighted consumer and producer surpluses. Let d_1 be the distribution weight for consumers, and d_2 the weight for producers. Then, $Q \cdot Dp \, d_2 - C \cdot Dp \, d_1$ is the weighted private sector effect. This effect is expressed in terms of domestic prices. To obtain the social welfare effect of the rise in price in terms of the numeraire, we must divide both the weighted producer and consumer effects by v. The main effect would then be $Q \cdot Dp/v \cdot d_2 - C \cdot Dp/v \cdot d_1$, or:

$$\text{Net gain in surplus} = (Q \cdot d_2 - C \cdot d_1)Dp/v \tag{7.3}$$

Equation (7.3) can be simplified by defining a as the proportion of production that is domestically consumed, i.e. $a = C/Q$. Restating this as $C = a \cdot Q$ enables us to simplify equation (7.3) to form:

$$\text{Net gain in surplus} = (d_2 - a \cdot d_1)Q \cdot Dp/v \tag{7.4}$$

The change in export earnings

The rise in the price of rice will affect the level of export earnings. The amount will depend on the elasticity of world demand for rice, η_w. From an elementary economics course we know that these earnings go up if the elasticity is less than unity. This is the reason that, in order to predict the change in export earnings, S & T use the following:

$$\text{Gain in export earnings} = (1 - \eta_w) \, X \cdot Dp \tag{7.5}$$

The derivation of equation (7.5) is explained in the Appendices. Note that the change in export earnings is automatically expressed in terms of the numeraire.

The change in consumer expenditure

There will be an effect of the price rise on the amount of domestic expenditure devoted to rice, and hence spent on other goods. Again we need to know the relevant elasticity. Define by η_d the domestic demand elasticity for rice. Expenditure on rice will rise by $(1 - \eta_d) C \cdot Dp$; therefore the expenditure on other goods will fall by $-(1 - \eta_d) C \cdot Dp$. But this time the change is in domestic terms. To convert this to the free foreign exchange equivalent, S & T multiply this change by a weighted average of shadow to market prices, β_1. The weights for β_1 are given by the share of the increased expenditure on rice devoted to each other good. The resulting expression is

$$\textit{Fall in consumer expenditure} = -(1 - \eta_d) \, C \cdot \beta_1 \cdot Dp \quad \textbf{(7.6)}$$

What equation (7.6) tells us is that when, for example, the expenditure on rice rises by a certain amount, the expenditure on all goods other than rice falls by that amount; β_1 translates the whole bundle of forgone domestic expenditures into terms of the numeraire.

The change in producer expenditure

Corresponding to the consumer expenditure change, there will also be a producer expenditure change, $Q \cdot Dp$. Any increased earnings by rice producers will mean a reduction in expenditure by producers on all other products. Since the bundle of goods that non-rice producers no longer spend their money on is unlikely to be the same as for consumer expenditures, S & T use β_2 as the weighted average of domestic to shadow prices for the producer expenditure reduction. The producer expenditure fall will then be

$$\textit{Fall in producer expenditure} = Q \cdot \beta_2 \cdot Dp \quad \textbf{(7.6)}$$

Cost of the increased domestic production

Any extra domestic production required by the increased demand for rice will raise costs, and detract from social welfare. Define by e the elasticity of domestic supply. The increase in domestic output in monetary terms, $Q \cdot Dp$, must be multiplied by e to obtain the increase in money costs measured in terms of local prices, i.e. $e \, Q \cdot Dp$. In terms of the numeraire, the extra costs are

$$\textit{Increased production costs} = \alpha \cdot e \, Q \cdot Dp \quad \textbf{(7.7)}$$

where α plays a role similar to β_1 and β_2 and α is the weighted average of shadow to market prices of the bundle of goods that are now no longer

produced, the weights being the share of costs that each input represents. (Different inputs affect some outputs more than others, so we
need to know which input costs are altered the most.)

7.2.2   The general S & T formula for shadow prices

All five components of the shadow pricing formula are expressed in
terms of the numeraire. They can be summed to obtain the aggregate
effect on social welfare of the rise in price of rice. The only difficult
point to understand is the sign that will be attached to each component
in the aggregation process. The components have been described in
terms of their effects on free foreign exchange. It is necessary to trans-
late these effects to their corresponding impacts on social welfare.

The object of the whole exercise is to record the welfare effect of
raising the price of rice to free this resource for use on the public
project. In other words, we are trying to estimate the loss of welfare
occasioned by the project use of rice. Any gains in free foreign exchange
reduce the size of the welfare loss, and any reductions in free foreign
exchange increase this loss. Thus, the first two components, by leading
to gains in terms of the numeraire, are to be added in the aggregation
process, while the last three components, by leading to reductions in
terms of the numeraire, are to be subtracted. The change in welfare,
DW, from aggregating the five components becomes

$$DW = -(d_2 - a \cdot d_1) \, Q \cdot Dp/v - (1 - \eta_w) \, X \cdot Dp$$
$$- (1 - \eta_d) \, C \cdot \beta_1 \cdot Dp + Q \cdot \beta_2 \cdot Dp + a \cdot e \, Q \cdot Dp$$

or, on simplification

$$[C = a \cdot Q, \text{ and } X = Q - C = (1 - a)Q]$$

$$DW = [e \cdot a - (1 - a)(1 - \eta_w) + a \cdot \eta_d \cdot \beta_1 + (\beta_2 - d_2/v)$$
$$+ a(\beta_1 - d_1/v)] \, Q \cdot Dp \qquad \text{(7.8)}$$

The definition of a shadow price is the change in welfare, DW, divided
by the change in the resource availability, Q. (Note that Q is already
defined as the *change* in rice use. Strictly, then, Q should be denoted
DQ.) From equation (7.8) one therefore derives the general shadow
price formula:

$$DW/Q = [e \cdot a - (1 - a)(1 - \eta_w) + a \cdot \eta_d \cdot \beta_1 + (\beta_2 - d_2/v)$$
$$+ a(\beta_1 - d_1/v)] \, Dp \qquad \text{(7.9)}$$

(S & T tell us (p. 144) that the five components combined into equation
(7.9) correspond to the basic shadow price relation, given in the last

chapter as $\lambda = DQ_g + H/W_g$. The net gain of producer and consumer surplus, the first component, corresponds to H/W_g, while the sum of the other components defines DQ_g.)

The final step is to convert the shadow price formula into the relevant accounting ratio, as in equation (7.1). Equation (7.9) determines the numerator in this ratio. The denominator is the new market price, after the rise to facilitate the project use of the resource. S & T use a weighted sum of the expenditure changes of X, C and Q to represent the new market price, where the weights are given by the appropriate elasticities. The new domestic price would then be

$$p = (\eta_w \cdot X + \eta_d \cdot C + e \cdot Q) \, Dp \qquad (7.10)$$

If we again use the relations $C = a \cdot Q$ and $X = (1 - a) \, Q$, this simplifies to

$$p = [e \cdot a + (1 - a)\eta_w + a \cdot \eta_d] Dp \qquad (7.11)$$

The accounting ratio for any category of commodity is obtained by dividing equation (7.9) by (7.11) to produce

$$\lambda/p = [e \cdot a - (1 - a)(1 - \eta_w) + a \cdot \eta_d \cdot \beta_1 + (\beta_2 - d_2/v)$$
$$+ a(\beta_1 - d_1/v)] / [e + (1 - a)\eta_w + a \cdot \eta_d] \qquad (7.12^*)$$

7.2.3 *Tradables with and without infinite elasticities*

The first set of special cases of the general shadow pricing formula that we shall consider involves traded goods. In the process we deal with the first two categories of commodity identified in Chapter 6.

Category 1: Tradables with infinite elasticities

For any kind of tradable, the consumption share of domestic output is zero, which makes $a = 0$. If the elasticity of world demand (η_w) approaches infinity, equation (7.12) is dominated by the size of η_w on both the numerator and the denominator. The value of the accounting ratio for commodities equals unity. This means that shadow prices are given by their domestic prices. Since S & T also assume that world prices and domestic prices are equal, the shadow prices are also equal to their world prices. This confirms the L & M shadow pricing rule given in the last chapter.

Category 2: Tradables with less than infinite elasticities

For tradables with less than infinite elasticities on world markets, S & T assume that both the domestic demand and the domestic supply are very inelastic, i.e. e and η_d approach zero. In addition, they set $\beta_2 = d_2/v$. This means that they are assuming that the social cost of a transfer to producers (given by β_2) is equal to the benefits (given by d_2/v). This makes the net transfer to producers, $\beta_2 - d_2/v$, disappear. (Note that this is like the assumption used to define the critical consumption group c^* in Chapter 3. There we had $\beta = d/v$.) With these values, and with $a = 0$, equation (7.12) simplifies to

$$\lambda/p = -(1 - \eta_w)/\eta_w = 1 - 1/\eta_w \tag{7.13}$$

It is shown in the Appendices that the right-hand side of equation (7.13) equals the marginal revenue divided by the domestic price. In which case the accounting ratio for tradables with less than infinite elasticities has a simple interpretation. The less elastic is demand, the more like a monopolist is the rice producer. As a monopolist would use the marginal revenue rather than the price to set its optimal output, S & T recommend the world price rule be replaced by a marginal revenue rule for commodities in category 2. The new rule is marginal revenue divided by p because it is the accounting ratio that is being considered.

7.2.4 Non-tradables

For any non-tradable good, category 3, the consumption share of domestic output is unity, which makes $a = 1$. Using this value for a in the general accounting ratio formula produces

$$\lambda/p = [e \cdot \alpha + \eta_d \cdot \beta_1 + (\beta_2 - d_2/v) + (\beta_1 - d_1/v)]/[e + \eta_d] \tag{7.14*}$$

Consider two cases. In the first, the domestic supply elasticity, e, approaches infinity. The size of $e \cdot A$ dominates the numerator, and e dominates the denominator. So the limiting value of the accounting ratio is α. S & T call this the marginal social cost (MSC) case. In the second, e approaches zero. If the producer transfer $(\beta_2 - d_2/v)$ and the consumer transfer $(\beta_1 - d_1/v)$ can both be ignored (set to zero), the value of equation (7.14) reduces to β_1. S & T call this the marginal social benefit (MSB) case. The task now is to explain the meaning and measurement of these two cases.

To understand the role of the two cases, we need to go back to first principles. As stated in Chapter 1, in a competitive market (and where distribution can be ignored) the social value is reflected in the market

price. The consumer/demand price (MSB) is the same as the producer/
supply price (MSC). So either the MSB or the MSC can be used to
measure the social value. But when there is some distortion in the
market, there is a divergence between the two, and a choice has to be
made. Should one use the MSB or the MSC?

The correct procedure depends on whether the resource being used
for the public project will replace existing consumption, or will be
satisfied by extra production. If the former, the MSB is the correct
approach; and, if the latter, then the MSC is appropriate. What is
required to value a non-traded good is a detailed analysis of the source
(consumption or production) of the particular good.

To illustrate how the source can be determined, consider the analysis
by Irvin (1978, p. 104) for electricity which is thought to be a typical
non-traded good. The supply of electricity can be characterised as one
where there are constant marginal operating costs up to a capacity level,
where the marginal costs then become effectively infinite (the marginal
cost curve becomes vertical). Irvin considers two possibilities:

1. When the existing demand for electricity is low (below the capacity
level), any extra demand due to the public project can be met out of
spare capacity, i.e. by producing more. Here one should use the marginal cost of supply to value the electricity, i.e. use the MSC.

2. If, instead, the existing demand for electricity is at the capacity level,
demand will cut the marginal cost curve on its vertical part. Any extra
use by the project would come at the expense of existing consumers.
Thus the cost is the marginal value placed by consumers. One needs to
look at the demand curve to value the electricity, i.e. use the MSB.

Clearly, these two possibilities simply correspond to the two S & T
cases outlined earlier. When demand is such that the capacity is reached,
the supply elasticity must be zero; and when production is below capacity, the marginal costs are constant, which makes the supply elasticity
approach infinity. But, what the Irvin example shows is how it can come
about that the relevant elasticities will be one of the two extremes.

S & T (p. 92) consider that in the long run, none of the increased
use for a public project will come at the expense of consumption. They
therefore recommend (p. 125) that in general the infinite elasticity case
be assumed to apply. This makes the MSC the basic approach to shadow
pricing for non-tradables, and α the appropriate accounting ratio.
However, following L & M, S & T do not suggest that the output conversion factor be used to measure α. This is considered to be too
aggregate a measure of the accounting ratio. Instead, they outline a

disaggregation procedure, which means that each commodity gets its own conversion factor.

The disaggregation procedure involves decomposing the non-traded input into its constituent parts and valuing each at its accounting ratio. There are four main constituents:

Traded: Use the accounting ratio based on border prices.

Taxes: The accounting ratio is zero (no resources are involved).

Primary: Mainly relates to labour. Use the shadow wage rate formula, and divide this by the market wage.

Non-traded: Decompose it into its four constituent parts.

Some practical problems arise for the fourth constituent, where a non-traded good depends on other non-traded goods. The main problems are as follows:

1. When, for example, electricity depends on transport, and transport depends on electricity, the two accounting ratios should be determined simultaneously.
2. When one non-traded good depends on another, and that other non-traded good itself depends on others, a short-cut procedure is often adopted. This involves finding an average conversion factor for all goods, and using this for all rounds of decomposition after the first.

7.2.5 Potentially traded goods

The fourth S & T category of commodities, goods that due to tariffs and quotas are not currently being traded, are treated according to the likelihood of the trade barrier existing in the future. If the trade barrier is thought temporary, then the commodity can be regarded as a traded good, while if the barrier is thought permanent, the commodity can be regarded as non-traded, and decomposed as above.

7.3   Measurement practice

The following applications are all based on Ahmed's (1983) study of accounting ratios in Thailand (first mentioned in Chapter 4). Thailand had some monopoly power in its major export, rice. Ahmed recognised that if the price of rice was not constant, then using the world price (based on the assumption of perfectly elastic demand) would not be appropriate. His study illustrates how accounting ratios were obtained for tradables with infinite elasticities, tradables using the general shadow pricing formula, and non-tradables using the decomposition procedure.

7.3.1 Obtaining accounting ratios for tradables

In the last chapter it was pointed out that a traded good was a mix of the good itself and domestic margins involved in the importation/exportation process. Even in the absence of these domestic margins, the accounting ratio for a tradable would not be unity because of taxes and subsidies that may be imposed by the government.

Recall from the discussion of the consumption conversion factor in Chapter 1, that an import tax adds to the domestic price relative to the world price, while an export tax lowers the domestic price. So, for any taxed importable, the accounting ratio would be given by $1/(1 + t_m)$, and for a taxed exportable, the accounting ratio would be $1/(1 - t_x)$. In Thailand, the average rate of tax on imports was 15.92%, and the average rate of tax on exports was 5.67%. Consequently, the average accounting ratio for an import was 0.86 and 1.06 for an export. This illustrates the general rule of accounting ratios for tradables under taxation; the accounting ratios for importables are greater than unity, while those for exportables are less than unity. The exception to this rule occurs when there are subsidies on exports. Here the accounting ratios would be greater than unity, seeing that a subsidy can be regarded as a negative tax. (That is, $1 - (-t_x) = 1 + t_x$ now appears on the denominator of the accounting ratio.)

7.3.2 An application based on the full shadow pricing formula

In Thailand the main export was rice, and this was considered to have some element of monopoly power. At the same time, any price rise for rice has repercussions on the rest of the domestic economy. This is the reason that Ahmed used the full S & T shadow pricing formula to find the accounting ratio for rice.

The version of equation (7.12) that Ahmed employed was

$$Accounting\ ratio = \frac{[e \cdot a - (1 - a)(1 - \eta_w)(1/(1 - t_r)) + a \cdot \eta_d \cdot \beta_1]}{[e + (1 - a)\eta_w + a \cdot \eta_d]} \quad (7.15)$$

This is the general formula where the producer and consumer transfers are ignored, and the export revenues are adjusted by a term $1/(1 - t_r)$ to record the fact that there is an export tax on rice, t_r.

The parameter values necessary to estimate equation (7.15) for Thailand were:

$$\eta_w = 4.0 \qquad e = 0.03 \qquad \eta_d = 0.4$$
$$a = 0.7 \qquad \alpha = 0.937 \qquad \beta_1 = 0.985 \text{ and}$$
$$t_r = 0.31.$$

The resulting accounting ratio for rice was equal to 1.11.

7.3.3 An application showing the decomposition procedure

Ahmed presents the full derivation of the accounting ratios for the three most important non-tradables in Thailand, namely construction, electricity and transportation. In Table 7.1 below, we highlight the case of construction (see Ahmed, 1983, Table 11). I have reclassified the entries in Ahmed's table so that they fit in with the decomposition headings outlined is section 7.2.4. Table 7.1 illustrates how the decomposition is to take place. There are four main steps:

1. From an input–output table one obtains the shares of all goods in the domestic market price of the particular commodity one is considering (in this case construction).
2. Then one assigns each input its relevant accounting ratio. For tradables, Ahmed used the simple tax formulae given in 7.3.1. For all non-tradables except the three main ones, an average for all products was used, equal to 0.92. (That is, the 'standard conversion factor' was 0.92.) For wages, one uses the SWR divided by the market wage. This was shown in Chapter 5 to also equal 0.92.
3. Next, the shares of market prices are multiplied by the accounting ratios, to obtain the socially weighted shares of the inputs into the market price.
4. Finally, one adds the socially weighted shares for all inputs to obtain the accounting ratio for construction. As we can see from Table 7.1, the accounting ratio for construction in Thailand was estimated to be 0.88.

7.4   Problems

The object of this section is to reinforce the understanding of the decomposition procedure. The task is to reproduce Ahmed's estimate of

Table 7.1 Derivation of accounting ratio for construction in Thailand

Constituent	Share of market price	Accounting ratio	Share at shadow prices
Traded			
Agriculture	0.00689	1.05	0.00723
Mining	0.04967	0.94	0.04669
Textiles	0.00094	0.75	0.00071
Wood products	0.00294	0.92	0.00270
Chemicals, etc.	0.03929	0.94	0.03693
Non-metallic products	0.08914	0.84	0.07488
Iron and steel	0.10690	0.91	0.09728
Other metal products	0.06133	0.84	0.05152
Machinery	0.04371	0.85	0.03715
Taxes			
Net indirect tax	0.01868	0.00	0.00000
Primary			
Wages and salaries	0.09868	0.92	0.09079
Operating surplus	0.21181	0.92	0.19486
Depreciation	0.03899	0.84	0.03275
Non-traded			
Other manufacturing	0.00006	0.92	0.00006
Public utilities	0.00414	0.92	0.00381
Construction	0.00028	0.92	0.00026
Trade	0.07816	0.92	0.07191
Transport, etc.	0.06272	0.87	0.05457
Services	0.02179	0.92	0.02005
Unclassified	0.00421	0.92	0.00387
Total	1.00000		0.88349

the accounting ratio for transportation (which actually appeared as an input in construction, so we know what the answer should be).

Background information

We list below the shares of all goods in the domestic market price of transport and their associated accounting ratios.

Product	Share	Accounting ratio
Agriculture	0.00048	1.05
Food manufacturing	0.00256	0.94
Textiles	0.01069	0.75
Paper and products	0.00389	0.92
Chemicals, etc.	0.00757	0.94
Petroleum and products	0.21606	0.95
Non-metallic products	0.00042	0.84
Metallic products	0.00128	0.84
Machinery	0.00210	0.85
Motor vehicles and parts	0.08555	0.73
Other manufacturing	0.00044	0.92

Product	Share	Accounting ratio
Public utilities	0.00454	0.92
Construction	0.00536	0.92
Trade	0.04867	0.92
Transport, etc.	0.03029	0.87
Services	0.03303	0.92
Unclassified	0.01016	0.92
Wages and salaries	0.19979	0.92
Operating surplus	0.21237	0.92
Depreciation	0.08991	0.84
Net indirect tax	0.03545	0.00

Note that the following items included above are traded inputs (the classification for all other goods has already been given in Table 7.1):

> Food manufacturing
> Paper and products
> Petroleum and products
> Metallic products
> Motor vehicles and parts

Questions

(a) Construct a table for calculating the accounting ratio for transport along the lines of Table 7.1. On the basis of this table, what is the value of the accounting ratio for transport in Thailand?

(b) The accounting ratio for construction in the figures given above was 0.92. This figure is the standard conversion factor. What is the rationale of using this figure? If the accounting ratio for construction was used from Table 7.1, based on the decomposition procedure, what difference would it have made to the calculated accounting ratio for transport?

(c) On the basis of your answer to question (b), is it always necessary to take the trouble to calculate precisely the accounting ratio for each input when one uses the decomposition procedure?

7.5   Discussion

Much of the discussion in the literature on non-tradables has been con-cerned with the original L & M methodology rather than the S & T extension. For example Warr (1982), in his survey of approaches to the shadow pricing of non-tradables, does not attempt to integrate the S &

T general formula into his analysis. (An exception is Tower and Purcel, 1986, pp. 114–16. They simply wish to emphasise that the elasticities and conversion factors used in the S & T general formula are general equilibrium ones that include non-compensated income effects.)

Nonetheless, there is an important issue relevant to both the L & M and the S & T versions that is covered in the literature. Irvin (1978, p. 105), on the basis of the work of Toye (1976) and FitzGerald (1977), draws attention to the problem of valuing a non-tradable when it is an output rather than an input. None of the authors is particularly clear on this subject because their arguments include basic misinterpretations of L & M, and consequently S & T. So we need to clearify matters before we can assess the validity of the arguments being made.

The issue, as they express it, involves the distinction between a non-tradable that is an input into a tradable product, and a non-tradable that is a final output. For the former, the decomposition procedure can be used. But, for the latter, the decomposition procedure cannot be used. The alternative is to use domestic prices. Because the L & M approach wishes to avoid using valuations derived from domestic prices, they allege that the whole L & M procedure breaks down. (Both Irvin and FitzGerald explicitly include S & T with L & M on this.)

Two points need to be made concerning this version of the issue:

1. The distinction between a non-tradable being an input or an output is not the same as that made by L & M, which involves distinguishing the source of the good being used by the public sector. The real division is between a good coming at the expense of consumption, or coming from an increase in domestic production.

2. Even if all goods that come at the expense of consumption can be called outputs, it is not true that S & T recommend using domestic prices for these cases. As we saw in section 7.2.4, the accounting ratio for these goods is given by the conversion factor β_1. (FitzGerald, p. 368, acknowledges that L & M also suggest using a conversion factor such as β_1.) It is true that one only obtains β_1 by ignoring distribution transfers, and this is also what happens when one uses market prices. But one is free to use the full formula for the MSB given by equation (7.14) if one wishes.

There are two aspects of the argument by Irvin (*et al.*) which are not simple misinterpretations and which require further discussion. The first concerns the judgement by S & T that the decomposition procedure is to be the generally applicable method of valuation for non-tradables.

The second relates to whether β_1 can be used as the accounting ratio for non-tradable outputs.

7.5.1   The applicability of the MSC method

Toye asserts that in only one in a hundred cases would it be appropriate to use the MSC (decomposition procedure) to value non-tradables. It is claimed that most cases would be non-traded outputs, such as health and education, where it is the domestic use value that needs to be obtained. Non-tradable inputs would be rare.

This is a proposition on which it is difficult to pass judgement. It would seem to be invalid, because many public projects in LDCs are intermediate goods (roads, tractors and irrigation) and therefore of the nature of inputs. Certainly, most of the cases cited in this text are of this type. But the point is that the reason there are so few applications of non-tradables of the final output type may be precisely that it is hard to evaluate them!

On this matter, it is safe to take the middle ground. LDCs spend less (absolutely and proportionately) on welfare programmes (health, education, etc.) than do developed countries. Non-tradables as final outputs for the public sector would not be as common as Irvin *et al.* suggest, though S & T probably do overstate the generality of the MSC approach. Given that the MSB method will often have to be used in practice, the next aspect becomes important.

7.5.2   The validity of the MSB method

The crux of the whole debate is contained in the specification of the type of non-traded output with which Irvin *et al.* are concerned. It is *public sector* output that they have in mind. Even if one accepts all the assumptions on which the derivation of β_1 was based, they question the relevance for public sector non-tradables of multiplying the domestic market price by β_1.

The main point can be uncovered by considering a simple example. Assume that the item to be valued involves providing health services in Kenya. Let these services be summarised by a quantity index, such as the number of days in a hospital, and let the hospital charge Kenyan £100 per day. The price charged by the public sector is not likely to be a market clearing price. If the Kenyan £100 price is arbitrary, what is the significance of scaling it down by β_1? Say β_1 has been correctly estimated to be 0.5. The social value of a hospital day would be cal-

culated to be Kenyan £500. But if the price charged could just as well
have been Kenyan £200 per day, then the social value would have to
have been assessed as Kenyan £100. This is so even though the 'true'
social worth of the service has not been altered.

While it does pose a meaningful question, there is a straightforward answer that is consistent with the principles of project appraisal
espoused in this text. We have argued that any project should be assessed on the basis of accepting existing constraints. In this case, the
constraint is that the project evaluater does not have control over the
pricing policy for the project. But whatever the charge that others have
decided for the project, the project has to be assessed on the basis of
this figure. In the S & T general accounting ratio formula there is provision for the size of the expenditure effects by domestic producers and
consumers. These effects are real even though the price that sparked
off these effects was set arbitrarily.

We can draw an analogy with the reasoning used in the determination of the SWR. The wage given for employment on the project may
not be socially optimal. The project evaluater still has to look at the
effects of the actual wage being offered. If the project wage offered
is high relative to the marginal product of labour, consumption will
be reduced. This certainly is a legitimate social cost within the S & T
methodology, irrespective of how the actual wage being offered was
determined.

Appendices

The appendices to this chapter simply provide some of the missing steps
in the derivation of two key results.

Deriving the gain in export earnings

Define the export earnings by R, which is the product of the price of the
product, p, and the quantity sold, X. That is,

$$R = p \cdot X \tag{7.16}$$

Take the total differential of R:

$$dR = p \cdot dX + X \cdot dp \tag{7.17}$$

Divide and multiply $p \cdot dX$ on the right-hand side of equation (7.17)
by $X \cdot dp$:

$$dR = (p \cdot dX/X \cdot dp) X \cdot dp + X \cdot dp = (p \cdot dX/X \cdot dp + 1) X \cdot dp \tag{7.18}$$

By the definition of the price elasticity of demand for exports,

$$\eta_w = -p \cdot dX/(X \cdot dp) \tag{7.19}$$

Substitute equation (7.19) into (7.18) to obtain

$$dR = (-\eta_w + 1) X \cdot dp \tag{7.20}$$

which is the same as equation (7.5) in the text.

Deriving the marginal revenue rule

The definition of marginal revenue, M_R, is the derivative of total revenue, R, with respect to quantity (in this case it is the quantity of the export, X):

$$M_R = dR/dX = d(p \cdot X)/dX \tag{7.21}$$

Using the product rule equation (7.21) becomes

$$M_R = p \cdot dX/dX + X \cdot dp/dX = p[1 + (X \cdot dp)/(p \cdot dX)] \tag{7.22}$$

Substitute the definition of the price elasticity of world demand from equation (7.19) into (7.22) to produce

$$M_R = p (1 - 1/\eta_w) \tag{7.23}$$

Finally, divide both sides of equation (7.23) by p to obtain the result we are seeking:

$$M_R/p = (1 - 1/\eta_w) \tag{7.24}$$

The right-hand side of equation (7.24) is the same as for equation (7.13). So the left-hand sides of the two equations must be the same. That is, the accounting ratio for an exportable with a less than infinite elasticity of demand equals the marginal revenue divided by the price.

8

The standard conversion factor and the shadow exchange rate

8.1   Introduction

In this chapter we complete the analysis of shadow pricing and in the process provide the final piece of the S & T puzzle. We will end up with the first of the formulae given for particular parameters in Chapter 3, i.e. equation (3.7), which defined the consumption conversion factor β. The analysis will, therefore, have turned full circle. We cover parts of Chapters 9 and 12 of S & T. The notation will be defined as we proceed.

When a private firm makes a sale overseas, it has a readily available guide as to what a US dollar is worth in terms of the domestic currency, and vice versa. That guide is the official exchange rate. As pointed out in Chapter 6, any taxes that exist do not lower the cost of anything the firm wishes to purchase domestically with that dollar. But the real (social) domestic cost of the use of foreign exchange is different for the government. Taxes are not a cost (in terms of forgone opportunities) and therefore the shadow price of foreign exchange differs from the official exchange rate. This needs to be borne in mind when we now analyse what the domestic currency is worth in terms of dollars, and what dollars are worth in terms of the domestic currency.

8.1.1   Definition of the SCF

The previous chapter described methods for deriving accounting ratios for non-tradables that were specific to a particular product, e.g. transport. However, it is often useful to have a more general version that can apply to any representative non-tradable. This is the notion of the standard conversion factor, SCF. An SCF was devised to apply to two main sets of circumstances:

1. For any minor non-tradable whose contribution to the project is so small that a more precise estimation would not affect the overall outcome to an appreciable extent, e.g. postage stamps.
2. Non-tradables that remain after one or two rounds of using the decomposition procedure.

The SCF can be defined as the ratio which translates the domestic price for any non-tradable into its border price value, so that the good can be expressed in terms of its real domestic price equivalent. For example, a two-shilling postage stamp obviously has a domestic value of two Kenyan shillings. But not all of this reflects real costs. A part may include domestic market imperfections in the production of postage stamps. Say, a half of the cost reflects inefficiencies. Then the social value of the stamp would be one Kenyan shilling. This can be expressed alternatively using words we have used many times before in our equations. The two shillings in terms of domestic values have a value of one shilling in terms of the numeraire (if the conversion factor is one-half).

From this definition of the SCF we can now see than S & T have, in effect, been working with two other kinds of conversion factor applying to groups of commodities; β was a conversion factor which applied to any consumption good, and α was a conversion factor which applied to any domestic output produced. So we can look upon the SCF as a more general version of α or β. It applies to any non-tradable, irrespective of whether it is a consumption or production good (or a mix of the two).

8.1.2 Definition of the SER

The shadow exchange rate, SER, can be defined as that rate of exchange which accurately reflects the consumption worth of an extra unit of foreign exchange in terms of the domestic currency. Say an extra US dollar is earned by the public project. What domestic consumption value would it buy? If, on average, the dollar could purchase five Kenyan shillings-worth of domestic output, then the SER would be that one dollar is worth five Kenyan shillings.

It is often useful to divide the SER by the official exchange rate, OER. This expresses the value of the SER in terms of dollars. If the OER is that one dollar is convertible into four Kenyan shillings, then the ratio *SER/OER* is 5/4 or 1.25. What this means is that a dollar of foreign exchange has a domestic purchasing power equivalent of 1.25 dollars. It can be considered that there is a 25% premium on a dollar earned abroad and spent at home. That is, the domestic economy would add to its nominal value a further 25% in terms of taxes and other kinds of non-resource, monetary effects.

8.1.3 Relation between the SCF and the SER

Since the SCF and SER perform similar functions, they can be related as follows:

$$SCF/OER = 1/SER \text{ or } SCF = OER/SER \qquad (8.1^*)$$

This reciprocal relation between *SCF* and *SER* will be referred to a number of times. It is therefore useful to have a simple demonstration of its validity. This is provided in the Appendix. For the above example, where *SER/OER* was 1.25, the value for *SCF* would be 1/1.25, or 0.8.

The importance of equation (8.1) is that it shows that there are two separate ways available of estimating the SCF: either it can be measured directly, as will be explained in section 8.3.2 of the applications, or else indirectly, via an estimate of the SER. The S & T approach uses the indirect method and this is explained in the next section.

8.2   S & T's methods

We start by identifying the basic ingredients of an SER. These are used to form the simplest version of the SER, which is the UNIDO formula. We then proceed to a special kind of SER, the free trade exchange rate (FTER). This is the formula recommended by Bacha and Taylor (1971). Finally, we present a simplified version of the FTER – the S & T formula.

8.2.1 The UNIDO SER formula

Let us go back and reconsider the figures used in section 8.1.2. A dollar was earned by the project and it was assumed to have a purchasing power of five Kenyan shillings. This means that the dollar can be spent on an imported good *j* (say, a pack of cigarettes) that has a price of five Kenyan shillings. That is, the domestic price of the cigarettes, p_j, is five Kenyan shillings. With the OER equal to four Kenyan shillings to the dollar, the official cif cost of the cigarettes, p_j^*, is four Kenyan shillings. So, when we said that *SER/OER* is 5/4, we were stating that

$$SER/OER = p_j/p_j^* \qquad (8.2)$$

It is a simple matter to generalise this procedure to the case where a number (m) of different imported goods are purchased with the foreign exchange, for then we need to take a weighted average of the domestic to world price ratios for each of the m goods:

$$SER/OER = \sum_1^m f_j \cdot (pj/p_j^*) \qquad (8.3)$$

where f_j is the proportion of the foreign exchange earned that is spent on import j.

When we allow for part of the foreign exchange to be spent on x would-be exports (as well as on the m imports), *SER/OER* is a weighted average of the domestic to world prices ratios for all $m + x$ traded goods. That is,

$$SER/OER = \sum_1^m f_j \cdot (p_j/p_j^*) + \sum_{m+1}^{m+x} f_j \cdot (p_j/p_j^*) \qquad (8.4)$$

where f_j is now the share of the foreign exchange earned which is spent on the jth tradable. The SER constructed in this way is the UNIDO formula for the shadow price of foreign exchange (see their equation 16.2).

8.2.2 The FTER formula

We have emphasised in the previous two chapters that the determination of any shadow price (and here we are considering the shadow price of foreign exchange) is dependent on the constraints imposed upon the government. In this section we will cover S & T's analysis of the implications for the SER of two kinds of constraint, a balance-of-payments constraint, and trade restrictions.

Devaluation and the SER

In our analysis of the shadow price for tradables (section 6.5.2 and the Appendix), we considered the balance-of-payments adjustment process required by the project's demand for an imported input. In their analysis of the SER, S & T (pp. 93–4) focus on the same kind of balance-of-payments implications (constraint) posed by the project's use of foreign resources. They consider using devaluation as a way of dealing with the balance-of-payments deficit that would result (assuming there was an external balance prior to the project being considered).

When there is a devaluation, the price of imports rises relative to exports. With money wages fixed, people can purchase fewer tradables, and the external deficit falls. With real wages declining, more non-tradables will be produced and this again helps the balance of payments.

S & T consider that the main effects of the devaluation are to be found in shadow price changes other than for foreign exchange. With *w* falling relative to domestic prices, the accounting ratio for labour (*SWR* divided by *p*) declines. This fall, coupled with the increased production of non-tradables referred to above, means that the decomposition procedure would have to be reworked. In sum, the effect of the devaluation will be mainly on the MSCs of non-tradables rather than on the SER.

Free trade and the SER

The FTER can be defined as that exchange rate which would rule if all protectionist barriers were eliminated. With all restrictions on trade removed, the accounting ratios for tradables would be affected as well as those for non-tradables. The removal of tariffs would raise the ratios for imports, and the removal of subsidies would lower those for exports. These changes in social prices would be accompanied by changes in domestic market prices. The quantities of the tradables produced would alter and this would in turn change the composition of the goods included in the UNDIO SER formula.

The extent of the change in the composition of tradables would depend on the responsiveness of consumers and producers to the market price changes, i.e. the elasticities of import demand (η_j) and export supply (e_j). When these elasticities are considered, one is dealing with what is known as the FTER, or the Bacha–Taylor SER. We use below the formulation of the FTER given in Balassa, 1974, equation (5):

$$FTER/OER = \frac{\sum_{m+1}^{m+x} e_j \cdot X_j \, (1 - t_j) + \sum_{1}^{m} \eta_j \cdot M_j \, (1 + t_j)}{\sum_{m+1}^{m+x} e_j \cdot X_j + \sum_{1}^{m} \eta_j \cdot M_j} \tag{8.5}$$

where X_j is the expenditure on export *j*, M_j is the expenditure on import *j*, and t_j is the relevant import or export tax. Equation (8.5) can be regarded as replacing the f_j shares in the UNIDO formula with the e_j and η_j elasticities (and using expenditures – prices times quantities – rather than simply prices).

S & T work with a simplified version of the FTER. This replaces the commodity-specific elasticities and taxes with an average for all commodities. With *e* as the average export demand elasticity, η as the average import supply elasticity, t_x as the average export tax, and t_m as the average import tax, the S & T version takes the following form:

$$FTER/OER = \frac{e \cdot X(1 - t_x) + \eta \cdot M(1 + t_m)}{e \cdot X + \eta \cdot M} \qquad (8.6)$$

Irvin (1978, p. 107) points out that the FTER has special relevance in the S & T context for the category of potentially traded goods. For these goods, we need to know whether existing restriction policies on trade are to continue. If they are, the potentially traded goods are to be treated as non-tradables; and if the restrictions are to be removed, then the goods are to be treated as tradables. But if all protectionist policies are removed, there are some general equilibrium effects which have to be analysed. There are two important aspects: (a) the set of traded and non-traded goods alters; (b) there is a change in the structure of domestic prices, and hence the pattern of consumption is altered. The FTER does try to accommodate the first aspect, while only reworking the decomposition procedure (and the accounting ratio for labour) will allow for the second aspect.

8.2.3   The S & T formula

Since the concern is with providing an (indirect) estimate of the SCF and not the SER, it is the reciprocal of equation (8.6) that S & T actually present. That is,

$$OER/FTER = \frac{e \cdot X + \eta \cdot M}{e \cdot X(1 - t_x) + \eta \cdot M(1 + t_m)} \qquad (8.7^*)$$

S & T (p. 96) consider one final simplification. 'In the event that no information is available on the elasticities, a reasonable approximation is to assume the elasticities are the same.' With $e = \eta$ in equation (8.6), and using equation (8.1), we obtain

$$SCF = \frac{X + M}{X(1 - t_x) + M(1 + t_m)} \qquad (8.8)$$

But, as the right-hand side of equation (8.8) is the same as the right-hand side of equation (3.7), their left-hand sides must be equal. We therefore end up with the interesting result that

$$SCF = \beta \qquad (8.9)$$

We can now give an alternative interpretation of the formula for the consumption conversion factor that we used to start off the detailed analysis of parameter values given in Chapter 3. Parameter β is an oversimplified version of the reciprocal of the Bacha–Taylor FTER!

The only outstanding issue is to examine to what extent β is a good approximation of this particular SER. S & T consider alternative values for e and η in equation (8.7) that range between 1 and 6 (where $M = X$, $t_m = 0.3$, and $t_x = -0.05$). As the ratio *OER/FTER* only varies between 0.79 and 0.92, S & T conclude that equation (8.7) is not very sensitive to different assumptions concerning the elasticities.

However, S & T (p. 96, fn 17) point out two main differences between the SCF and the ratio OER/FTER – i.e. equations (8.7) and (8.8) – that do not relate to the elasticities. First, the SCF includes the effects of tariffs and quotas, while the FTER excludes these restrictions. In short, the Xs and Ms may not be the same in the two expressions. Secondly, the definitions of the taxes in the two formulae are not the same. The SCF allows for sales taxes, while the FTER only includes taxes or restrictions relating to foreign trade.

8.3   Measurement practice

The following applications illustrate both direct and indirect methods for estimating the SCF.

8.3.1 An indirect estimate of the SCF for Turkey

Mashayekhi (1980), in his study of shadow prices for Turkey, used the oversimplified FTER formula to estimate the SCF, as in equation (8.8). That is,

$$SCF = \frac{X + M}{X(1 - t_x) + M(1 + t_m)}$$

There are four variables in this formula that need to be quantified, X, M, t_x and t_m. Mashayekhi took the average values for the years 1974–8. The trade figures are in millions of US dollars.

$X + M = 6,595$: The balance of trade was in deficit throughout the period, with a cif figure for imports equal to 4808, and a fob figure for exports equal to 1,787.

$(1 + t_m) = 1.91$: Imports had five different types of taxes on them:

1. Customs duty.
2. Stamp duty.
3. Customs surcharge.

4. Quay duty.
5. Production tax.

All these taxes combined to set the average import tax rate at 31.0%. In addition, Turkey had a number of non-tariff restrictions, rationing and exchange controls that Mashayekhi interpreted as acting like an imperfect tax system. This required adding a 'premium rate' to imports of 60%. The total import tax rate was therefore 91%, being the sum of the explicit tax (31%) and the implicit tax (60%).

$(1 - t_x) = 1.076$: Exports in Turkey were eligible to receive a rebate of 7.6%, which means there was a negative tax on exports. Since the formula contains $-t_x$, with t_x negative, we have to *add* the rebate.

Substitution of the above values for the four variables into the SCF formula produces this estimate for Turkey:

$$SCF = \frac{6595}{1787\,(1.076) + 4808\,(1.91)} = 0.59$$

The SER corresponding to this SCF is 1.69 (1/0.59) times the OER. This made the SER equal to 47.2 Turkish liras to the dollar. Mashayekhi regarded this as a good estimate because it was very close to the effective market rate that followed a series of substantial devaluations in Turkey.

8.3.2 A direct estimate of the SCF for Kenya

Instead of using the SER concept, S & T (p.130) suggest an alternative estimation procedure for the SCF. This concentrates on the role of the SCF as a typical accounting ratio. For the SCF to be considered typical, it should be the accounting ratio that would relevant on the average. By estimating the accounting ratios for a large number of goods, and then taking the average (or some other statistical measure of central tendency) one can obtain a direct measure of the SCF.

Scott, MacArthur and Newberry (1976) used this direct method in their study of land resettlement in Kenya (1976: Table 10 on pp. 203–5 contains accounting ratio estimates for 126 goods). A summary of the results is presented in Table 8.1. When a distribution has a number of extreme values, the average is a poor representative of the data. Extreme values are particularly evident with the accounting ratios for imports. In such cases, the median is a better guide as to what is typical. Consequently, Scott *et al.* used the median to summarise the accounting ratios for each distribution identified in Table 8.1. The median for all categories combined is 0.8. This, then, is the estimate of the SCF.

Table 8.1   Accounting ratios for goods and services in Kenya

Category	Median	Standard deviation	Lowest	Highest
Traded exports	1.00	0.25	0.52	1.42
Traded imports	0.86	0.25	0.43	1.87
Consumption	0.82	0.14	0.45	1.00
Non-traded	0.77	0.06	0.62	0.90
All combined	0.80	0.21	0.43	1.87

Alternatively, we can say that the SER for Kenya was 1.25 times the official exchange rate.

Aside from providing the SCF estimate, Scott *et al.* use their results to make two interesting observations.

1. An illuminating way of looking at the median values of accounting ratios for any of the categories is to view them as reflecting 'effective rates of protection'. A value of 1 can be interpreted as no protection, less than 1 is positive protection, and greater than 1 is negative protection. Consistent with many effective rates of protection studies, imports in Kenya were protected (the median is 0.86) while exports were not (the median was equal to 1). This is what one expects with import substitution policies.

2. An issue separate from that of central tendency is the dispersion around the median. All other things being equal, the greater the standard deviation or the range (the difference between the highest and lowest values), the less representative is the median. The export and import accounting ratios have large standard deviations (both equal to 0.25) and the range for imports is particularly high at 1.44. This means that one has to measure their accounting ratios carefully. On the other hand, the accounting ratios for non-tradables have little dispersion (the standard deviation is 0.06 and the range is 0.28). It is this close grouping that makes it sensible to adopt the short-cut procedure of taking a single ratio for all of them (i.e. 0.8).

It is instructive to consider why the dispersion is so low for non-tradables. Recall that the main S & T method for deriving the accounting ratio for a non-tradable was to decompose the good into its four constituents (traded, taxes, primary and non-traded). The resulting accounting ratio is a weighted average of the accounting ratios for the four constituents. It is a basic principle in statistics that the standard deviation of population averages is much less than the standard deviation of the population as a whole. Thus it is to be expected that the standard deviation for non-tradables would be lower, as it involves just such an averaging procedure.

8.4   Problems

By now all the essential ingredients to the S & T methodology have been covered and one is in a position to undertake a complete project appraisal from start to finish. The data is based on the Pakistan tractor project study by Tyler (1979). Do not be too concerned about reproducing precisely Tyler's set of figures because (a) the data is not always the same as for Tyler, and (b) showing an understanding of the principles of project appraisal is more important.

Background information

Table 8.2 shows the distribution of income in the project area before and after the introduction of the tractors. The 202 big farmers increased their acreage at the expense of the 879 small farmers who were effectively dispossessed. The small farmers became unemployed and 'lost' all their income. However, their consumption did not fall to zero as they received 100 rupees per head as assistance from their relatives.

Of the 2,236 full-time workers existing prior to the introduction of the tractors, 828 became unemployed and received the same amount of family assistance as the small farmers, 912 continued as full-time workers, and 496 obtained positions as casual labour, earning the average casual labour income of 844 rupees. The 660 casual workers existing prior to the project were relatively unaffected. All of these changes are summarised in Table 8.3 for the categories affected by the project. Information is also given about household size and consumption/saving behaviour. Average consumption per head in the economy as a whole was 552 rupees. Table 8.4 provides figures for the project inputs and outputs in terms of domestic prices (in thousands of rupees per year).

Table 8.2   Distribution effects before and after the Pakistan tractor project

Category income	Number	BEFORE		Number	AFTER	
		Average income (rupees)	Total income (1,000s)		Average income (rupees)	Total income (1,000s)
Big farmers	202	8,990	1,816	202	27,153	5,485
Small farmers	879	1,923	1,690	0	0	0
Full-time workers	2,236	1,404	3,139	912	1,404	1,280
Casual labour	660	844	557	1,156	844	976
Receivers of land rent	?	?	691	?	?	691
Government tractor Fuel tax						1,495
Total income			7,893			9,927

Table 8.3 Summary of the effects on the four affected groups in the Pakistan tractor project

Category	No. of households	Household size	Average household income	Average household saving	Average household consumption
Before					
Big farmers	202	8.5	8,990	1,970	7,020
Small farmers	879	4.5	1,923	151	1,772
Full-time workers	2,236	4.0	1,404	0	1,404
Casual workers	660	4.0	844	0	844
After					
Big farmers	202	8.5	27,153	1,970	25,183
Unemployed small farmers	879	4.5	0	0	450
Full-time workers	912	4.0	1,404	0	1,404
Casual workers	1,156	4.0	844	0	844
Unemployed full-time workers	828	4.0	0	0	400

Table 8.4 Inputs and outputs in domestic prices for the Pakistan tractor project

Additional inputs		Additional outputs	
Traded:		Traded:	
Cash crop inputs	485	Cash crop outputs	3,409
Tractor fuel	369	Other	612
Tubewell running costs	867		
Non-traded:		Non-traded:	
Livestock fodder	−58	None	
Tractor repairs	324		
Additional value added:	2,034		
Total	4,021	Total	4,021

The items listed took place for each of seven years. Note that the additional value added of 2,034 is the difference between total income after (9,927) and total income before (7,893) the project, as itemised in Table 8.2. All traded inputs connected with the project listed in Table 8.4 have included in their values a tariff which is 90% of the domestic price figure recorded. There were no other domestic cost components connected with the tradables. An independent study estimated the SCF to be 0.7.

The initial capital cost, which was incurred a full year before any of the ongoing input/output effects, was 5,231 thousand rupees (the cif price converted to domestic prices at the OER). As the tractors were imported and there was an import levy of 1,010 rupees, the total capital cost was 6,241 thousand rupees.

Pakistan financed the purchase of tractors by a loan from the World Bank at a rate of 10% per annum. The marginal rate of return on public investment in Pakistan at the time was also 10%. The government of Pakistan has shown a varied emphasis on economic growth in the past. At times it has valued a rupee to itself at 1.5 times that of a rupee to private sector consumption at the average level of consumption, while at other times this value was as high as 4.0. While concern over the distribution of income did exist, it had not been acute. So it is expected that the 'typical' World Bank weighting parameter be used. During the project period, the economy as a whole had a trade balance (the level of exports equalled the level of imports). The average tariff rate on imports was 40% and average export duties were 20%.

Question

The World Bank has commissioned you to prepare a report to make an assessment of the actual introduction of tractors into a project area in Pakistan. Present your appraisal separately in both economic efficiency and in social terms. You are expected to explain fully and justify the assumptions you use. In your summary of the effects of the tractor project, please include some comments on whether any major considerations have been excluded from your calculations.

8.5   Discussion

As Scott (1974, p. 182) points out, the problems encountered in estimating the SCF (SER) are the same as those in estimating shadow prices generally. The following discussion therefore looks at the SCF in the light of the previous S & T analysis of shadow prices.

8.5.1   The validity of using the FTER as a basis for the SCF

We have stressed many times the presumption that project appraisal is to be carried out accepting existing constraints on government control over the economic and political environment. In this context it is strange to accept the FTER as a basis for the SCF, seeing that it assumes the elimination of all restrictions on international trade. The correct starting point would seem to be the UNIDO formula which presupposes the continuation of the government constraints on trade. Strictly, then, the S & T formula presented in equation (8.8) should be considered an oversimplified version of the UNIDO formulation and not the Bacha–Taylor SER. A comparison of equations (8.4) and (8.8) shows that the oversimplification stems from two differences between S & T and UNIDO (apart from the reciprocal dimension discussed in the next chapter):

1. The S & T version uses as weights the existing shares of total imports or exports devoted to a particular good, while the UNIDO formulation uses the shares spent from the increased foreign exchange earned.
2. The UNIDO version divides each good's domestic price by the world price and then sums, while the S & T version sums all domestic prices and then divides by the sum of all world prices.

Of course, the point just made assumes that one is using the indirect method to estimate the SCF. If one uses the direct method, there is just one difference between the UNIDO and the S & T formulations. The UNIDO version takes a weighted average of the accounting ratios, while the S & T version uses the simple average (strictly, the median) of the accounting ratios.

8.5.2 The appropriateness of using β as a measure of the SCF

It was stated in the last chapter that the fundamental problem of the S & T approach to estimating shadow prices for non-tradables was thought to arise when one is dealing with non-tradable public outputs. We suggested that this problem was overstated if one is aware that S & T have a method for dealing with these cases, i.e. using β_1 as the accounting ratio. But the use of the S & T SCF seems to blur many issues. The problem lies in using β as the SCF, as will now be explained.

Instead of using the decomposition procedure for small non-tradables, one is to use the SCF which, if one uses β as the SCF, means using β. When β is not much different from β_1 (and, in fact, S & T suggest on p. 127 using β as the MSB), one is using the MSB to measure the MSC! At a minimum, this vitiates S & T's claim on p. 125 that the MSC should be the method for estimating the accounting ratios for non-tradables 'unless there is specific information to the contrary'.

It seems desirable to keep a clear separation between β and the SCF. One way of doing this is to follow the lead of Mashayekhi (1980) in his study of shadow prices in Turkey. Although he does actually use equation (8.8) to estimate the SCF, Mashayekhi (p. 22) uses a slightly different version for calculating β. This employs only those exports or imports devoted to consumption. Mashayekhi's version can be expressed as

$$\beta = \frac{X_c + M_c}{X_c(1 - t_{xc}) + M_c(1 + t_{mc})} \tag{8.10}$$

where X_c is consumption exports, M_c is consumption imports, t_{xc} is the tax rate on consumption exports and t_{mc} is the tax on consumption imports.

Equation (8.10) is a natural definition of β given that it is the *consumption* conversion factor. However, for Turkey, there was very little difference in the SCF estimate using equation (8.8) and the β estimate using equation (8.10). The SCF was 0.8, while β was 0.79 (again using the 60% premium rate on imports).

8.5.3   *Whether to include tradables in the SCF*

Bhagwati and Srinivasan (1981, p. 397) question the inclusion of tradables in the list of goods which are to determine the average/median under the direct method for estimating the SCF.

They first equation the logic of using tradables in an index which is supposed to reflect a typical non-tradable. However, this point is easily countered when we recall from section 8.3.2 that the decomposition method (which is the recommended approach for dealing with non-tradables) basically relies on a weighted average of traded goods.

Bhagwati and Srinivasan raise a second point which is more valid (though, strictly, it does not relate specifically to the issue of whether to include tradables in the SCF). When there is interdependence among shadow prices, as with transport depending on construction and construction depending on transport, one can hardly use the accounting ratio of transport (whose precise decomposition is known) in the SCF to determine the accounting ratio for construction (whose precise decomposition is unknown).

Appendix

The only task in the appendix is to verify the relation between the SCF and the SER given in the text.

The inverse relation between the SCF and the SER

Consider the case of a single tradable which does not have any domestic taxes on it. Its domestic price, p, will then be the world price, p^*, expressed in domestic terms by the SER. That is,

$$p = p^* \cdot SER \tag{8.11}$$

The SCF, where there is a single good, is (using the direct estimation method) the AR of the particular tradable, which was defined in Chapter 7 as the ratio of the world to the domestic price. This means

$$SCF = p^*/p \tag{8.12}$$

Substituting for p from (8.11) into the denominator of equation (8.12) produces the inverse relation we were seeking:

$$SCF = p^*/(p^* \cdot SER) = 1/SER \tag{8.13}$$

PART 2
Further issues in project appraisal

9

Comparison of methods I

9.1　Introduction

This is the first of two chapters dealing with alternative methods of project appraisal. There are three main methods: the UNIDO, the L & M, and the Bruno & Kruger approaches (hereafter B & K). For the purposes of this chapter, S & T's work will be identified with the L & M method (for the reason explained in section 9.1.2).

Apart from showing what alternative methods are available and indicating their relative merits, this chapter serves a more fundamental purpose. It explains clearly the basic problem which any comprehensive method of project appraisal is required to solve. Thus one obtains a greater appreciation of exactly why project appraisal was developed in the first place.

In the last chapter we showed the inverse relation between the SCF and the SER. This relation is exploited in this chapter to show the general equivalence between the L & M and UNIDO methods. However, we now also consider situations where this inverse relation does not hold. Identifying the circumstances under which the conditions hold is the main task of this chapter.

The theory underlying this chapter comes from Lal (1974) and Irvin (1978, pp. 82–91). Rather than invent numbers as these authors do, we will illustrate the main points by referring to the Stern (1972) case study with which we are already familiar. For simplicity, we can assume that all projects last just one year. There will then be no need to consider discounting.

9.1.1   Which methods will be compared

Although three main methods exist, there are really only two alternative procedures that need to be compared, i.e. L & M and UNIDO.
This is because, as we shall see in section 9.3.1, the B & K method can
be regarded as a variant of the UNIDO approach. However, given the
emphasis placed by the international trade literature on the Bruno &
Kruger method, we will examine B & K further in the next chapter.

9.1.2   Basis of the comparison

The basis of comparison between L & M and UNIDO will be in terms
of the choice of numeraire. Obviously, there are many other differences
between the two approaches, but we concentrate only on the numeraire
issue for two main reasons:

1. Some differences between L & M and UNIDO have become out-
dated. For instance, the original L & M (1969) manual did not allow
for (intragenerational) distributional considerations, while this was
included in the revised L & M (1974) version.

2. Many of the other differences are not relevant for us because we are
not dealing in this text with the 'pure' L & M method. We are examining the S & T version which is really a compromise method. For example, the SWR differs between the two main approaches (L & M and
UNIDO). However, S & T follow neither (i.e. they include the disutility
of effort effect which does not appear in either L & M or UNIDO).

   Because the numeraire is the basis of comparison, and S & T share
the same numeraire as L & M, we can equate S & T with L & M in this
chapter. As both L & M and UNIDO include distributional weights and
a premium on investment, we can make our comparisons abstracting
from these issues.

9.1.3   Nature of the market imperfection

In Chapter 1 we pointed out that one of the reasons for undertaking a
social rather than a private evaluation of a project is the presumption
that market imperfections are large (and largest in LDCs). The following analysis will concentrate on just one cause of market imperfections,

i.e. protectionism. A tariff will be imposed on domestic imports. It must not be forgotten, however, that in Chapter 6 we derived the shadow price for tradables in a setting where there were other causes of market distortion (as in the Diamond and Mirrlees theorem where no lump sum income taxes exist, and commodity taxes have to be imposed on domestic prices to achieve efficiency and distributional objectives).

9.2   The main methods

Before outlining each of the main methods, we will present what Irvin calls a rudimentary approach to solving the basic problem. It is then a simple matter to see how the main methods improve on the rudimentary approach.

Consider a project which produces an export good (X) and uses both domestic inputs (D) and foreign inputs (M): X and M are measured in border prices (dollars), while D is expressed in domestic prices (shillings). As M is imported, its domestic price includes a tariff. The project has to be evaluated in the light of the tariff distortion. All methods of project appraisal recognise that the tax is not a real cost of production. The tax needs to be subtracted from the domestic price of the import, which leaves us with the border price of M. The social net benefits would then be

$$S = \$ X - \$ M - D \text{ shillings} \qquad (9.1)$$

One immediately sees in equation (9.1) the basic problem to be solved. The traded goods are expressed in different units (currencies) from the domestic input. A rudimentary approach would convert the dollar prices at the official exchange rate (OER) to produce an outcome expressed entirely in shillings. The social net benefits of the project would then be

$$S = X \, (OER) \text{ shillings} - M \, (OER) \text{ shillings} - D \text{ shillings} \qquad (9.2)$$

The drawback with the rudimentary approach is that the OER is, like any market price, subject to distortions. The OER may not, therefore, be a good guide to the social value of foreign exchange. Recall that we started our analysis with the assumption that there was a tariff. We know, then, that the domestic price structure is distorted, there being too much internal use of domestic production. Because there is this over-use of domestic resources, other methods of project evaluation have been devised in order to prevent tradables being undervalued and domestic production being overvalued.

9.2.1 The UNIDO method

The UNIDO solution is to scale up the values for the tradables. This requires finding the domestic purchasing power equivalent to the dollars associated with the tradables. In other words, UNIDO use the SER. With the SER replacing the OER, the social net benefits become

$$S = X \, (SER) \text{ shillings} - M \, (SER) \text{ shillings} - D \text{ shillings} \qquad \textbf{(9.3)}$$

The social net benefits in equation (9.3) are, like equation (9.2), expressed in shillings. But S will be larger under the UNIDO method if the project is a net contributor to foreign exchange (i.e. $X > M$). This follows because the SER is larger than the OER (when the domestic currency is overvalued).

9.2.2 The L & M method

L & M tackle the problem from the reverse direction. They concentrate on the overvalued domestic production. The value of D is scaled down to provide its value in terms of foreign exchange, which is considered more valuable. As the nature of the domestic input is unspecified, we can use the SCF as the relevant conversion factor. In which case the L & M social net benefits (S^*) become

$$S^* = \$X - \$M - \$D \, (SCF) \qquad \textbf{(9.4)}$$

The social net benefits are now in dollar units. But this in itself is not of any consequence. For we can, as we did when expositing the L & M approach, express values in terms of the domestic currency by using the OER. The L & M social evaluation based on equation (9.4) would then appear as

$$S^* = X \, (OER) \text{ shillings} - M \, (OER) \text{ shillings}$$
$$- D \, (SCF \cdot OER) \text{ shillings} \qquad \textbf{(9.5)}$$

9.2.3 The Bruno & Kruger method

Rather than deal with net benefits solely in terms of domestic prices, or solely in terms of border prices, B & K deal with domestic prices relative to border prices. In this way they are effectively dealing with the concept of a foreign exchange rate. There are two exchange rates involved in their method. The first is the exchange rate generated by the project itself, which is called the 'domestic resource cost' in the literature. The project transforms domestic inputs in terms of shillings (given by D) into foreign exchange earnings in terms of dollars (given by $X - M$). The ratio $D/(X - M)$ can be regarded as the domestic cost per unit of foreign exchange that the project produces. The second exchange rate is the one that assesses the desirability of obtaining dollars, i.e. the SER. If the benefit (desirability) of obtaining the dollars is greater than the cost of producing them via the project, then the project is worthwhile. The social evaluation of the project entails checking that

$$SER > D/(X - M) \tag{9.6}$$

This comparison deals directly with the problem of the overvaluation of domestic production (undervaluation of tradables) caused by the tariff, for if domestic production is overvalued, projects that produce dollars will be 'cost effective' (see Chapter 12).

9.3 Comparing the methods

The first task will be to dismiss B & K as an independent project appraisal method. Attention will then be given to a comparison between UNIDO and L & M. The comparisons are made at two levels. We start by showing the general equivalence between the two methods. Then we proceed to deal with any differences that may arise from the detailed implementation of the two methods.

9.3.1 Bruno & Kruger and UNIDO

The B & K method can be regarded as a version of UNIDO. They use exactly the same kind of information as UNIDO, so their approach cannot be considered an independent method. To see this, let us reconsider the UNIDO formulation given by equation (9.3). The social net benefits would be positive ($S > 0$) provided that

$$X\,(SER)\ \text{shillings} - M\,(SER)\ \text{shillings} - D\ \text{shillings} > 0 \tag{9.7}$$

This can be rearranged as follows:

$$X\,(SER)\ \text{shillings} - M\,(SER)\ \text{shillings} > D\ \text{shillings}$$
$$X\,(SER) \qquad - M\,(SER) \qquad > D$$
$$(X - M)\,(SER) \qquad > D$$

which results in

$$(SER) \qquad > D/(X - M) \tag{9.8}$$

Equation (9.8) is exactly the B & K method set out in equation (9.6). The only difference involved in using B & K is in the way they re-arrange the information. Lal (1974) points out that most economists are familiar with the NPV and IRR criteria. The B & K method has the disadvantage of unfamiliarity, and no compensating advantages.

9.3.2   UNIDO and L & M in outline

In comparing UNIDO and L & M (or S and S^*) the important aspect is not that one outcome is measured in shillings and one is measured in dollars, for we have already seen that L & M's project evaluation can be expressed in terms of shillings – equation (9.5) can replace (9.4). What is notable is that the two methods are using different numeraires. UNIDO are using domestic prices, while L & M are using world prices. The issue then is whether there is any material difference involved with using the alternative numeraires.

Under certain conditions (to be identified now and examined in the section 9.3.3) the two methods are equivalent. It is not that the numerical outcomes are identical, but the two methods will approve (and reject) the same sets of projects and give identical rankings, for one outcome is a simple proportional relation to the other outcome, as we shall now demonstrate.

Let us see what happens when the UNIDO criterion is multiplied by OER/SER. Equation (9.3) becomes

$$S \, (OER/SER) = X \, (OER) \text{ shillings} - M \, (OER) \text{ shillings}$$
$$- D \, (OER/SER) \text{ shillings} \qquad \textbf{(9.9)}$$

When we compare equation (9.9) with equation (9.5) we see that

$$S \, (OER/SER) = S^* \text{ if (and only if) } SCF = 1/SER \qquad \textbf{(9.10)}$$

Equation (9.10) states that provided that the UNIDO's SER is the reciprocal of L & M's SCF, S and S^* are proportionally related (with OER/SER the proportionality factor). That there would be a reciprocal relation between SER and SCF was demonstrated in the last chapter. Equation (8.1) stated

$$SCF = OER/SER \qquad \textbf{(9.11)}$$

This is precisely the reciprocal relation required in equation (9.10), except for the inclusion of OER on the numerator. However, the ex-clusion of OER from equation (9.10) can be easily explained. Equation (9.5), which was used to establish the relation in equation (9.10), was the L & M version (9.4) multiplied by the OER. So we had already allowed for the OER. (We had to use the OER to convert the dollar amounts into shillings, which was the currency outcome under UNIDO.)

To illustrate the equivalence between the two numeraires, let us reconsider the Kenya small-holder tea project. The skeleton appraisal had tea exports of 41m lb, the tea price using *OER* was three shillings, there were no imports, labour costs were 153.4m shillings, and the *SCF* was 0.75. The OER was automatically incorporated into the calculations. For the current exercise, we need to make the OER explicit. The OER will be taken to be eight shillings to the dollar. In terms of equation (9.5), the L & M criterion would have produced

$X(OER)$ = 123m shillings   (41m × 3 shillings)
$M(OER)$ = 0m shillings
$D(SCF)$ = 115m shillings   (153.4m shillings × 0.75)

and

S^* =   8m shillings   (123m − 115m shillings)

(Note that this is the same outcome as for S & T in Chapter 6, seeing that eight Kenyan shillings are equal to 0.4 Kenyan pounds.)

Now let us make the evaluation from the point of view of UNIDO. To use their method we need to know the price of tea in dollars. Since the price of tea was three shillings using the OER, the dollar price must have been $\frac{3}{8}$, i.e. 0.375 dollars per lb. This makes the export earnings for the 41m lb equal to 15.375m dollars. The only additional information required involves the SER. Let the SER for Kenya be 10.67 shillings to the dollar. Inserting the relevant information into equation (9.3) produces

$X(SER)$ =   164m shillings   (15.374m × 10.67 shillings)
$M(SER)$ =   0m shillings
D = 153.4m shillings

and

S = 10.6m shillings   (164m − 153.4m shillings)

The numeraires are different, so the magnitudes of the two outcomes do not correspond. But, by multiplying S (10.6m) by OER/SER (8/10.67 = 0.75) we can actually get identical numerical outcomes (8m). That is, $S × 0.75 = S^*$.

The conclusion is that the two methods produce evaluations which are, in general, very similar. The choice of numeraire will not, by itself, decide the fate of any project.

9.3.3   *UNIDO and L & M in detail*

From the outset, we must emphasise the conditional nature of the equi-valence result. As specified in equation (9.10), the two methods differ only by the proportionality factor provided that the SCF is the reci-procal of the SER. It is only in the special case where the SER was 10.67 shillings to the dollar that the UNIDO outcome could be trans-formed into the L & M outcome; 10.67 shillings to the dollar was the 'right' amount for *SER* because, in line with equation (9.11), the re-ciprocal of *SCF* (0.75) was 1.33, and 1.33 multiplied by *OER* (eight shillings to the dollar) results in an *SER* of 10.67 shillings to the dollar. For any other magnitude of *SER*, the two outcomes would not be the same.

The main issue of the choice of numeraire then reduces to one of de-termining the circumstances under which the two methods would, and would not, use the reciprocal relation between the SER and the SCF. The condition corresponding to the fulfilment of the reciprocal relation is that the marginal trade bill must correspond to labour's forgone pro-duct. The rest of this section is devoted to an explanation of what this condition is actually stating. We first deal with the condition from the UNIDO point of view.

The UNIDO SER formula was given in Chapter 8 as

$$SER/OER = \sum_{1}^{m} f_j \cdot (p_j/p_j^*) + \sum_{m+1}^{m+x} f_j \cdot (p_j/p_j^*) \qquad \textbf{(8.4)}$$

where the f_js were the shares of any additional foreign exchange earned spent on tradable j, and the p_j/p_j^*s were the ratios of domestic to world prices (the inverses of the S & T accounting ratios). As a first appro-ximation, we can imagine UNIDO using average ratios for imports and exports. The UNIDO SER formula would simplify to the following:

$$SER/OER = f_X \cdot (p_X/p_X^*) + f_M \cdot (p_M/p_M^*) \qquad \textbf{(9.12)}$$

where f_X is the share spent on exports as a whole, f_M the share spent on imports as a whole, and the bracketed terms are the average ratios for exports and imports respectively. In this form, the ratios given in Table 8.1 can be used (based on Scott, MacArthur and Newberry's 1976 study of land resettlement in Kenya). (Note, the SCF suggested by the cal-culations of Scott *et al.* was 0.8, which is reasonably close to the 0.75 used by Stern.) The average (median) accounting ratio for exportables in Kenya was unity. Its inverse, p_X/p_X^*, which appears in equation (8.4), must also be unity. The median accounting ratio for importables in Kenya was 0.86. Its inverse, p_M/p_M^*, is 1.16. The shares can be assumed to take a 50/50 split (i.e. $f_X = f_M = 0.5$). Using these values the UNIDO SER for Kenya becomes

$$SER/OER = 0.5\ (1) + 0.5\ (1.16) = 1.08 \qquad (9.13)$$

One would *not* then obtain the same result as with the L & M method, for their *SER/OER* was 1.33 (10.67/8).

The first idea contained in the equivalence condition is that the products (and their shares) appearing in the UNIDO SER formula given by equation (8.4) must be the *marginal* ones that correspond to the particular project being evaluated. The wage income earned on the project is spent on a whole bundle of goods, not all of which are tradables. The non-tradables have lower accounting ratios, which makes their inverses (p_j/p_j^*) higher. This explains why the UNIDO SER as measured by equation (9.12) produces a ratio of 1.08 which is lower than the 1.33 of L & M. It excludes the non-tradable components. A *project-specific* SER must be used by UNIDO to satisfy the equivalence condition.

When D contains inputs other than labour, the differences between the two methods become even larger. For instance, the Kenya tea project involved transporting the tea by rail to Mombasa in order to ship the tea overseas. The decomposition procedure applied to rail transport showed that rail had a 38.6% tradable component. For the UNIDO method to accommodate this effect fully, not only would the SER have to include the non-tradable rail transport as one of the goods, but it would also have to alter the base to which the SER applies. That is, the first part of equation (9.3) has $X - M$ times the SER. The foreign exchange reduction caused by the tea transportation needs to be deducted from the direct $X - M$ effect.

The main conclusion can now be stated. If the equivalence relation is to hold, UNIDO have to trace through not just the direct foreign exchange effects of the project, but also the indirect foreign exchange effects embodied in the L & M decomposition procedure. In practice, one can expect UNIDO to fail to carry out such a full foreign exchange analysis. Hence, we can regard L & M as the complete method of project appraisal, and the UNIDO approach as an approximation to the L & M method.

The reasoning behind this conclusion can be reproduced by looking at the equivalence condition from the L & M point of view. When D contains labour as the only domestic input, one can regard the SCF as a part of an SWR formula, i.e. $SWR = SCF \cdot w$. This SWR is like equations (5.8) and (5.9), with the SCF taking the place of the conversion factors, β and α respectively. Actually, Ahmed's (1983) study of the SWR in Thailand (reported in section 5.3.1) used precisely the formula $SWR = SCF \cdot w$, seeing that he used an average conversion factor to replace α. With this interpretation, $SCF \cdot w$ represents labour's forgone marginal product. The goods forgone by not using labour on small-holder tea plantations would be the tradables generated by the tea project, i.e. $X - M$. By putting $SCF = 0.75$, Stern is stating that the tradables are 1.33 (1/0.75) times more valuable than the domestic resource. If UNIDO were to use an SER/OER value of 1.33, then the marginal trade bill that they would be employing would be labour's forgone product, as stated in the equivalence condition.

But when D consists also of non-labour domestic inputs, non-tradables are a part of labour's forgone marginal product. There would not be any reason for the reciprocal relation between the SCF and the SER, seeing that the UNIDO SER formula is defined in terms of tradables only. As pointed out by Scott (1974), the UNIDO formula excludes unskilled labour and domestic distribution margins, elements which contain domestic consumption and which would thus be scaled down under L & M. One would expect their accounting ratios to be lower, making SER/OER higher than under L & M, and hence its reciprocal – which is effectively the UNIDO SCF – will be smaller than the L & M SCF.

It is true that there is always going to be a figure for SER/OER that will make the UNIDO outcome numerically the same as the L & M outcome. But let us see what this implies. In general, D will consist of labour, consumption and non-tradables. The L & M (and S & T) method would use the output conversion factor (α) for valuing labour, the consumption conversion factor (β) for valuing consumption, and the decomposition procedure for non-tradables. In Chapter 7 it was explained that using the decomposition procedure was like producing a particular conversion factor for each non-tradable. The decomposition procedure thus generates a whole set of conversion factors in addition to α and β. What all this means is that UNIDO is using one parameter to pick up the effects of a large number of conversion factors employed by L & M. Without actually estimating all of the conversion factors, how can the correct average figure be calculated by UNIDO?

Because one cannot expect UNIDO to calculate all the L & M conversion factors to obtain the necessary weighted average, we again reach the main conclusion that the UNIDO approach is an approximate version of the L & M method. We restate the conclusion as follows. Although the two methods can be considered to be equivalent in principle, the key difference lies in the level of disaggregation. L & M use a series of conversion factors while UNIDO effectively use but one omnibus conversion factor.

9.4   Problems

Even when the UNIDO and L & M methods are equivalent, there is still a further issue involved with the way that the methods allow for the tariff. Both methods follow the rudimentary approach in that they do not treat the tax as a real cost. This deals with the issue from a social point of view, but not from a private perspective. The tax still has to be paid by the private sector. The problems which follow are designed to show that the private viewpoint must also be considered in the making of a social evaluation, when the private sector is responsible for undertaking the project.

Stern's (1972, p. 110) study of the Kenya tea project was the first to identify the general issue, and the data comes from this source. Brent's (1988) analysis of the Farmers Home Administration's (FmHA) decisions regarding the Farm Ownership Loan Programme provides the basis for the specific questions asked and their suggested resolution.

Background information

One way of looking at the new issue is to recognise that there are distribution dimensions to project appraisal separate from that of income redistribution. They involve (a) the distribution of gains between the private and public sectors, and (b) the distribution of gains within the private sector, i.e. between the agents that carry out the project and those that do not. It is this second dimension we wish to emphasise here. Both dimensions are related to the types of taxes used by the fiscal branch of the government. As usual, we shall assume that the fiscal branch is outside the sphere of influence of those carrying out the project evaluation.

For the Kenya tea project, the existence of tariffs is the main reason for the difference in return between the private and public sectors. This difference corresponds to the different returns obtained at market and at shadow prices. The KTDA's charge (implicit commodity tax) is the

Table 9.1   Rates of return regarding the Kenya tea project

	%
Kenya tea project IRR at shadow prices	38.8
Kenya tea project IRR at market prices	22.0
Kenya tea project IRR to growers	13.9
Government cost of borrowing	10.0

reason for the difference between the returns to the private sector and to the growers who undertake the tea project.

The data for the Kenya tea project, which can be used to illustrate the new distribution dimension, are presented in Table 9.1.

Questions

(a) Using the IRR criterion, show that the Kenya tea project was socially worthwhile.

(b) Using the IRR criterion, was the Kenya tea project worthwhile from the growers' point of view, assuming that they would have to pay 15% interest on any private loans?

(c) On the basis of your previous two answers, would the tea project that was socially worthwhile actually be undertaken by the private growers if they had to provide the finance?

(d) Would the tea project actually be undertaken by the private growers if they could borrow from the government at the government's own cost of borrowing? What then is the major difference for project appraisal between the government undertaking a project itself and relying on the private sector to undertake the project?

9.5 Discussion

This chapter was mainly concerned with establishing, and examining, the equivalence between the UNIDO and the L & M methods. The first task of this section will be to provide some general comments on this equivalence in light of some of the empirical work. The second task will be to point out the incompleteness of both methods with regard to the ways in which they correct for tariff distortions.

9.5.1 Equivalence between UNIDO and L & M in theory and practice

The literature on this subject (see, for example, Balassa, 1974 and Irvin, 1978) concludes that UNIDO and L & M are equivalent in theory, but differ in practice.

There is a very simple reason that the equivalence condition holds. Although UNIDO claim to be using domestic prices as their numeraire, this is not entirely valid. By deducting the tariff and working with X

− *M*, UNIDO are immediately focusing on the foreign exchange effects of a project (albeit only the direct foreign exchange effect). Moreover the benchmark they use in their SER formula is world prices. In equation (8.4) we see that the UNIDO domestic prices are divided by their border prices to form their accounting ratios, the p_j/p_j^*. In these circumstances, it would be surprising if there were no correspondence between the two methods.

Let us turn now to the issue of the two methods differing in practice. We can see from the previous chapter that as far as the S & T version of L & M is concerned, there is considerable overlap in practice between the two methods. S & T used a version of the SER as the main way to estimate the SCF. Clearly, the theoretical debate over whether it is necessary to estimate separately an SER is redundant if, in practice, an SER is used in a method which uses world prices as the numeraire. There does therefore seem to be some equivalence in practice. (It is true that UNIDO do not use an SCF in their case studies in Part IV of their Guidelines. However, they do not in any of the four cases presented there actually use their formula to find the SER.)

The main reason that one should consider this chapter on a comparison of methods is to provide some insight into the origins of project appraisal. There is not much point in seeking general theoretical advantages of one method over another, when the theory and the practice overlap so much.

9.5.2   The need to include a loan decision in project appraisal

Both UNIDO and L & M deduct the tariff from domestic prices when trying to estimate the real (social) cost of a taxed importable. This ensures that foreign goods will not be undervalued relative to domestic production. But this does not make the tax disappear for the private sector. For an agent undertaking the project which the public sector wishes to foster, the tax is something that reduces its private (financial) return. If this return is not sufficient to cover its cost of capital, the private agent will not undertake the project. This occurs despite the fact that the project is socially worthwhile. (In formal economic terms, we have what is known as an 'incentive compatibility problem'.)

The problems set in section 9.4 supplied an example of just this eventuality. It also suggested the solution. The government needs to provide credit for projects that would otherwise fail private criteria. Brent's (1988) study of FmHA farm ownership decisions illustrates the general methodology. There was a two-step project decision package which the government (Department of Agriculture) needed to follow. In the first step, the decision was made as to whether a farm should be bought. This is the expenditure decision proper. For this decision, if it was privately profitable, it was also socially worthwhile. Distributional weights did not affect the decision. The second step occurred when the farm was socially desirable, but privately unprofitable. A loan decision then had to be made. The loan was socially worthwhile only if the expenditure part of the decision package passed a joint efficiency and distribution criterion based on a zero interest rate repayments assumption.

This two-step decision-making process should become a standard part of project appraisal in developing countries, irrespective of the method to which one wishes to adhere. We have pointed out in Chapter 6 that shadow pricing was to be considered in the context of optimal policy for a mixed economy. In LDCs, the public sector shares are smaller than in developed countries. There is therefore more reliance on the private sector to undertake the projects. In these circumstances, the incentive incompatibility problem is more likely to occur.

9.5.3   Other problems of using shadow rather than market prices

Heggie (1976) points out operational difficulties similar to the incentive compatibility problem just referred to in the last section 9.5.2. Management may have day-to-day control problems when they are required to plan investments using shadow prices, for they may need to use different prices in their management decisions. To illustrate his argument, Heggie used the case of Port Louis in Mauritius. On the basis of shadow prices, the port was more labour-intensive than it would have been if market prices had been used. The SWR was 0.37 to 0.62 times the market wage. What prices should it actually charge when managing the port? If market prices were charged for the users of the labour, which entails a higher price, it would be just as if the users were paying a tax, and would be resisted. Moreover, private operators may start up cheaper, but duplicate services. This would not only be a waste of resources in itself, but also it would cause the usage estimates made in the investment decision to be violated. If, on the other hand, accounting prices were charged, the port could undercut private competitors and force them out of business. The lowest-cost producer for the nation may not be the public producer.

One possible solution suggested by Heggie was to charge the market price for the users of labour and give them, either directly or indirectly, a subsidy. This is like the recommended solution to the incentive compatibility problem which involved subsidised loans. Heggie was not optimistic over the extent to which there would be inter-government cooperation to implement these subsidies. No matter what the outcome in the Mauritius case, the general problem remains. L & M and UNIDO advocate deducting distortions from market prices for investment purposes, but offer no guidance as to what prices to use at the operational level.

10
Comparison of methods II

10.1 Introduction

The last chapter concluded that the DRC method was a particular formulation of the UNIDO approach to project appraisal. As such, it did not warrant special consideration, especially from the point of view of the choice of numeraire. Nonetheless, international trade theory has become increasingly interested in developing and using the DRC concept. So further discussion of the DRC approach as a method of project appraisal seems useful.

Linked to the work on the DRC have been studies of the 'effective rate of protection' (hereafter ERP). Since there is this link, it is convenient to deal with the ERP approach in this chapter as well. Again we will consider it only from the point of view of it constituting a potential project appraisal method.

Much of the analysis of this chapter is based on Srinivasan and Bhagwati (1978). We use their notation as far as possible, though we do state how this relates to the notation used in Chapter 9.

10.1.1 The basic DRC method

In chapter 9 we presented Lal's (1974) version of the DRC criterion as

$$SER > D/(X - M) \tag{10.1}$$

where the DRC was the ratio of domestic inputs D (measured in local prices) to foreign exchange earnings $X - M$ (measured in terms of the main foreign currency, assumed to be dollars). Here we wish to generalise this measure of the DRC ratio.

Assume that there are two traded goods (X_1 and X_2) and a domestically produced export good (X_3) which is the public project. There are two domestic inputs, capital (K) and labour (L). The respective world prices of the three goods are p_1^*, p_2^* and p_3^*; their market prices are the ps without the asterisks. There is a tariff on X_1 and X_2 at different rates. The domestic factor prices are r (the rental price of capital) and w (the wages paid to labour).

A simple definition of the DRC is as follows:

$$DRC = \frac{\textit{Value added at market prices}}{\textit{Value added at world prices}} \tag{10.2}$$

where 'value added' is the difference between the value of what a project produces and the value of any inputs purchased from elsewhere. Value added will be considered here per unit of output of the public project (X_3). How one measures value added depends on the technological characteristics of the project. We shall assume that the public project uses X_1 as an input.

Value added at domestic prices is just the value of the payments made to domestic capital and labour. This follows from the familiar identity used in elementary macroeconomics to derive national income which states that value added is

Value of sales − *Value of purchases* = *Sum of factor incomes* **(10.3)**

In our case there is one purchased input (X_1) and two factors (L and K). Equation (10.3) for X_3 then takes the form:

$$p_3 \cdot X_3 - p_1 \cdot X_1 = w \cdot L + r \cdot K \tag{10.4}$$

Dividing equation (10.4) by X_3 produces

$$p_3 - p_1 \cdot (X_1/X_3) = w \cdot (L/X_3) + r \cdot (K/X_3)$$

or

$$p_3 - p_1 \cdot f_1 = w \cdot l_3 + r \cdot k_3 \tag{10.5}$$

where f_1 is the share of X_1 in X_3, l_3 is the share of L in X_3, and k_3 is the share of K in X_3. Value added at domestic prices is therefore given by $w \cdot l_3 + r \cdot k_3$.

Value added at world prices can be found from the left-hand side of equation (10.5) by replacing the market prices (the ps) by their world prices (the p^*s) to obtain $p_3^* - p_1^* \cdot f_1$.

The DRC based on equation (10.2) appears as

$$DRC = \frac{w \cdot l_3 + r \cdot k_3}{p_3^* - p_1^* \cdot f_1} \tag{10.6}$$

Table 10.1   DRCs for tradables in Turkey

Export industries		Import-substitution industries	
Glassware	11.2	Cooling unit	24.7
Window glass	12.0	Electric motor	20.5
Radiators	14.0	Fertiliser, sodium phosphate	98.1
Nylon	12.1	Fertiliser, ammonium nitrate	63.6
Tomato canning	14.5	Truck tyres	97.9
		Passenger tyres	102.5
		Kraft paper	20.1
		Plastic	292.5
		Electric cables	49.2

Since $D/(X - M)$ equals D/X_3 divided by $(X - M)/X_3$, Lal's formulation corresponds to equation (10.6) with $D/X_3 = w \cdot l_3 + r \cdot k_3$ and $(X - M)/X_3 = p_3^* - p_1^* \cdot f_1$.

Krueger (1970) estimated the DRCs for a number of industries in Turkey for 1965. Her results are in Turkish lira per dollar. One set of DRCs (corresponding to column 1 of her Table 3) are presented in Table 10.1. To find out whether the import-substitution policies that were being encouraged in Turkey were socially worthwhile, we need to apply the criterion given in equation (10.1). This involves testing whether the DRC for a commodity is lower than the SER. Krueger did not explicitly provide an estimate for the SER. But, in her policy analysis, she did consider rates that were twice and thrice the OER, which was 9 Turkish lira to the dollar. We can consider TL18 = $1 and TL27 = $1 as alternative estimates of the SER. Table 10.2 shows the social desirability of the commodities at these SER.

Table 10.2 supports the critical verdict made by Krueger of import-substitution policies in Turkey. With a 100% premium on foreign exchange (SER of TL18 = £1), an expansion of any of the exports would be socially worthwhile, while none of the existing import-substitution could be justified. Only with a 200% premium on foreign exchange would three of the nine import-substitution products be considered worthwhile. The rest could not be justified at either of the exchange rates considered.

10.1.2 The basic ERP method

Recall from Chapter 9 that the main distortion that warrants a social rather than a private evaluation of a project is the existence of tariffs. It is the tariff on X_1 that is used as an input in the public project which now concerns us. The ERP is a calculation that tries to measure the

Table 10.2 Applying the social criterion to Turkish tradables using alternative estimates of the SER

	Social evaluation at TL18 = $1	Social evaluation at TL27 = $1
Export industries:		
Glassware	Accept	Accept
Window glass	Accept	Accept
Radiators	Accept	Accept
Nylon	Accept	Accept
Tomato canning	Accept	Accept
Import-substitution industries:		
Cooling unit	Reject	Accept
Electric motor	Reject	Accept
Fertiliser, sodium phosphate	Reject	Reject
Fertiliser, ammonium nitrate	Reject	Reject
Truck tyres	Reject	Reject
Passenger tyres	Reject	Reject
Kraft paper	Reject	Accept
Plastic	Reject	Reject
Electric cables	Reject	Reject

'true' or effective magnitude of this tariff. The official size of the tariff may be 25% – but, if most of the production from the public project is contributed by imports, the domestic resources are being protected at a rate much higher than 25%.

Following Bhagwati and Desai (1970, p. 336), the ERP can be defined as the incremental value added due to the tariff divided by the value added at cif prices. Incremental value added is the difference between value added at domestic and at import prices. The ERP can therefore be stated as

$$ERP = \frac{Value\ added\ at\ market\ prices\ -\ Value\ added\ at\ world\ prices}{Value\ added\ at\ world\ prices} \quad (10.7)$$

The relevance of an ERP calculation for project appraisal can be seen by rearranging equation (10.7). Dividing both terms on the right-hand side by the value added at world prices produces

$$ERP = \frac{Value\ added\ at\ market\ prices}{Value\ added\ at\ world\ prices} - 1 \quad (10.8)$$

Using equation (10.2), this simplifies to

$$ERP = DRC - 1 \quad (10.9)$$

The ERP can, therefore, rank projects just like the DRC providing we modify the criterion slightly. The DRC must be less than the SER for a socially worthwhile project. We can use equation (10.9) to restate this

Table 10.3   Nominal and effective tariff rates for import-substitution industries in Turkey

	Nominal tariff (%)	Effective tariff (*ERP*)
Cooling unit	62	80
Electric motor	71	66
Fertiliser, sodium phosphate	71	186
Fertiliser, ammonium nitrate	27	925
Truck tyres	131	170
Kraft paper	77	?
Plastic	102	916
Electric cables	82	147

criterion as requiring that $ERP + 1 < SER$ for a socially acceptable project.

Since we have applied the DRC criterion to the Turkish tradables, we already know which products would be worthwhile expanding or contracting. However, we can use the corresponding Krueger's ERP calculations given in Table 10.3 above as corroborative evidence of the problems posed by tariffs in the context of project appraisal. Table 10.2 has told us that producing ammonium nitrate fertiliser is not a worthwhile activity. Let us use the figures in Table 10.3 to see precisely why it is that the domestic production of fertiliser should be discouraged. Recall that one of the basic ideas behind the S & T (and L & M) project appraisal methodology is that the foreign exchange effects be used to determine the net benefits of projects. It is in this respect that the effective tariff rate is important. Notice from Table 10.3 that although the nominal tariff on ammonium nitrate fertiliser is only 25%, the ERP is much greater at 925%. This large value indicates that very little of the production of this fertiliser comes from domestic resources. The foreign exchange gain is, therefore, very small. Consequently, the activity fails to generate much net benefits from a project appraisal standpoint.

10.2   Comparing the methods

The previous section has presented the main ideas behind the DRC and the ERP from a project appraisal perspective. The international trade literature has, however, considered a number of different variants of these measures. In order to make comparisons among the project appraisal methods we need to be careful to identify exactly which version one is considering. To this end, we begin our analysis by specifying three different measures of the DRC. We then outline how a standard project appraisal would evaluate product X_3. From there it is a simple matter to see whether any of the variants that are commonly included in a DRC or ERP calculation correspond to the project appraisal criterion.

10.2.1 Alternative DRC measures

Srinivasan and Bhagwati have identified six alternative measures of the DRC. Here we focus on three of these. The main differences arise from the particular specification of the numerator of the expression given in equation (10.6):

$$DRC = \frac{w \cdot l_3 + r \cdot k_3}{p_3^* - p_1^* \cdot f_1}$$

The w and r on the numerator of equation (10.6) can be specified in terms of (a) 'first-best' factor prices, (b) 'second-best' factor prices, or (c) market factor prices. Each of these specifications will be described in turn.

A 'first-best' situation was described in Chapter 6 as one where the government is pursuing its objectives subject only to a production constraint. There is no tariff to contend with in this context. Product prices will be the social prices, p^*. The factor prices would be those that correspond to a distortion-free situation, which we can label w^* and r^*. With these product and factor prices, the DRC equation (10.6) would become

$$DRC_1 = \frac{w^* \cdot l_3 + r^* \cdot k_3}{p_3^* - p_1^* \cdot f_1}$$

(10.10)

In the 'second-best' situation that we will be considering, there will be a tariff as well as the production constraint which limits the government furthering its objectives. Since production does not take place at first-best levels, factor usage will be different and so will be factor prices. Let us represent the wage and rental income that corresponds to the second-best factor proportions by w'^* and r'^*. We have shown in Chapter 6 that even in a second-best world the correct shadow prices are the world prices. The DRC would then appear as

$$DRC_2 = \frac{w'^* \cdot l_3 + r'^* \cdot k_3}{p_3^* - p_1^* \cdot f_1}$$

(10.11)

The third variant that we will be considering uses the factor payments which exist with the tariff distortion. These factor prices are, of course, the market prices. We will represent the market wage by w' and the market rental income by r'. The product prices will be the same as for the other two variants, as it will be assumed that these are the ones which firms actually face when involved with sales and purchases of traded goods. The third DRC measure takes the form:

$$DRC_3 = \frac{w' \cdot l_3 + r' \cdot k_3}{p_3^* - p_1^* \cdot f_1} \tag{10.12}$$

10.2.2 A social project appraisal

A social evaluation would judge product X_3 worthwhile provided that the social value of the output was greater than the social value of all the inputs. Social value would be determined on the basis of the shadow prices for the outputs and inputs. Product X_3 is worthwhile if

$$p_3^* \cdot X_3 > w'^* \cdot L_3 + r'^* \cdot K_3 + p_1^* \cdot X_1 \tag{10.13}$$

Dividing through by X_3, and using the same notation for shares of X_3 as before, we obtain

$$p_3^* > w'^* \cdot l_3 + r'^* \cdot k_3 + p_1^* \cdot f_1 \tag{10.14}$$

When we subtract $p^*_1 \cdot f_1$ from both sides of equation (10.14), our social criterion turns into

$$p_3^* - p_1^* \cdot f_1 > w'^* \cdot l_3 + r'^* \cdot k_3 \tag{10.15}$$

10.2.3 The DRC as a project appraisal

If it were the case that the project X_3 was marginal, the left-hand side of equation (10.15) would equal the right-hand side. In which case,

$$p_3^* - p_1^* \cdot f_1 = w'^* \cdot l_3 + r'^* \cdot k_3 \tag{10.16}$$

Dividing both sides by $w'^* \cdot l_3 + r'^* \cdot k_3$ results in

$$\frac{p_3^* - p_1^* \cdot f_1}{w'^* \cdot l_3 + r'^* \cdot k_3} = 1 \tag{10.17}$$

Using equation (10.6), the left-hand side of equation (10.17) equals the reciprocal of the DRC. Hence, the project appraisal criterion given by equation (10.15) is satisfied only if the DRC, as measured by equation (10.17), is less than unity. This confirms the result shown in Chapter 9 which stated that the DRC was a special way of arranging the determinants of a project appraisal (using the UNIDO methodology).

While there is this equivalence between a project evaluation and a DRC calculation, only version DRC_2, the 'second-best' DRC measure, will provide the same rankings.

10.2.4 The ERP as a project evaluation

Srinivasan and Bhagwati point out that the standard ERP calculation uses market prices to measure the factor payments. The typical ERP would specify the relevant value added as

$$ERP = \frac{w' \cdot l_3 + r' \cdot k_3}{p_3^* - p_1^* \cdot f_1} - 1 \qquad (10.18)$$

This produces the result

$$ERP = DRC_3 - 1 \qquad (10.19)$$

In the standard case, then, the ERP fails to work with the 'right' information, i.e. it uses DRC_3 rather than DRC_2. Consequently, the ERP will not provide rankings that correspond to a project appraisal.

The obvious question to ask is why the ERP uses an inappropriate numerator in its calculations. The answer that Srinivasan and Bhagwati provide is that the users of the ERP method think it is more 'objective' to work with market factor prices rather than their social counterparts. The view that project appraisal is not objective has been discussed fully in section 1.6.2 of Chapter 1. Here all we need to point out is that if we thought that market prices were appropriate indicators of social value, project appraisal would not have been developed in the first place.

10.3   Measurement practice

Monson and Pursell (1979) extended the notion of a DRC, which is normally applied to goods, to provide an assessment of services. In particular, they wished to evaluate an import-substitution activity on the Ivory Coast, which involved training local labour to replace previously imported skilled labour. Because the industrial sectors of many LDCs are dominated by multinational corporations, and their educational systems are just starting to expand, LDCs employ many foreign nationals. European expatriates constituted around 70% of the modern sector managerial and technical labour force on the Ivory Coast. Indigenisation (replacing foreign employees with locals) is therefore a basic component of the development process. In addition, with the industrial and agricultural sectors of LDCs being evaluated in terms of their contribution to foreign exchange, an evaluation of educational expenditures allows a comparison to be made with projects in these other sectors.

10.3.1 The DRC used to evaluate indigenisation on the Ivory Coast

The DRC was viewed as a special kind of cost–benefit ratio. Costs and benefits comprise two categories, domestic resources and foreign exchange effects. Hence total benefits, B, are the sum of domestic benefits, B_1, and foreign exchange benefits, B_2. That is, $B = B_1 + B_2$. Similarly, on the costs side, $K = K_1 + K_2$, where K are the total costs, K_1 are domestic costs and K_2 are foreign exchange costs. Rather than divide K by B (as with a cost–benefit ratio), the DRC divides net domestic costs by net foreign exchange benefits, to form

$$DRC = \frac{K_1 - B_1}{B_2 - K_2} \tag{10.20}$$

As an investment criterion, it is based on the cost–benefit ratio rationale. Recall that from Chapter 2, this ratio (strictly, the reverse of this ratio) was appropriate when a funds constraint existed. The DRC version focuses on there being a shortage of just one source of funds, i.e. foreign exchange.

In the context of the Ivory Coast indigenisation effort, the specifications of the benefits and costs were:

B_1: Expenditure of domestic resources per expatriate.
K_1: Domestic resource training costs per successful trainee;
forgone earnings per successful trainee;
alternative earnings per successful trainee.
B_2: Expenditure on tradables in border prices per expatriate;
savings per expatriate replaced.
K_2: Foreign exchange training costs per successful trainee.

These specifications acknowledge the fact that some effects take place during the training period, while others occur once the labour substitution has taken place. An adjustment had to be made for the possibility that it would take more than one local to replace one expatriate.

The resulting DRCs for four different occupational categories are included in Table 10.4 (Table 4 of Monson and Pursell). The results correspond to the case where previously given foreign educational aid would not be continued, and where educational requirements for occupations were set by Ivory Coast national planners. The table shows

Table 10.4 DRCs of indigenisation efforts on the Ivory Coast at various discount rates

Occupation		SDR	
	5%	11%	17%
Office labour	0.322	0.762	1.589
Supervisors	−0.477	−0.332	−0.085
Technicians	−0.382	−0.180	0.157
Managers	−0.261	0.158	1.326

that at the rate of 11%, which was thought to be the most suitable discount rate, all occupation categories had DRC values well below unity. Training labour for expatriate replacement on the Ivory Coast was therefore socially beneficial.

10.4 Problems

The problems in this section are aimed at examining one of the implications of the Monson and Pursell indigenisation study just outlined. The focal point is the existence, interpretation and evaluation of activities with negative DRCs. For a full analysis of statistical and economic causes of negative DRCs, see the appendix to Chapter 17 of Bhagwati and Desai (1970, pp. 363–7).

Background information

Table 10.4 contains most of the relevant information. The only other point to be aware of is that for supervisors and technicians, B_1 was greater than K_1. This was largely due to the fact that expenditures by expatriates on tradables were so large. Foreign exchange net benefits were positive for all occupation categories.

Questions

(a) Were net domestic costs positive or negative for supervisors and technicians? Were their respective DRC ratios positive or negative?

(b) Would it have been more socially beneficial to have had positive net domestic costs for supervisors and technicians? Thus, is it ever socially desirable to have projects with negative DRCs?

(c) On the basis of your answers to the previous question, rank the four occupational categories in terms of their DRCs using the 11% discount rate.

10.5 Discussion

Now that we have a good idea about the workings of DRC and ERP methods, it is time to make an assessment of them from a project appraisal standpoint. Before this assessment will be undertaken in section 10.5.2, it is first necessary to dispose of a common argument made in favour of the DRC method.

10.5.1 Whether the DRC method can avoid using an SER

It is often thought that the DRC method has advantages over other project appraisal criteria on the grounds that it alone does not need to estimate an SER. Monson and Pursell are one of the latest to make this claim. They use it to justify their adoption of the DRC method to carry out their indigenisation study. They point out that UNIDO needs an SER, and L & M need an SER equivalent, i.e. their conversion factors, while the DRC can proceed without it. It is instructive to consider Warr's demonstration of why this claim is invalid (1983).

Warr starts his analysis by showing that the DRC is really just another 'switching value' – the value of a parameter that makes the NPV equal to zero. To see this, consider an NPV calculation based on the UNIDO method. This converts foreign exchange effects into domestic price equivalents using an SER. The foreign exchange effect has been defined in this chapter as $p_3^* \cdot X_3 - p_1^* \cdot X_1$, and the domestic effect was represented by $w^* \cdot L_3 + r^* \cdot K_3$. The NPV investment criterion would take the form

$$NPV = (p_3^* \cdot X_3 - p_1^* \cdot X_1)\, SER - (w^* \cdot L_3 + r^* \cdot K_3) \qquad \textbf{(10.21)}$$

Setting the NPV equal to zero in equation (10.21), we obtain

$$SER = \frac{(p_3^* \cdot X_3 - p_1^* \cdot X_1)}{(w^* \cdot L_3 + r^* \cdot K_3)} \qquad \textbf{(10.22)}$$

But the right-hand side is equal to the *DRC*. Thus the *SER* equals *DRC* when *NPV* equals zero. In other words, the *DRC* is the switching value for the *SER*.

Warr then proceeds to analyse the claim that although an SER is necessary to decide whether a project is socially desirable or not, an SER is not necessary to rank mutually exclusive projects. So, for example, if a country really needs a highway, choosing the alternative with the lowest DRC will lead to the best highway design. Warr's insight is to recognise that in equation (10.21), the NPV is linearly related to the SER. There is a positive slope, given by $(p_3^* \cdot X_3 - p_1^* \cdot X_1)$, and a negative intercept, given by ($w^* \cdot L_3 + r^* \cdot K_3$). Defining the slope by b and the intercept by a, we simplify equation (10.21) to make it appear as

$$NPV = -a + b \cdot SER \tag{10.23}$$

Let there be two mutually exclusive projects, 1 and 2. The counterparts of equation (10.23) for the two projects would be

$$NPV_1 = -a_1 + b_1 \cdot SER \text{ and } NPV_2 = -a_2 + b_2 \cdot SER \tag{10.24}$$

Provided that the two projects do not have the same slope, the two straight lines in equation (10.24) will intersect. Call the SER value where they intersect SER^*. For SER values less than SER^*, one project will have the higher NPV; and for values higher than SER^*, the other project will have the higher NPV. One cannot rank the two projects unless one knows whether the 'true' SER is greater or less than SER^*. We can, therefore, conclude that the alleged claim for the superiority of the DRC method is invalid. The precise value for SER needs to be known for ranking projects, as well as deciding whether they are socially worthwhile.

10.5.2 An assessment of the DRC and ERP methods

We begin our assessment of the DRC and ERP methods by focusing on fundamental weaknesses which they both have in common. Then we deal with each method separately.

Common weaknesses of both methods

The main limitation of the DRC and ERP approaches can be seen by considering the following statement by Srinivasan and Bhagwati (1978) concerning their work on these two concepts:

> Finally, it is also clear that implicit in our analysis is the assumption that problems of income distribution and savings can be tackled through deployment of appropriate non-distortionary instruments. Obviously, if this is not possible, the shadow prices will have to be calculated afresh by introducing additional constraints which reflect the feasible set of public policy instruments.

What this is saying is that both DRC and ERP calculations ignore distributional considerations and place no premium on savings. We have stated in Chapter 1 that central to any project appraisal methodology for LDCs is the idea that an allowance must be made for both income distributional outcomes and the effect on savings. This means that the two methods, as currently formulated, are efficiency approaches and do not attempt to evaluate social outcomes. Why anyone would want to evaluate an indigenisation activity on the Ivory Coast, which is such a basic component of the development process in Africa, without considering these two ingredients is hard to understand.

The other main weakness of the DRC and ERP methods is equally basic. They are both, as typically formulated, one-period measures that ignore discounting. (However, this is not the case for the Monson and Pursell study, which did use a multi-period version using a discount rate.)

The DRC as a method of project appraisal

A DRC calculation has the further problem of having such a narrow focus. It looks at the size of domestic resources given up per unit of foreign exchange earned. It is only in these terms that the ratio makes sense. One cannot add to, or subtract from, the numerator or denominator and retain its distinctive meaning.

To help understand this limitation better, let us consider one of the policy implications made by Monson and Pursell in their indigenisation study. It is a very common finding of cost–benefit studies of higher education in LDCs that many of the direct costs of receiving the education (e.g. food and lodging) are financed by the government. The social net benefits are, therefore, much less than the private net benefits (those received by the person being educated). This result was also observed in the Ivory Coast indigenisation programme. The private cost–benefit ratio was half that of the social cost–benefit ratio. But the point is that to obtain this important result, Monson and Pursell had to leave their DRC framework and resort to one of the more fundamental investment criteria. Private and social cost–benefit ratios have meaning. There can be little meaning attached to a 'private' DRC ratio. A private individual would have no reason to make such a calculation.

The ERP as a method of project appraisal

If a DRC calculation is to be considered a very restricted project appraisal procedure, an ERP calculation has to be considered to be outside the realm of project appraisal. The distinctive characteristic of a bird is that the animal has feathers. When a chicken is plucked, it loses its identity as a bird. An ERP is a 'plucked' project appraisal. Not only does it ignore distributional issues and make no special allowance for savings, but (as we saw in section 10.2.4) it also avoids using shadow prices for factor prices. It is just these considerations (intergenerational weighting, social valuing public income, product and factor outputs) that this book has been analysing. Without these ingredients, there is no need for project appraisal.

This is not to say that there is no value in an ERP calculation. We are just saying that it does not constitute a legitimate project evaluation method. An ERP calculation indicates the real size of the market distortion caused by a tariff. This information is useful in the fight to try to have the tariff removed. But project appraisal works on the assumption that these distortions will not be removed in the life of the project. It therefore tries to neutralise the effect of tariffs rather than eradicate them. Thus, the two areas of study have set themselves very different tasks.

11
Allowing for risk

11.1 Introduction

This chapter covers the material in Chapter 5 of S & T. S & T devote only three pages to this subject, when there is much that needs to be explained. Certainly, no project appraisal can be considered complete without some sensitivity analysis of the key parameters that have played the largest role in determining the final outcome. Therefore this chapter will follow the lead of Chapter 2 by presenting all the results stated by S & T and, in addition, filling in the words of explanation and providing numerical examples of the main concepts used. Just as with Chapter 2, the problems faced are basically the same for a private firm as for the government carrying out a social appraisal. The only difference is that the firm will be calculating its IRR based on private revenues and costs, while the government will be forming its IRR based on social benefits and costs.

Much of this chapter is based on the case study by Pouliquen (1970) of the Mogadiscio port project in Somalia. This study was especially devised to uncover some of the ways that risk analysis could be incorporated into project appraisal. Initially a conventional evaluation was made using best estimates. However, this ran into a number of difficulties which a risk analysis could best remedy. The existing lighterage port was to be replaced by a project consisting of a two-berth, deep water port. The success of the project depended on a large number of factors on both the demand and the supply sides.

Table 11.2 below contains the main results. On the basis of the best estimates for each component in the evaluation, the IRR was 12.2%. The cost of capital in Somalia was considered to be 8%. The project seemed to be acceptable. But much of the data was considered suspect and based on optimistic projections. When least favourable estimates were chosen, the IRR dropped to 2%. Ideally, one would prefer to know the likelihood of the least favourable circumstances actually prevailing. Thus, the Mogadiscio port project was judged to be a good project for which to employ risk analysis – a method which seeks to ascertain the probability that any outcome will result.

11.1.1 The distinction between risk and uncertainty

In a general sense (first recognised by Dorfman, 1962) risk and uncertainty are present whenever one has to consider more than one possible outcome for a project evaluation. If one can obtain estimates of the probabilities that are to be attached to the possible outcomes, then one is dealing with risk. When the probabilities are unknown, one is dealing with uncertainty. This is the basic difference between the two concepts, and this is why Knight (1921) has called risk 'measurable uncertainty'.

Let us illustrate these two definitions. A project transforms inputs into outputs. This transformation process is not usually under the full control of the project supervisor. So there will be a range of outcomes that correspond to any one given input level. For the Mogadiscio port project, an important input was gang labour productivity, and the outcomes were the numbers of tons a gang could unload from a ship per hour. For these outcomes to constitute a risk situation, we need also to know the probabilities with which every outcome will occur. Pouliquen reports the information contained in Table 11.1 regarding gang labour productivity. Thus, when one is in a risk situation, one is dealing with a probability distribution, i.e. the range of outcomes and their associated probabilities.

If we did not know the relevant probabilities, the situation would have been one of uncertainty. Probabilities are usually obtained from

Table 11.1 Probability distribution of gang labour productivity in Mogadiscio port project

Possible outcomes (tons per gang-hour)	Probability
5–6	0.03
6–7	0.08
7–8	0.15
8–9	0.25
9–10	0.25
10–11	0.16
11–12	0.08

past experience by looking at the frequency with which any particular event occurred. For example, if one were evaluating a dam for irrigation purposes, one would want to know how much and how often it rained: that is, past rainfall figures would indicate the probabilities. But, if one thinks that the climate is changing, past experience would not be a good guide. We would then be uncertain as to the dam's water storage potential.

In this chapter we concentrate on risk only. The circumstances where risk is the appropriate situation are much more frequent than one would expect from just considering its definition. This is because one is not limited to past occurrences in order to obtain estimates of the probabilities. One can base the probabilities on subjective feelings of the project decision-maker. For example, even though the climate may have changed (which makes past frequencies of rainfall unreliable estimates of future rainfall probabilities), the decision-maker for a dam project could still take a personal view of what the chances of rainfall will be and base the estimates of probabilities on these hunches.

Note that in Pouliquen's study subjective probabilities are used, being the judgements of experts connected with the operations of other ports (although he does point out on p. 3, fn 1, that 'all "subjective" judgements that we are likely to obtain from experts are based on some sort of "objective" experience'.) Techniques for handling uncertainty do exist (see, for example, Dorfman, 1962). But they do not yet play a major role in project appraisal practice. (The main World Bank study on uncertainty is by Reutlinger, 1970.)

11.1.2 How not to deal with risk in project appraisal

Before explaining legitimate methods of allowing for risk, it is instructive to consider three main responses to risk that should not be followed.

1. One should not just present the best estimate of the NPV. Recall that the NPV was given in Chapter 2 as

$$NPV = \sum_{t=0}^{t=T} S_t/(1 + r)^t \tag{11.1}$$

This is a single figure. As such, it does not allow for the existence of alternative outcomes and (by the general definition given above) it does not consider risk. Moreover, there is no precise statistical statement of what the 'best' estimate constitutes. Is it the mean, the median, the mode, or none (or all) of these? We have no guarantee that the best estimate is representative of the range of possible outcomes.

2. One should not present an estimate of the NPV that consists of the most unfavourable figure for each element in the NPV. Again this is a single figure, and does not allow for alternative possible outcomes. In addition, the NPV figure so generated is ultra-conservative; it may have only the remotest possibility of occurring. (This point is demonstrated in the results for the Mogadiscio port project given later.)

3. One should not add a 'risk premium' to the discount rate and use as the criterion

$$NPV = \sum_{t=0}^{t=T} S_t/(1 + r + u)^t \tag{11.2}$$

where u is the risk premium. This is wrong for three main reasons: first, it just scales down the NPV best estimate – what is needed is an allowance for the dispersion around the best estimate; second, it assumes that risk increases over time (this is demonstrated in the Appendix) – when this is not the case, it discriminates unfairly against long-lasting projects; and third, it combines two concepts that should be kept separate – time discounting and allowing for risk.

11.2 Risk methods

We first outline the two risk methods mentioned by S & T, and then proceed to analyse the main general criteria for dealing with risk.

11.2.1 Sensitivity analysis

One way of allowing for risk has been used many times in the applications used in previous chapters. A sensitivity analysis was carried out to accompany the best estimate, that is, the project evaluator would vary the magnitudes of key variables by a certain percentage to see how sensitive the results were to this variation. For example, in the Ivory Coast indigenisation study presented in the last chapter, the best estimate for the social discount rate was 11% and this indicated a worthwhile project. Then values 50% smaller and larger were tried to see if the outcome were altered. When final outcomes (the project decisions) are not altered, the best estimate is not considered controversial. It can be adopted without the need for precise justification. But when a final outcome is altered by an alternative value, then a detailed defence of the estimation procedure behind the best estimate must be made.

To see the strengths and weaknesses of sensitivity analysis, consider the alternative IRRs found for the Mogadiscio port project shown in

Table 11.2 Sensitivity analysis of the IRR for the Mogadiscio port project

Parameter varied	*IRR* using best estimate	*IRR* using lowest value	*IRR* using highest value	% *IRR* change to 10% change in best estimate
1 Cost of project	12.2	10.8	12.9	8.20
2 Gang productivity	12.2	14.2	7.3	4.10
3 Reduced damages	12.2	13.6	10.8	3.28
4 Ton cargo average	12.2	13.3	11.2	3.28
5 Unnecessary staff	12.2	10.7	11.9	1.64
6 Road transport costs	12.2	11.5	13.0	0.82
7 Ship working day, cargo	12.2	12.5	11.9	1.64
8 Years of life of asset	12.2	12.3	10.9	0.82
9 Imports growth rate	12.2	13.0	11.8	0.82
10 Investment costs avoided	12.2	12.4	11.9	0.82
11 Ship working day, banana	12.2	12.3	12.1	0.82
12 Maximum banana traffic	12.2	12.1	12.1	0.82
13 Exports growth rate	12.2	12.5	12.1	0.00
14 Banana growth rate	12.2	12.2	12.6	0.00
15 Maintenance of materials	12.2	12.1	12.4	0.00
16 Men in gang, cargo	12.2	12.1	12.3	0.00
17 Men in gang, banana	12.2	12.2	12.3	0.00
18 Men in transit sheds	12.2	12.2	12.3	0.00
19 Men doing maintenance	12.2	12.2	12.3	0.00
20 Miscellaneous cost	12.2	12.2	12.2	0.00
21 Banana charge	12.2	12.2	12.2	0.00
22 Port charges	12.2	12.2	12.2	0.00
23 Export/import charges	12.2	12.2	12.2	0.00
24 Men in warehouses	12.2	12.2	12.2	0.00
25 Men in administration	12.2	12.2	12.2	0.00
26 Elasticity of demand	12.2	12.2	12.2	0.00
27 Ship charges	12.2	12.2	12.2	˙0.00

Table 11.2 (based on Table 2 of Pouliquen, 1970). One important advantage of undertaking a sensitivity analysis is that it identifies those variables that should be analysed further to obtain more reliable estimates. There were twenty-seven components in the evaluation whose values were considered questionable. The effect on the IRR of a 10% change in the value of the best estimate is shown in the last column of Table 11.2. It shows that only seven of the twenty-seven components crucially affected the IRR outcome (cost of the project, productivity of labour, value of an average ton of cargo, percentage of the tonnage that would be saved through reduction in damages, growth rate of imports, value of a ship working day, and the life of the assets). Only these seven components warrant further investigation.

The other main advantage is that a sensitivity analysis acts as an aid to the management of a project. It indicates critical areas that require close supervision in order to ensure that the project will have a favourable outcome. For example, in the port project, gang productivity (component 2) was crucial. Since this component was so pivotal, it would be worthwhile to hire a supervisor to ensure that gang productivity did come up to its best estimate.

On the other hand, a sensitivity analysis does have three main drawbacks:

1. When the key variables are varied by a given percentage (10% in the port project), it is not clear whether this contains the likely variation of the variable. A 10% variation may cover 90% of the area of one variable's probability distribution; while for another variable the same 10% variation may cover only 20% of the area. In the latter case, most of the probable range of outcome is being overlooked.

2. Following on from the first point, there is the problem that a sensitivity analysis does not tell us the probability of obtaining any particular result. How likely is it that components will be 10% higher or lower?

3. A sensitivity analysis does not show the combined net effect of changing all variables simultaneously. For instance, we know that if gang productivity (component 2) were 10% lower, the IRR of 12.2% would be 4.1% lower. This assumes that all other components were held constant at their best estimate values. But what would be the outcome if port capacity were also 10% lower?

11.2.2 Risk analysis

Risk analysis was initiated in order to combat the drawbacks of sensitivity analysis. There are four main stages in the undertaking of a risk analysis. These are the steps necessary to construct a probability distribution for the outcomes as a whole. Each step will be illustrated with respect to the port project and will be explained in turn.

Disaggregating the benefits and costs

One needs to disaggregate because it is often difficult to form judgements about outcomes that depend on the combined effect of a number of separate influences. For instance, the engineer on the port project was unable to specify alternative values that the costs could take. However, when total costs were split into labour costs that depended on labour productivity, the engineer could use his past experience to state that gang productivity varied between 5 and 12 tons per gang hour.

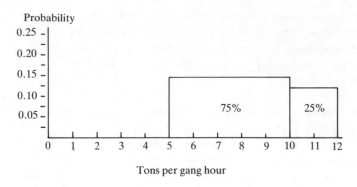

Figure 11.1 *The initial distribution of labour productivity*

Assigning probabilities

Given that only seven components were crucial. Pouliquen directed attention at finding distributions for these. Two methods were used on the port project. The first method uses a priori reasoning to suggest a particular, well-known (classical) form for the probability distribution. Thus a normal distribution was assumed for the value of a ship working day, the value of an average ton of cargo, and the percentage reduction in damages, and the chi-square distribution for the cost of the project. The other method is to use the active participation of the appraiser to form rectangular stepped distributions. This second method was used for the life of assets, the import growth rate and labour productivity. Here we illustrate the second method for the labour productivity component.

We have already stated the engineer's view that gang labour productivity lay in the range of 5–12 tons per gang hour. Because 10 tons was the best estimate, the range was split into two around 10, i.e. 5–10 and 10–12. The procedure works as follows. First, a qualitative judgement is made. The question is asked whether the two ranges of outcomes are equally likely to occur, or whether one is more probable than the other. The engineer thought that the lower section was more likely to occur than the upper section. Then a quantitative judgement is made. A precise figure is assigned to the relative likelihoods. On the basis of the engineeer's experience, productivity was 75% of the time in the lower range and 25% in the upper range. The initial distribution was as illustrated in Figure 11.1. The probabilities are related to the areas. Thus, 75% spread over five units gives a probability of 0.15 per unit in the lower range, and 25% spread over two units gives a probability of 0.125 in the upper range.

The procedure proceeds by refining the initial judgements to con-

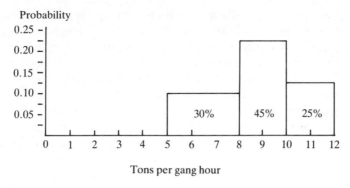

Figure 11.2 *The subsequent distribution of labour productivity*

centrate on ever smaller intervals. The lower interval was subdivided into two sections, 5–8 and 8–10. The engineer then made the necessary qualitative and quantitative judgements. The upper section was allocated 45% of the 75%, while 30% of the 75% was allocated to the lower section, which made the new distribution appear as illustrated in Figure 11.2. Continuing as before, the sections were split up into ever smaller intervals, until the engineer no longer felt that one part of the range of outcomes was any more, or any less, likely to occur than another part of the range. The final distribution, after two further rounds of subdividing intervals, took the form illustrated in Figure 11.3. This is the distribution from which Table 11.1 was constructed.

Allowing for correlations

Many of the components may be correlated (components vary with each other in a systematic way). For example, labour productivity and

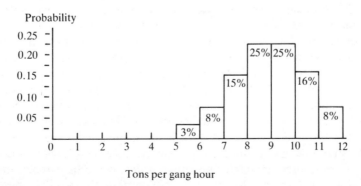

Figure 11.3 *The final distribution of labour productivity*

port capacity were positively correlated; the larger the port capacity, the more tons one could expect to obtain from a gang hour. The existence of correlations has an important bearing on the distribution of final outcomes. It is a well-known result of statistical theory that even though the underlying distributions of the components may not be normal, providing the components are independent, the overall distribution of the outcomes that depends on all the components will still take the form of a normal distribution. However, if independence does not exist (there are correlations among components) the variation in one component will not offset the variation in another. Normality cannot be assumed, and some other way needs to be found to form the overall distribution of IRRs. This is why the fourth stage comes into being.

Pouliquen stated that forming the correlations was not an easy step because engineers are not accustomed to looking at production relationships in this way. Nonetheless, the judgement of the engineer was invoked to obtain correlations for those pairs of components which were expected to have the largest correlation. Besides labour productivity and port capacity, positive correlations were expected for banana gang productivity and general cargo gang productivity, and the number employed in a transit shed and in a warehouse.

Simulation

The final stage involves undertaking a simulation (using the 'Monte Carlo approach'). This uses the probability distributions of the components, and the correlations among them, to form a distribution for the outcomes. The method is straightforward. The computer is asked to generate a set of random numbers for each of the components. On the basis of the values for the components, the overall outcome is determined: that is, an IRR figure is obtained. The computer then specifies another set of random values for the components, which leads to another IRR figure. The computer continues to generate random numbers, and hence IRR figures, until the analyst considers that a large enough sample has been formed. For the Mogadiscio port project, 300 IRR figures were obtained. The cumulative distribution of these IRR figures is presented in Table 11.3 (based on Figure 3 of Pouliquen). The table shows for each IRR the probability of getting at least as much as this figure. There is (effectively) no chance of earning an IRR less than 5% or greater than 16%. The distribution has a mean of 10.6% (i.e. there is a 50% chance of an IRR of 10.6% occurring).

We shall now use Table 11.3 to show the advantages of a risk analysis over a sensitivity analysis. Basically, a risk analysis enables precise probability statements to be made concerning the results previously

Table 11.3 The cumulative distribution of IRRs for the Mogadiscio port project

IRR	Cumulative distribution (%)
5% and less	0.00
6% and less	0.01
7% and less	0.06
8% and less	0.15
9% and less	0.28
10% and less	0.40
11% and less	0.54
12% and less	0.68
13% and less	0.80
14% and less	0.90
15% and less	0.98
16% and less	1.00

presented. Using the completed risk analysis for the port project allows us to say the following:

1. The best estimates for all components led to an IRR of 12.2%. Table 11.3 indicates that there is a 70% chance that the IRR will not be that high. This finding alone justified the mission's feeling that the Mogadiscio port project was a risky project, and that the best estimates gave a false impression of the likely outcome.

2. The worst case scenario for each component produced an IRR of 2%. Since there is virtually no chance of obtaining a value below 5%, the ultra-conservative approach leads to an outcome too remote to consider.

3. The switching value for the IRR was 8% (the same value as the cost of capital in Somalia). However, the chance of the IRR being below 8% is relatively small; it has a 15% probability of occurring.

Aside from giving greater precision to the sensitivity results, a risk analysis also indicates the degree of distortion that is involved in a sensitivity analysis which only varies one component at a time, holding all others constant. This procedure ignores the correlation among components. The importance of recognising correlations can be illustrated by one other finding from the risk analysis. When one ignores the correlation between the productivity of labour and port capacity, the probability that the IRR was less than 10% was 15%. But, as we can see from Table 11.3, when one includes the positive correlation between these two components, the probability that the IRR was less than 15% rose to 40%.

11.2.3 General criteria

Risk analysis gives a clearer picture of what the probabilities are when undertaking a project. But it does not say anything about how to choose among projects with different degrees of risk. To help deal with this choice, general risk criteria were developed. The main criterion is the expected (present) value rule, and most of this section will concentrate on the rationale and applicability of this decision rule. We start by explaining the mechanics of the expected value rule. Then we introduce the idea of variance (variation about the expected value) and analyse whether decisions can be made which allow for both the expected value and the variance. Finally, we deal with the proposition that public projects need only consider the expected value and can ignore variance.

The expected value rule

The expected value (*EV*) approach looks at all the possible outcomes and weights each by the probability of the outcome occurring. *EV* is therefore the weighted sum:

$$EV = \sum [\text{Probability}] \cdot [\text{Outcome}] \tag{11.3}$$

The *EV* is equivalent to the mean, as it is the value for the outcome that would be obtained on average. That is, if one sampled from the range of outcomes an infinitely large number of times, this is the value that one would observe on average.

The probability distribution for IRRs was given in Table 11.3. We present the same information in non-cumulative terms in Table 11.4. To be able to calculate *EV*, we need the outcomes as precise figures rather than as intervals. For this purpose, the mid-points in Table 11.3

Table 11.4   Probability distribution of IRRs for the Mogadiscio port project

Possible outcomes (*IRR*s)	Mid-point	Probability
5–6	5.5	0.01
6–7	6.5	0.05
7–8	7.5	0.09
8–9	8.5	0.13
9–10	9.5	0.12
10–11	10.5	0.14
11–12	11.5	0.14
12–13	12.5	0.12
13–14	13.5	0.10
14–15	14.5	0.08
15–16	15.5	0.02

can be used to indicate the outcomes. The *EV* for the IRR in the case of the Mogadiscio port project would then be as follows:

$$EV = (0.01)(\ 5.5) + (0.05)(\ 6.5) + (0.09)(\ 7.5)$$
$$(0.13)(\ 8.5) + (0.12)(\ 9.5) + (0.14)(10.5)$$
$$(0.14)(11.5) + (0.12)(12.5) + (0.10)(12.5)$$
$$(0.08)(14.5) + (0.02)(15.5)$$

i.e.

$$EV = 10.64$$

This confirms that the mean value for the port project IRR was 10.6. Clearly, the best estimate of 12.2 was different from the IRR value that one would expect to find. (As the modal value was between 10 and 12, the best estimate was not the most likely IRR value either.)

Allowing for variance

The expected value was 10.64, but how representative is this mean value of the whole distribution? To answer this question one needs to look at the degree of variation about the mean. The greater this variation, the less representative is the mean value. The usual measure of mean variation is reflected in the concept of the variance (Var), which is defined as:

$$\text{Var} = \sum [\text{Probability}] \cdot [\text{Outcome} - \text{Mean outcome}]^2 \qquad \textbf{(11.4)}$$

For the port project, the variance was as follows:

$$\text{Var} = (0.01)(-5.14)^2 + (0.05)(-4.14)^2 + (0.09)(-3.14)^2$$
$$(0.13)(-2.14)^2 + (0.12)(-1.14)^2 + (0.14)(-0.14)^2$$
$$(0.14)(\ 0.86)^2 + (0.12)(\ 1.86)^2 + (0.10)(\ 2.86)^2$$
$$(0.08)(\ 3.86)^2 + (0.02)(\ 4.86)^2$$

i.e.
$$\text{Var} = 5.23$$

The variance is the square of the standard deviation. Using my calculation the standard deviation is 2.3. However, Pouliquen states that the standard deviation for the port project was 2.5. His figure is more accurate than mine since I transformed a continuous distribution to a discrete one (in order to aid the exposition).

The full picture concerning risk for the port project is that the mean value was 10.64 and the variance was 5.23. The basic issue now is how to choose among projects with different mean and variance values. For two projects with the same variance, one selects the project with the higher expected value. But which project should one choose if there is a project which has a lower expected value and also a lower variance? Unfortunately, as will now be explained, there is no accepted way of combining the two characteristics of a probability distribution.

Let us represent IRR outcomes by the variable x. Say one wishes to state that social utility U is positively related to the mean outcome x^*, and negatively related to the variance. One could write U as

$$U = ax^* - b \, \text{Var} \, x \tag{11.5}$$

where a and b are positive constants. This can be called a 'gambler's utility function'. As the variance of x is given by $(x - x^*)^2$, equation (11.5) can be rewritten as

$$U = ax^* - b(x - x^*)^2$$

or

$$U = ax^* - bx^{*2} - b(x^2 - 2xx^*)$$

$$\left. \vphantom{\begin{array}{c} 1 \\ 1 \\ 1 \end{array}} \right\} \quad \textbf{(11.6)}$$

It is the expression in the brackets of equation (11.6) which poses the fundamental problem. It states that when outcomes are above a certain level (x is greater than the square root of $2xx^*$) utility will decline with further rises in x. This implies that a rich person or nation (operating at high levels of x) would be less likely to get involved with risky ventures than a poor person or nation! There is plenty of empirical evidence contradicting this implication. Thus a utility function of the form of equation (11.6) is not a good representation to use to describe risk decision-making behaviour.

The argument for ignoring variance in public projects

Given the difficulty in combining notions of risk and variance, it would be very convenient if there were a proposition that argued that one need not consider variance in public projects. It turns out that such a proposition does exist. This proposition is called the Arrow–Lind theorem. Arrow and Lind (1970) give a detailed proof of the proposition. Here we give a more intuitive explanation, based on two ideas behind the theorem, 'risk pooling' and 'risk spreading'.

An insurance company eliminates an individual's risk by pooling the effects of many persons. If there is a one in a million chance that a person's house will burn down, and there are one million persons in a society, there is expected to be one house burned down each year. If a house is worth $100,000, then society expects to lose $100,000 each year. By each individual paying a premium of 10 cents, which is a certain loss, one can avoid a risky situation which could involve a $100,000 loss.

Although the public project evaluator usually will not be able to contract out a project's risk to an insurance company, risk pooling may still be relevant if there are a large number of independent projects to be undertaken by the government, for then projects which realise more than their expected value will be offset by projects which realise less than their expected value. Mean values dominate the outcomes, and variances can be ignored. However, up till now, developing countries undertake just a few large projects and risk pooling is not an important consideration in practice.

Much more relevant to project appraisal practice, and the logic behind the Arrow–Lind theorem, is the idea of risk spreading. This works by the government involving more persons in the outcome of the project than would be the case if the project were undertaken by a private investor. If an investment has a 50% chance of producing net-benefits of two million dollars, and a 50% chance of losing one million dollars, then a single, private investor stands to gain a lot or lose a lot. But if the investment is made by the government on behalf of a society with a million people, who agree to share outcomes equally, then there is a 50% chance of a $2 per person gain and a 50% chance of a $1 per person loss. The important point is that even though the variation of project outcomes is the same in the aggregate irrespective of who undertakes the project, government involvement would spread the risk and thereby make it smaller on a per person basis.

The reason that the size of the per person risk is important is because (in economic theory) there is assumed to be an asymmetry between the value of equal-sized gains and losses. A risk-averse person would value a million-dollar gain at less than a million-dollar loss. A loss of this size would probably drive the individual into poverty; while the gain would not add satisfaction to the same degree. If the million-dollar gain was considered one-third as much as the million-dollar loss, the project would not be considered worthwhile for an individual investor. It would then be 'too risky'. But, if the government was involved, and the number of people in the society was great, the per person loss would not drive individuals into poverty. A $1-gain would be effectively worth as much as a $1-loss, and the project would be perceived to be worthwhile (net benefits per person would be $1). The risk element is so small that it can be ignored.

The Arrow–Lind theorem, by justifying the ignoring of variance, has been hailed (by Tresch, 1981, p. 512) as providing one of the few instances where public investment decision-making is simpler than private investment decision-making. However, there are some reservations to be made, even within the confines of an efficiency-only approach.

1. When pure public goods are involved (such as defence) benefits per person are not reduced no matter how many persons are involved.
2. When taxes are not shared out equally, per person costs may not fall equally when the number of people involved increases.

To these efficiency reservations must be added a distributional qualification. Throughout this text, and central to the S & T approach, is the splitting of the effects of a project into its impact on particular income groups. The more we disaggregate in this way, the less we can regard different individuals' gains and losses as offsetting, and the more we must recognise the need to allow for variance.

   To conclude, when distributional objectives are considered important, the Arrow–Lind theorem does not apply. Some allowance for variance must be made. Because there is no generally accepted criterion for combining an allowance for variance with a regard for the expected value, we shall consider in the discussion section whether there are any viable *ad hoc* methods for allowing for risk.

11.3   Problems

Reference has already been made to Knight's classification of risk as measurable uncertainty. Knight also pointed out that because risk is measurable, it is also insurable. Once insured, the risk becomes a certain cost, equal to the premium paid. Risk becomes just like any other cost of production. It no longer requires separate consideration. The problems that follow are based on this type of reasoning. The only difference is that it is shown that it is not always necessary to go to an insurance company to remove the risk. The problems are based on the data from the Mogadiscio port project. The risk concerning labour productivity is the main focus of the analysis.

Background information

The Mogadiscio port project involved constructing a breakwater, two berths, two transit sheds, storage area and office accommodations. The port was expected to last forty years. The cost of the project was estimated at $14.6 million. There were three main benefit categories: (a) savings in cargo handling cost; (b) savings in the reduction of damages; and (c) savings in ship-turnaround time. Pouliquen does not state the expected benefits and costs over the life of the project. However, he does inform us (on p. 7) of the gross benefits for the first seven years. They are around $2 million per year. Assume that $1.8 million are the net benefits per year over the full life of the project (except for year zero when the capital costs are incurred). (Note that the figure of 1.8 million makes the IRR just above 12%, which is Pouliquen's outcome for the IRR.)

Questions

(a) Calculate the NPV for the port project assuming a discount rate of 10%. (Hint: the NPV of a $1-stream for forty years at 10% is $9.78.)

(b) Assume that when labour productivity is at its lowest (five tons per gang hour) annual net benefits fall by $400,000 below what they otherwise would have been. Would the port project be worthwhile at this lower level of labour productivity?

(c) Say a gang supervisor can be found who could guarantee that labour productivity would be at the best estimate level (ten tons per gang hour) and charges $100,000 per year for carrying out the supervision. Would hiring the supervisor be worthwhile?

(d) On the basis of your answer to the previous question, need there be any risk to the project on the account of adverse labour productivity?

11.4 Discussion

This is not the place to present a critique of risk theory in the context of project appraisal. (Useful surveys are provided in Dasgupta, 1972, Chapter 8 and Lind, 1982, Chapter 2.) Instead, I will limit the discussion to two suggestions for improving the practice of allowing for risk in project appraisal.

11.4.1 Allowing for risk in the form of a separate project appraisal

Pouliquen's idea of hiring a supervisor to ensure that labour productivity is not below expectations is worth generalising. As we saw in the problems, the idea is like the Knight strategy of reducing a risky outcome to a certain cost. If the main project is worthwhile when this cost has been deducted, then for the assessment of the project itself, risk does not have to be considered further. The only issue is whether one wishes to incur the extra cost to remove the risk. This can be considered as a 'secondary project', on which a decision can be made separate from that for the main project.

Secondary projects to reduce risk can take different forms. One could actually take out an insurance policy to protect against an adverse eventuality (e.g. using Lloyd's of London to insure against shipping accidents). Or else one could, as with the hiring of the port supervisor, undertake an activity that directly affects the outcome of the main project. One could also think about initiating a new project which is not a part of the main project but obtains positive returns in states of the world where the main project receives negative returns.

The principle involved can be seen clearly by considering exactly why the hiring of a port supervisor reduces the risk of the main project. In the problems we found that the NPV for the port project is $3 million (if the best estimate is used for labour productivity) and it is −$0.912 million if labour productivity is at the lower end of its range. Thus, the main project produces $3 million in 'good times' (states of the world where the best estimate occurs) and −$0.912 million in 'bad times' (states of the world where the lowest estimate occurs). The hiring of the supervisor has a cost in present value terms of $0.978 million and a benefit in present value terms of $3.912 million (the forgone adverse effect in the main project). The cost has to be paid even if good times would have occurred for the main project in the absence of the supervisor. The secondary project, therefore, produces net benefits of $2.934 million ($3.912 − $0.978) during the bad times for the main project, and − $0.978 million during the good times for the main project (when a supervisor would not have been needed). Note that the gains and losses for the secondary project occur in the opposite time periods to that of the main project. When the main project loses, the secondary project gains, and vice versa. The joint outcome of the main and secondary projects are summarised in Table 11.5. This shows that when both projects are implemented, the joint NPV is $2.022 million in either state of

Table 11.5 NPVs for the port project for alternative states of the world (levels of labour productivity)

	States of the world	
	Main project has labour productivity below its best estimate	Main project has labour productivity equal to its best estimate
Main project *NPV*	− $0.912 million	+ $3.000 million
Secondary project *NPV*	+ $2.934 million	− $0.978 million
Joint *NPV*	+ $2.022 million	+ $2.022 million

the world. The outcome has no variation and risk has been eliminated.

From the previous example one can see the property that a new project (which is not part of the main project) must have. Its outcomes must be negatively related to the outcomes of the main project in order to remove the risk. For this reason the modern theory of finance defines the riskiness of an asset (project) in terms of covariance rather than variance. (Covariance is how the variances of different projects are associated.) An asset having a large variance is risky only if its outcomes are positively related to other assets. If it has a negative covariance the riskiness of the whole group of assets (the projects in a development plan) is actually reduced. An example of a new project which would remove the risk from the port project is one that aims at developing a domestic import-substitution activity that prospers only when foreign trade is adversely affected.

11.4.2 The need to include confidence intervals in parameter estimation

There are a number of distinctions that need to be drawn concerning the causes of risk. Some variables in the S & T framework are value parameters, such as the distribution aversion parameter (n), while other variables are empirical by nature, e.g. the per capita growth rate (g). When one says that one is 'unsure' about the 'true value' of a variable, one is saying quite different things for the two kinds of parameter.

The lack of knowledge about the value parameters is due to a conceptual vagueness. One is unsure about making value judgements when welfare theory does not provide enough guidance to make precise statements. It is wise to provide a sensitivity analysis for the value parameters. Note that a risk analysis would not be appropriate here. One can hardly put a probability statement on, say, whether n is equal to 1 or 2.

On the other hand, the lack of knowledge of the empirical parameters has a much simpler explanation. Developing countries do not have sufficient data on which to form reliable estimates for many of these values. Most of the time, project evaluators just choose a best estimate for a parameter. This is understandable. But there is another distinction that needs to be made.

Some best estimates are, in fact, the only estimates available for a variable. When such parameters crucially affect the overall outcome for a project, further possible values must be sought. This is where risk analysis plays a role. But there are other best estimates that constitute a single-point estimate from a range of values that have occurred in the past. In these cases, project evaluators should not choose just one value (a 'point estimate') without acknowledging the existence of the others. One does this by forming confidence intervals around the point estimate. Constructing a confidence interval for empirical parameter estimates should become a standard part of project appraisal practice. There are 'bad' point estimates due to sampling error (there is so much variation in the sample that the 'true value' could just as well be zero as the best estimate value), and 'good' point estimates which are not due to sampling error ('statistically significant' estimates). For statistically insignificant estimates, the project evaluator needs to either find some more data, or use an alternative estimation technique. (Using an 'alternative estimation technique' involves either employing a different S & T formula to find a parameter, which relies on different variables and hence different data, or employing a different statistical/econometric technique.)

We can make the points just mentioned concrete by considering two parameter estimates used in the Ahmed study (1983) of shadow prices for Thailand.

First, the theory of Chapter 3 indicates that distribution effects should be included in a project evaluation. However, this suggests only that the inequality aversion parameter, n, should be greater than zero. S & T recommend a value for n equal to unity, so Ahmed's best estimate was $n = 1$. As n is a value parameter, with no conceptual certainty as to what precise figure to adopt, it was sensible for Ahmed to try a sensitivity analysis. He therefore also experimented with a value for n equal to 1.5.

Second, in the more complete method to find v, the marginal propensity to save/reinvest (s) plays a part (see equation 4.9); s is an empirical parameter whose value can be estimated from a sample of past observations. To find s for Thailand, Ahmed ran a regression of national income on savings for the years 1970–80. The point estimate was 29% and this was the only value that Ahmed considered. But the value of s varied throughout the eleven-year period. An estimate of this variation is given by the standard error for s. The value for this standard error was 0.05. With about 95% probability, one can say that the value for s is within plus or minus 2 times the standard error. Thus, with 95% confidence, s is between 28% and 30%. (Hence the 'confidence interval for s' is between 28% and 30%.) Any sensitivity analysis for s should involve the upper and lower bounds of the confidence interval.

We can conclude by summarising the three main results:

1. For value parameters, risk can be allowed for by using a sensitivity analysis.
2. Risk analysis is appropriate for empirical parameters when we have

knowledge of just a few of the possible outcomes and try to put probabilities on these outcomes. The probabilities are derived from the subjective evaluations of the project evaluator.

3. When there are a large number of known past outcomes for an empirical factor, one can adopt the standard methodology of statistics by assuming that the probabilities are given by a normal distribution. In which case one should derive a confidence interval for these parameter estimates and use them in any sensitivity analysis one may wish to make.

Appendix

There is just one proposition to demonstrate: how the existence of a risk premium in the discount rate is tantamount to assuming that risk increases over time. The demonstration is based on Sugden and Williams (1978, p. 41, and pp. 61–2).

How a risk premium assumes increasing risk over time

Recall from equation (11.2) that when there is a risk premium u added to the discount rate r, the social criterion is given by

$$NPV = \sum_{t=0}^{t=T} S_t/(1 + r + u)^t$$

Sugden and Williams show that $(1 - u)/(1 + r)$ is approximately equal to $1/(1 + r + u)$. Using this approximation, the criterion becomes

$$NPV = \sum_{t=0}^{t=T} S_t (1 - u)^t/(1 + r)^t \qquad \textbf{(11.7)}$$

Define u as the probability that a project will fail in any year of its life. Then $(1 - u)$ is the probability that a project will succeed. Thus, equation (11.7) can be interpreted as the expected NPV. As each year's social net benefits are conditional on the project surviving the previous year, this is why the expectation for any year is $(1 - u)$ raised to the power of t. The longer the time period, the larger is t, and the lower the value of the expectation of project survival. This means that the probability of success declines over time, the proposition we wished to establish.

12
Basic needs

12.1 Introduction

It was stated in Chapter 1 that aiming for economic development is the objective that is to define the net benefits for a project appraisal. In the 1960s development was associated with growth; while in the 1970s attention focused on growth and income distribution. Consequently, in S & T's text written in 1974, net benefits are specified in terms of efficiency and income equity.

Since the mid-1970s, many development economists (see, for example, Hicks and Streeten, 1979) have questioned whether these two social objectives are sufficient indicators of development. The main concern was that too much attention was given to income (both its growth and distribution) as the central concept. There are complaints with using income as an indicator, even if it is a poor group which is being assisted. There may be non-income dimensions to the welfare of individuals, such as their ability to read and write; and additional cash of the poor may be devoted to low nutritional foods, thus not leading to the health benefits that one would expect from rising incomes. The subject matter of this chapter will therefore revolve around the two themes of how to incorporate other indicators of development into project appraisal, and when to replace an individual's consumption choice with a social evaluation of consumption.

12.1.1 The basic needs concept

Hicks and Streeten interpret the basic needs approach as seeking to in-

224

corporate a concern for the alleviation of poverty into the specification of development. When in poverty one is deprived of certain essential/basic needs, such as health, education, food, water supply and sanitation. These basic needs can be reflected by various indicators. For example, health can be measured by life-expectancy, and education can be gauged by literacy levels. While income-based measures of development focus on total production and the distribution of income, the basic needs approach concentrates on the composition of production (health, education, etc.) and its beneficiaries.

One important advantage of some basic needs indicators is that they automatically incorporate distributional considerations, which is not true of income-based measures. For example, if the literacy rate is increased, this inevitably means that the distribution of education has improved, seeing that the proportion of beneficiaries has increased.

One obvious question to ask about the basic needs indicators is the extent to which they differ from the income-based measures of development. To answer this, Hicks and Streeten used the World Bank's social data bank to check the correlation between basic needs indicators and GNP per head. The results are reported in Table 12.1. We can see that there is a moderate average correlation (0.50) of the seven basic needs indicators and GNP per head when all countries are pooled, but the average correlation is low when we just consider developing countries on their own (0.25). This means that increasing a developing country's income will not necessarily satisfy basic needs. The two approaches are (somewhat) distinct. So the conventional project appraisal methodology based on the income concept will have to be adapted if one wishes to allow for basic needs.

Although the two approaches can be considered to be separate, Hicks and Streeten point out (p. 571): 'It has never been clear whether the search was for an alternative to GNP, or a complement or a supplement.' For project appraisal purposes, we will assume that the aim is to combine the two approaches in some meaningful manner.

Table 12.1 Correlations (r^2) of basic-needs indicators and GNP per head

Basic needs indicator	All countries	Developing countries	Developed countries
Expectation of life at birth	0.53	0.28	0.13
% of required calorie consumption	0.44	0.22	0.22
Infant mortality	0.42	0.34	0.25
Primary enrolment	0.28	0.24	0.05
Literacy	0.54	0.47	0.16
Average persons per room	0.58	0.08	0.29
% of houses without piped water	0.74	0.13	0.36
Average r^2 of all indicators	0.50	0.25	0.18

12.1.2 Cost-effectiveness analysis

The simplest way of integrating basic needs criteria into project appraisal is to use the cost-effectiveness approach. In this method, one first assumes that a particular objective is worthwhile, and then one tries to obtain the benefits at minimum cost (the least-cost technique is chosen as the most 'cost-effective' project). The method was first conceived in terms of objectives whose benefits were thought too difficult to evaluate, such as the value of a human life. Thus in the health field the aim is to save lives. Doctors are asked to find those treatments or procedures that save a life in the cheapest way. Cost-effectiveness is also used extensively for evaluating defence expenditures where, for example, the United States sets an objective to 'maintain a presence in the Middle East', and the military advisers have to select the least-cost way of achieving this goal. In the basic needs area, the approach has usually been adopted for nutrition schemes. For example, Reutlinger and Selowsky (1976) of the World Bank applied cost-effectiveness in terms of the fiscal cost of providing one extra calorie to a particular (target) group of consumers.

Although cost-effectiveness analysis is straightforward, Scandizzo and Knudsen (1980, hereafter S & K) point out that it does have a number of fundamental drawbacks when used for basic needs. There are four main difficulties:

1. The cost-effectiveness goal may not be attainable within the financial resources at the disposal of the government. If the goal is not attainable, then clearly there can be no least-cost project to choose. In the 1960s President Johnson pledged to eliminate poverty in the US. While the numbers below the poverty line were greatly reduced ten years later, poverty still existed. The eradication of poverty in its entirety is not therefore a goal that cost-effectiveness can handle at present.

2. Given the first difficulty, recognition should be given to the fact that some poverty will remain after the government project. In these circumstances, it is not sufficient to set as a goal the attainment of a feasible calorie target that is below the poverty level, for those persons who are furthest away from the targets should be given priority over those who are nearest to the target.

3. The target levels specified in a cost-effectiveness study are expressions of social preference. But no allowance is given for private preferences. These are also important because they determine the extent to which the rich exceed the target levels and the poor dip below the target levels.

4. Cost-effectiveness analysis only allows projects to be ranked for a single basic-needs indicator. How does one compare two projects, where one brings everyone up to a target calorie level, while the other achieves a certain literacy percentage level for the country?

S & K present a methodology for dealing with these deficiencies of cost-effectiveness analysis. This will be covered in section 12.3. First we shall outline an approach by Harberger which S & K consider to be a precursor to their work.

12.2 Harberger's approach

Harberger (1984) has a complaint about the use of distribution weights in project appraisal. The weights do not come from individuals' preferences but, rather, they are the decision-maker's articulation of social preferences. Harberger recommends that as an alternative, one consider the basic-needs philosophy, because he considers that this reflects individual preferences better.

12.2.1 Basic needs as a public good

Assume that society can be split into two groups, r the rich and p the poor. Altruism by the rich is the individual preference with which Harberger was concerned. However, wealthy individuals seem to be more concerned with certain basic needs of the poor, say their food consumption measured in calories, rather than their income, which reflects the total consumption possibilities of the poor. Let R be the food consumption target for the poor set by the rich, and D_p the private consumption demand by the poor. (Note: D in this chapter stands for demand and not for a finite change.) The difference between the target and what the poor actually demand is called the basic-needs gap, that is,

$$Basic\text{-}needs\ gap = R - D_p \qquad (12.1)$$

It is the preferences by the wealthy over this gap that defines the altruism. Let D_r represent the demand by the rich for the consumption of the poor. Since the wealthy feel worse off the greater the gap, and the gap is smaller the greater the private consumption demand by the poor (D_p), D_r is positively related to D_p. This positive relation defines the indirect (psychological) benefits by the rich for the consumption by the poor.

A pure public good is one in which consumption by any one group automatically leads to consumption by all groups. A loaf of bread is a private good, because the more one group consumes of it, the less is available for others, while defence is a public good, because any extra security received by one group from expenditures on defence will be received by everyone in the country simultaneously. As the consumption by the poor generates direct benefits for the poor and indirect benefits for the rich, consumption by the poor has the property of being a public good. Because consumption by the poor is a public good, the social demand curve is constructed in a particular way, as we now explain.

12.2.2 The social demand curve for a basic-needs good

The social demand is the total demand for all parties affected, the rich and the poor: that is.

$$Social\ demand = D_r + D_p \qquad (12.2)$$

The demand by the poor (D_p) is a function of the price of the consumption good, P (the price of food). When the price of food falls, the poor consume more. The more the poor consume, the greater are the indirect benefits to the rich. Thus, D_r is also a function of P. This means that we can construct a social demand curve for the consumption by the poor as a function of price. The social demand curve is presented in figure 12.1. For any unit of consumption by the poor, there are two groups that benefit. Total benefit (demand) is the sum of the two groups' benefits (demands). The social demand curve is thus the vertical summation of the demand curves by the rich and the poor. The social demand curve is shown by ABC in the diagram.

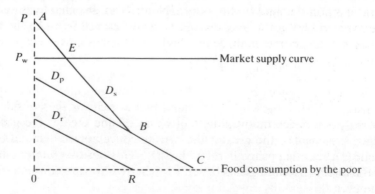

Figure 12.1 *The social demand curve for food consumption by the poor*

The market demand curve would be given just by D_p. This would not justify any food consumption by the poor, as D_p is below P_w (the world price for food) for all consumption levels. But, using the social demand curve, some consumption by the poor is warranted (determined by the intersection of the social demand curve and the market supply curve). Recognition of the basic-needs demand by the rich thus justifies socially financed increases in consumption of food by the poor. Social net benefits of a public food consumption project would be equal to the triangular area given by AEP_w. This area is the difference between the area under the social demand curve (total benefits) and the area under the supply curve (total costs) for the socially optimal level of consumption (given by the intersection of the social demand curve and the market supply curve, which is denoted by point E).

12.3 Scandizzo & Knudsen's approach

S & K's analysis is similar to Harberger's, except for two major differences. A different group is making the social evaluation on behalf of the poor, and attention is focused on the complete market for food, rather than just the food consumption by the poor. The implications of these two differences will be analysed separately in the next two sections.

12.3.1 Redefining the social demand curve

In the Harberger approach, the preferences (demand curve) of the rich determined how much should be added to the demand for food by the poor in order to form the social demand curve. In the S & K framework, it is a 'social agent' who is to supplement the demand by the poor. The social agent may be a representative of the rich. But the agent could just as well be a representative of a charitable organisation or a member of the government. If we represent by D_a the social agent's demand, the social demand is now defined by

$$Social\ demand = D_a + D_p \qquad (12.3)$$

Not only is a different entity helping to determine the basic needs demand, the basis is different. The social agent respects individual preferences when the private demand by the poor is above the target level R. But the agent does not fully accept private consumption behaviour whenever this entails consumption levels below the social target. Instead, the social agent imposes a desired consumption level exactly equal to R. This is achieved by the agent demanding an amount of food equal to the basic needs gap, $R - D_p$. What determines whether the consumption by the poor will be below R is the price of food (with the income and preferences of the poor taken as given). Let PR be the price at which the poor would choose precisely R. Then the social demand is formed in the following way:

$$P < PR : D_a = 0, \qquad \text{thus } D_s = D_a + D_p = D_p$$
$$P > PR : D_a = R - D_p, \text{ thus } D_s = D_a + D_p = R$$

A graphical representation of the S & K social demand curve is shown in figure 12.2. The splitting up of the social demand curve according to whether prices are above or below PR results in a kink at the target level of consumption. This is the reason that D_s is given by *abc* in figure 12.2. As before, government-financed food consumption projects would be socially beneficial. But this time the desired level is always at (or beyond) the target level of consumption, R.

12.3.2 Analysing the complete market

Using the social agent's demand instead of the preferences of the rich was the first difference between the S & K and the Harberger approaches. The other difference involves the specification of the quantity unit. Rather than focus solely on the consumption of the poor, attention is given to the market determination of food consumption, which

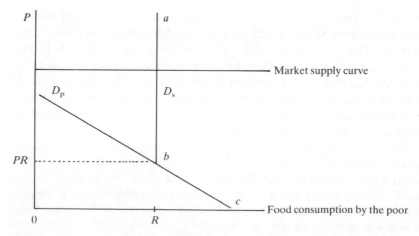

Figure 12.2   *The Scandizzo and Knudsen social demand curve for food consumption by the poor*

depends on the consumption behaviour of both the rich and the poor. Because it is aggregate demand that is being analysed, S & K can allow for the number in poverty (N) to vary with the price. In the process, as we shall now see, the social demand reflects the preferences of the group that is released from poverty by the marginal lowering of the price.

We again consider two groups (of equal number). This time we call the two groups 1 and 2, with group 2 richer than group 1 : D_1 is group 1's private demand for food and D_2 is group 2's private demand for food. (Note that a private demand makes no allowance for altruism.) The social demand curve is defined similarly to that given in equation (12.3), except that we allow the number in poverty to vary with the price charged. The social demand curve becomes

$$Social\ demand = R \cdot N + D_\mathrm{p} \tag{12.4}$$

where $R \cdot N$ is the social agent's demand and D_p is now the sum of the private demands of those who are not in poverty (consuming below the level of R).

An important point for the analysis is that there is a price of food at which even the richer group would be below the target level, R. Thus, N in equation (12.4) is a variable depending on the price of food. Define PR_1 as the price for food above which group 1 is in poverty, and PR_2 as the price above which group 2 is in poverty. The social demand curve (D_s) for various price intervals would be determined as follows:

$P > PR_2 : N = 2$ and $D_\mathrm{p} = 0,$ thus $D_\mathrm{s} = R \cdot N + D_\mathrm{p} = 2R$
$P < PR_1 : N = 0$ and $D_\mathrm{p} = D_1 + D_2,$ thus $D_\mathrm{s} = R \cdot N + D_\mathrm{p} = D_1 + D_2$
$PR_2 > P > PR_1 : N = 1$ and $D_\mathrm{p} = D_2,$ thus $D_\mathrm{s} = R \cdot N + D_\mathrm{p} = R + D_2$

The social demand curve is depicted by the double-kinked curve *abcd* in figure 12.3.

In figure 12.4 we reproduce the social demand curve from figure 12.3 and add the market demand and supply curves. The market demand curve is given by the line *ecd*. It is the horizontal sum of the two private demand curves, D_1 and D_2. Note that the line segment *cd* is a part of both the social and the market demand curves.

The market equilibrium would be at the intersection of the private market demand curve and the market supply curve. This happens to occur at consumption level $2R$ (in order to make the diagram easy to read). This does not mean that both groups are consuming the required level, for the deficiency by group 1 is exactly matched by the over-consumption by group 2.

The social equilibrium would be at the consumption level C^*, where the social demand curve intersects the market supply curve. This

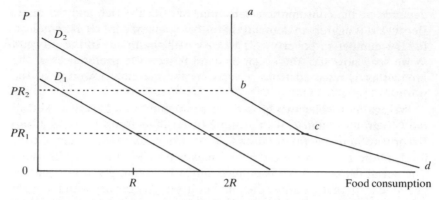

Figure 12.3   *The Scandizzo and Knudsen social demand curve for food consumption*

equilibrium is at a higher level of consumption than that given by the private market solution. There are social gains to be obtained by expanding consumption to level C^*, where group 1 will be consuming exactly R, while group 2 will be consuming more than the required level. The social gains can be measured by the difference between the total benefits and total costs over the additional consumption, given by the difference between C^* and $2R$. Note that this difference is the basic-needs gap of group 1. Benefits are given by the area under the social demand curve, and costs are given by the area under the market supply curve. Thus, the net benefits are represented in figure 12.4 by the area of triangle *bgh*.

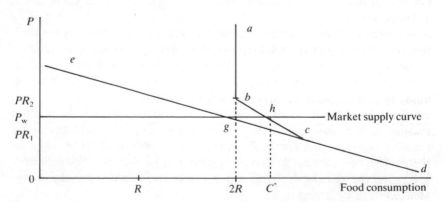

Figure 12.4   *The social demand curve and market equilibrium for food consumption*

The important point to understand about the way that the social gain of removing the basic-needs gap is being measured concerns the precise role played by the two groups. The size of the gap, and hence the size of the public food assistance project, is determined by the market behaviour (preferences) of the group in poverty, while the value to be given to the incremental consumption by the group in poverty is determined by the preferences of the group just above the target level (this is because the slope of the *bc* segment of the social demand curve is derived from the slope of demand curve D_2).

12.3.3 Applications of the social demand curve

There are three main ingredients of the social demand curve: (a) the food target, R; (b) the number below the target, N; and (c) the private food demand curves by those above the target level, D_p. The S & K measures of these ingredients, and the resulting estimates of the social demand curves, for six poor developing countries are presented in Table 12.2.

An expert committee of the Food and Agriculture Organisation (FAO) and the World Health Organisation (WHO) specified a calorie intake for an average man weighing 65 kilos to be 3,000 calories per day, and the relevant figure for a woman weighing 55 kilos was 2,200 calories. S & K defined R as having 10% (approximately 200 calories) below the average level. The private demand curves were estimated by a semi-logarithmic regression of calories on income. Calories were converted to the grain equivalent at the rate of 3.5 million calories per metric ton.

Based on the estimates of the social demand curve, S & K also estimated the net benefits to be obtained from a food distribution scheme (public project) which removes people from poverty. That is, S & K

Table 12.2 Estimates of social demand and its components for six poor developing countries

Country	Target population (N) (millions)	Private demand (millions metric tons)	Social demand (millions metric tons)
Bangladesh	48.5	15.3	16.6
India	152.8	137.0	146.0
Indonesia	58.3	27.9	30.1
Morocco	6.1	4.0	4.3
Pakistan	37.9	13.9	14.2
Sri Lanka	0.0	2.9	2.9

Table 12.3   Estimates of the net benefits of removing poverty

Country	Social gains ($US millions)	Social gains per capita ($/capita)	Social gains per capita in poverty ($/capita)
Bangladesh	95.4	12.0	19.6
India	148.1	0.25	0.7
Indonesia	232.4	1.8	4.0
Morocco	28.7	1.9	4.7
Pakistan	116.2	1.8	4.4
Sri Lanka	2.1	0.2	0.3

Note: Since Sri Lanka did not have anyone 10% below the average calorie target level, S & K raised the target for this country equal to 100% of the average level.

estimated the social gain triangle *bgh* of figure 12.4. The results are shown in Table 12.3.

12.4   Problems

Because the basic-needs approach uses the social demand curve to make the valuations of changes in outputs, it is using a different procedure for shadow pricing to the one used by S & T. In the problems that follow, we develop S & K's method for deriving shadow prices and compare this with S & T's methods.

Background information

Refer back to figure 12.4. The market price for food is determined by the intersection of aggregate private demand (curve *egd*) and the supply curve. As there are no taxes to consider, the market price is equal to the world price of food, P_w. But this does not necessarily mean that the world price is the shadow price. The shadow price is the social value of any particular food output level. By definition, the social demand curve records the amount of this social value. Whenever the market output is below the socially optimal level, the market price (and hence the world price) will be below the social value. In figure 12.4, C^* is the socially optimal level and $2R$ is the market equilibrium. At output level $2R$ (strictly, one unit greater than $2R$) the shadow price given by the height $b2R$ exceeds the world price by the amount *bg*. S & K provide estimates of this excess relative to the size of the world price. These estimates are presented in Table 12.4.

Table 12.4   Ratios of shadow prices to world prices

Bangladesh	6.30	Indonesia	1.75	Pakistan	3.35
India	1.15	Morocco	1.65	Sri Lanka	1.00

Questions

(a) As the world price is always equal to the market price in S & K's analysis, what could one call (using S & T's terminology) the shadow to world price ratios that appear in Table 12.4?

(b) To what is the shadow price equal at the social optimal level of output C^* in figure 12.4? Hence, what is the ratio of the shadow price to the world price at C^*? What is the size of the shadow to world price ratio at $2R$ relative to that at C^* (is it greater, smaller, or the same size)?

(c) How many groups are consuming below the poverty consumption level at C^* in figure 12.4? How many groups are consuming below the poverty consumption level at output level $2R$?

(d) On the basis of your answers to questions (b) and (c) what is the relation between the numbers in poverty and the size of the shadow to price ratio? Do the figures in Tables 12.2 and 12.4 support your postulated relationship?

(e) What price do S & T recommend be used to measure shadow prices? On the basis of your answer to question (d), can you suggest a general category of reason that their recommended shadow price methodology may need to be amended? Using the figures in Table 12.4, are the necessary amendments quantitatively significant?

12.5 Discussion

All of this section will be devoted to an evaluation of S & K's work on basic needs. We start by interpreting their basic-needs approach as a general project appraisal methodology. Since it is S & T's text that this book is concerned with, it is a comparison of the basic-needs approach and S & T's methods that provides the focal point. Then we proceed to examine various interpretations of S & K's contribution as an income distributional weighting scheme. Finally, we compare how S & K deal with the numbers in poverty relative to the approach recommended throughout this text, i.e. including a numbers' effect as a third element in the social objective function for project appraisal.

12.5.1 Basic needs and S & T's project appraisal methodology

Although not obvious at first glance, S & K's work is understandable within the framework of S & T's project appraisal methodology. The main social objectives for S & T are efficiency and distribution. These objectives are accommodated in the basic-needs approach in the following way. Economic efficiency is reflected in the private demand curves for food consumption. The greater consumer willingness to pay for a product (project), the greater is society's satisfaction from resource availability, holding income distributional issues constant. It is because demand curves do not recognise the inability to pay by poor consumers, who would otherwise greatly value the public project output, that income distributional considerations must be included to supplement the efficiency evaluation. S & T scale up the efficiency effect when the benefits go to low income groups. In the basic-needs approach the social value of consumption by the poor is added on to the efficiency effect. But, no matter whether one is augmenting the efficiency effect by multiplying by a factor greater than one, or adding a positive amount, the end result is that one is using a joint efficiency and distributional measuring rod for the social evaluation of projects.

However, there are three main differences between S & K's approach and that of S & T which are of major importance. These differences are over the choice of numeraire, shadow pricing and the saving premium.

One way of thinking about the choice of numeraire (see Yotopoulos and Nugent, 1976, pp. 381–91, and also Chapter 7 of this book) is in terms of the source of the resources used in the public project. If domestic suppliers are going to produce more of the resource as a replacement, then the supply price should be used to make the social evaluation of the resources. This is the basic S & T (and L & M) assumption. While if the resources for the public project are to be obtained by cutting back domestic consumption, which is the UNIDO assumption, then the demand price provides the relevant social valuation. The fact that S & K use demand curves based on willingness to pay to make their social evaluations means that they are implicitly following the UNIDO approach, which uses domestic consumption as its numeraire. As we know, S & T use public income (investment) as their numeraire.

Once one understands that S & K are using the demand price to make social valuations, it is clear why they do not always recommend using world prices as shadow prices for food projects. When the social optimal level of food consumption exceeds the market equilibrium level, the demand price will be higher than the supply price. When no domestic tariff exists, the supply price is equal to the world price. So the fact that the demand price is being used means that the S & K shadow price will be greater than the world price (whenever there is a group consuming below the target level).

S & K's work therefore provides a main reservation to the use of world prices, which was not mentioned in Chapter 6 when the general rationale for using world prices for tradables was being discussed. For food projects, the social demand price must be used to measure the value of the project output. S & K, in equation (18), provide a formula for calculating the elasticity of the social demand curve which depends on properties of the private demand curves, the distribution of income, and the ratio of those in poverty to the total population.

There is a major omission from S & K's analysis which any general project appraisal methodology should include, i.e. an allowance for a savings premium/consumption penalty. There is no counterpart for S & T's v in the S & K approach. Given that S & K implicitly adopt the UNIDO numeraire, their analysis should be extended to have a term which correponds to the UNIDO investment premium. Since the main aim of food projects is to stimulate consumption, an investment premium would have the effect of reducing somewhat the social desirability of food projects.

12.5.2 Basic needs and income distributional weights

Harberger (1984) considers the basic-needs approach as an alternative to using distributional weights, while Ray (1984, pp. 41–3) summarises S & K's work as implying a particular kind of income weighting scheme. These two interpretations of the basic-needs approach will be discussed in turn.

Basic needs versus distribution weights

Anyone who has followed the analysis of the social demand curve in Harberger's statement of the basic-needs approach, and who has read Hochman and Rodgers' (1971) justification for government redistribution of income in kind, will recognise that the two arguments are the same. It is because the donors (the rich) get satisfaction from the consumption of particular goods (food), rather than the total consumption by the poor (reflected by the money income of the poor), that it is more efficient for the government to assist the poor in kind (providing particular goods) rather than giving them cash hand-outs. It is therefore very confusing to state that the basic-needs approach provides an alternative to distributional weighting. It is less incorrect to say that the basic-needs approach tries to replace distributional weights based on money income by weights based on income in kind. However, if this were all that lay behind the basic-needs approach, we could end our discussion here for, in Chapter 3, we already pointed out that one

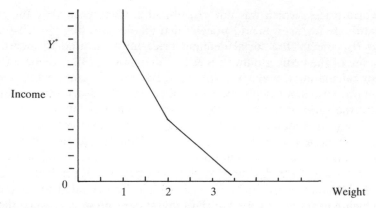

Figure 12.5   *Income weights and the basic-needs approach according to Ray*

weakness of the S & T conception of distributional weights was that it ignored redistribution in kind. We suggested that weights for both money income *and* income in kind be included in project appraisal, along the lines developed in Brent (1980 and 1986). There would be no real need to invoke the basic needs concept for this innovation. Before stating what I think is the fundamental message behind the basic-needs approach, let us look at Ray's interpretation of S and K.

Basic needs as a particular money-income weighting scheme

Ray summarises S & K's work as providing an alternative money income distributional weighting scheme. His summary is presented in the form of a diagram (his Figure 2) reproduced as figure 12.5. Ray explains that in the diagram: 'Y^* is the level of income at which all basic needs are fully met. The kinks represent income thresholds at which some of the basic needs are fully met.' He does not explain precisely how he constructed the diagram. From the shape of the curve, it would seem that what Ray has in mind is figure 12.4, which was S & K's construction of the social demand curve. He uses the diagram to make the observation that in the S & K approach, 'The effect of weighting will be greatly dampened in relation to the use of distributional weights in the constant-elasticity form.' For reference we also reproduce (as figure 12.6) the constant elasticity figure which we first presented in Chapter 3. Ray's interpretation of S & K appears therefore to consist of using the shape of the social demand curve to replace the constant elasticity curve for distributional weights attached to incomes.

The first point that needs to be made in assessing Ray's interpretation of S & K is that it is not inherently wrong. It is possible to consider distributional weights, which usually are applied to incomes, in the

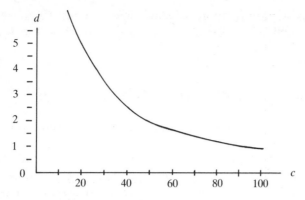

Figure 12.6 *S & T's constant elasticity function used for income distribution weights*

context of valuations of goods. Boadway (1975), following Feldstein (1972), has shown that one can construct a distributional weight for the commodity as a weighted average of the distributional weights to the incomes of the groups (where the weights are given by the proportion of total expenditure on food by the various income groups).

However, even if Ray could show precisely how he constructed his income weights from the social demand curve, his interpretation does a disservice to S & K: Ray's reader is left with the impression that all S & K are doing is replacing a smooth income distributional weighting function by a kinked weighting function. If this were all that they were saying then their work would be unexceptional. For it has been pointed out in Chapter 3 (based on the papers by Brent, 1980 and 1984) that S & T should follow the practice of Weisbrod (1968), who used discrete (and discontinuous) numbers rather than smooth (and continuous) functions for distributional weighting purposes.

In my opinion, S & K's work is a pioneering piece which has been grossly neglected by the project appraisal literature. What makes S & K's work such a significant contribution to project appraisal has very little to do with distribution weights *per se*. There are two contributions involved:

First, S & K provide one solution to a fundamental philosophical problem of public policy-making, i.e. how does one combine individual preferences and imposed preferences by government decision-makers acting for the 'social good'? Their solution is to give priority to individuals when basic needs are being met, and to give priority to the social decision-makers when consumption levels are below the social targets. This is an interesting compromise which is worthy of a full discussion (see Chapter 13 for an initial attempt to do this).

Second, S & K are the first to try to bring a concern for poverty explicitly into a project appraisal calculation rather than use cost-effectiveness analysis. This contribution will be discussed in the next section.

12.5.3 Poverty, the numbers effect and basic needs

In the introduction we stated Hicks and Streeten's interpretation of the basic-needs philosophy. The essential idea was to introduce a concern for poverty into development policy. It seems to me that this is what S & K have achieved. Sen (1976) identified three dimensions which need to be included in any comprehensive index: the size of the poverty gap, the numbers below the poverty line (called the 'head count'), and the distribution of income among those below the poverty level. S & K's approach accommodates all of these dimensions. The poverty gap was the magnitude that determined the social agent's demand, and the kinks in the social demand curve were dependent upon the numbers moving out of poverty. Concern over the distribution among the poor is partially reflected by the fact that the groups that are in greatest need contribute the largest to S & K's social demand curve.

The issue to be decided is how best to incorporate the various dimensions of poverty (in particular, the numbers in poverty, N) into project appraisal. That is, should we follow S & K and use N in joint combination with efficiency, E (in the form of willingness to pay), to help determine social net benefits, S, or is it more useful to include N as an additively separable component of S? My view is that the latter course is the more fruitful approach. Let me now try to defend this position.

The major problem with combining a concern over N and a desire for E is that one is obscuring the basic trade-off that is involved with policy-making decisions. Usually a decision-maker has to choose more of one objective at the expense of another. The weights in a project appraisal reflect the relative importance of the various objectives. It has been argued in Chapter 3 that it is best that any weights be made explicit in a project appraisal. In S & K, the weights are implicit, as we explain below.

In the S & K approach they first combine N with distributional factors to form a joint weight on these two objectives. This joint weight is implicit in S & K's construction of the social demand curve. When we examine precisely the nature of this joint weight we see that it is actually a variable weight. It varies with the extent of poverty. When all groups are below the poverty line (R), the social demand curve is vertical, which means an infinite weight is attached to increases in food consumption. To see this, refer back to figure 12.4 and imagine the market demand *egd* intersecting the market supply curve to the left of point *g* (a level of consumption below 2*R*). Any increase in consumption which results from the public project would be aggregating under a social demand curve that has no upper bound. Hence, its value would be infinite. When no group consumes less than *R*, the joint weight drops to zero, and efficiency is the sole index of the social net benefits. In between *R* and 2*R*, the weight falls with the preferences of group 2 to their own consumption of food. (It appears that it was to achieve less extreme values for the implicit weight that S & K switched the focus of their analysis from the consumption of food by the poor to the complete market for food.)

The nature of the trade-off is obscured not only by S & K's weights being implicit, but also by the fact that (as we have just seen) an infinite weight is used for a certain range of consumption. Adopting an infinite weight is tantamount to avoiding the trade-off issue. It gives priority to one objective for all values of the other. (Note that here we are not going against the earlier conclusion that Ray and Harberger are wrong to interpret S & K's work as one of income distributional weights. The weight we are discussing is the one attached to the joint income distribution and poverty objective relative to the efficiency effect.)

How, then, would explicitly allowing for *N* as a third social objective improve matters? In the S & T methodology, there are two social objectives, efficiency and distribution. These are additively separable factors in the social criterion. That is, *S* was given by

$$S = E - C(\beta - \omega) \tag{12.5}$$

If we introduce *N* (the numbers *no longer* in poverty) into the social criterion, also in an additively separable fashion, it would appear as

$$S = E - C(\beta - \omega) + a_N \cdot N \tag{12.6}$$

where a_N is the weight to the number no longer in poverty.

In this framework, we can see precisely what impact the concern for poverty was having on the social outcome. The aim to remove poverty would be an extension to, rather than a replacement for, S & T's methods. S & K's ideas could still be helpful in that if we knew their social demand curve, we could estimate *N* for different levels of the public food project. We would then know the values for *N* to insert into equation (12.6).

To complete the argument we need to say something about how the weight a_N can be obtained. Strictly, we would try to estimate the social value of removing someone from poverty. In the absence of such an estimate, we can use an idea adapted from Harberger (1984). He was concerned that in including income distributional objectives into project appraisal, one might be investing more resources than would be entailed in devising a direct food transfer to the undernourished. If it costs, say, $2,000 dollars per year to provide a food transfer, then $2,000 is the value to be placed on the public project effect that takes a person out of poverty. That is, a_N is $2,000. But note that this is a lower bound to the weight on N. If we assume (as we do throughout this book on project appraisal) that other government instruments will not be changed, the value of removing poverty will be greater than the cost of removing poverty.

13
Summary and conclusions

13.1   Introduction

The most useful way of summarising the subject matter of this book is to work through the practice project approach from start to finish. Such a summary helps one identify the key factors in project appraisal and confirms the applied/applications emphasis of the text. The appraisal basically relates to the case study by Tyler (1979) of the purchase of tractors in Pakistan. The rest of this chapter is organised around the calculations developed for the practice project appraisal. In section 13.2 we focus on the main components in the practice study and use this opportunity to provide an assessment of both the theory and the practice. Section 13.3 elaborates on a number of themes that have spanned more than one chapter. By analysing recurring themes one can see more clearly the fundamental methodological issues in project appraisal. Finally, the problems in section 13.4 present a number of essay questions to test the general understanding of the reader on all the main subject areas. There is no need for a separate discussion section as comments, criticisms and suggestions will be given as we proceed throughout the chapter.

13.2   Working through the practice project appraisal

The S & T approach involves making a social evaluation of a project on the basis of

$$S = E - C \left(\beta - d/v\right) \qquad (13.1)$$

243

The data has already been provided in section 8.4.1 of Chapter 8. We start with the efficiency calculation and then obtain the social outcome. We provide a summary at the end.

The efficiency calculation

The efficiency calculation involves taking the additional inputs and outputs given in Table 8.4, which are measured in market prices, and multiplying them by their accounting ratios, so that they will be expressed in shadow price terms. The additional outputs are all exported and do not have any price distortions. The accounting ratio for these outputs is equal to unity. Multiplying 4,021 (all monetary values are in thousands of rupees) by 1 leads to a social value of output equal to 4,021 per annum. The world price value is 4,021 (the fob export price times the number of physical units) expressed in units of the local currency by way of the official exchange rate.

There are two kinds of input for the tractor project, traded and non-traded. The traded inputs have an accounting ratio of unity if there are no distortions. However, we are told that there is a tariff of 90% of the domestic price quoted. This makes their accounting ratio equal to 0.10. The traded inputs then have a social value of 0.10 times 1,721 (the sum of the domestic values for the three imports), which is equal to 172.1 per annum. The non-traded inputs, which in net terms amount to 266, do not have any information as to how they can be broken down (in order to use the decomposition procedure). Since we are told the standard conversion factor, we can use its value to apply to the non-traded inputs. That is, the SCF of 0.7 becomes the accounting ratio. Note that by using the SCF, we are effectively using the marginal social value approach to valuing non-tradables. Multiplying 266 by 0.7 produces a social value for the non-traded inputs equal to 186.2 per annum. The total social value for the traded and non-traded inputs is 172.1 plus 186.2, which is 358.3 per annum.

The efficiency net benefits for any year are therefore equal to 4,021 (the value of outputs) minus 358.3 (the value of inputs), i.e. 3,662.7. These net benefits accrue for each of seven years into the future, starting in year 1. Since they relate to the future they must be discounted to obtain their equivalent present values. Once discounted, they can then be summed and compared with the capital cost of the tractors which takes place in year zero. The tractors had a world price value (and hence, a shadow price value) of 5,231. (This capital cost figure can be interpreted as applying an accounting ratio of 0.83 – i.e. 5,231/6,241 – to the market price of the tractors.) The necessary calculations to form

Table 13.1 The efficiency NPV for the Pakistan tractor project (based on data assumed in Chapter 8)

Year	Efficiency net benefits (E)	Discount factor (at 10%)	Today's value (at 10%)
0	−5,231	1.000	−5,231
1	3,662.7	0.909	3,329.4
2	3,662.7	0.826	3,025.4
3	3,662.7	0.751	2,750.7
4	3,662.7	0.683	2,501.6
5	3,662.7	0.621	2,274.5
6	3,662.7	0.564	2,065.8
7	3,662.7	0.513	1,879.0
		NPV at 10% =	+12,595.4

the efficiency net present value are shown in Table 13.1 (which follows the format presented in Table 2.4). The discount rate used in this table is 10%. There are two reasons why this is the appropriate rate to use:

1. The S & T social discount rate is the accounting rate of interest. It is the rate that the public sector should use to ration its available funds. If (as is assumed for the Pakistan tractor project exercise) the marginal rate of return on public investment is 10%, then any additional funds that are being used for the new project have an opportunity cost of 10%.
2. When the available funds come from abroad, the opportunity cost of funds is expressed in terms of foreign exchange. Since S & T's numeraire is free foreign exchange, it immediately follows that the foreign loan rate charged is their social discount rate. The practice project appraisal tells us that 10% is the rate charged by the World Bank who is financing the loan. So 10% is the SDR for the Pakistan tractor project.

Table 13.1 shows that the net present value of the tractor project in efficiency terms is 12,595.4. Since this is a positive figure, it passes the NPV investment decision rule. The country has a larger net output with the project than without it. Given the penchant of the World Bank for using rates of return in its reports, it is necessary also to present the final outcome as an IRR. The relevant calculations for the IRR are shown in Table 13.2. The upper value (R_U) for *IRR* is shown as 70% and the lower value (R_L) is 65%. Using Gittinger's interpolation rule – see equation (2.6) – *IRR* is 68%. Since this greatly exceeds the cost of capital of 10%, the tractor project also passes the IRR investment decision rule expressed in efficiency terms.

Table 13.2   Calculating the IRR for the Pakistan tractor project (based on data assumed in Chapter 8)

Year	Efficiency net-benefits (E)	Discount factor (at 70%)	Today's value (at 70%)	Discount factor (at 65%)	Today's value (at 65%)
0	−5,231	1.000	−5,231	1.000	−5,231
1	3,662.7	0.588	2,153.7	0.625	2,219.6
2	3,662.7	0.346	1,267.3	0.391	1,344.2
3	3,662.7	0.204	747.2	0.244	816.8
4	3,662.7	0.120	439.5	0.153	494.5
5	3,662.7	0.070	256.4	0.095	300.3
6	3,662.7	0.041	150.2	0.060	183.1
7	3,662.7	0.024	87.9	0.038	109.9
		NPV at 65% =	−128.8	*NPV* at 60% =	+237.4

The social calculation

The social evaluation starts with the efficiency outcome, E, and adjusts it for the distributional consequences, $-C\,(\beta - \omega)$. The distribution adjustment itself can be split into two. First, there is the change in consumption, C; then there is the weight to be attached to the consumption change, $\beta - \omega$. The consumption change is summarised in Table 13.3, the weights are presented in Tables 13.4 and 13.5, and the weighted consumption change is shown in Table 13.6. There will be two social outcomes as two alternative values for v will be tried. The social (combined efficiency and distribution) NPV outcome for the case where v = 4 appears in Table 13.7.

The information necessary to calculate the consumption change was given in Table 8.3. The consumption change is different for each of the four groups affected, i.e. 202 big farmers, 879 small farmers, 496 full-time workers becoming casual workers, and 828 full-time workers becoming unemployed. (Note that the 660 original casual workers and 912 of the 2,236 full-time workers were unaffected.) The difference between the various groups' before and after consumption is given below.

Table 13.3 reports the widely different consumption experiences of the four groups. The big farmers gained enormously, but all the other groups were faced with large reductions in their consumption levels. How socially significant these consumption differences are to be judged depends on the weights attached to them. The estimates of the weights will now be explained.

Since $\omega = d/v$, there are three variables to estimate in order to find the weight to consumption for each group, i.e. β, d and v. These three variables will be examined in turn.

Table 13.3 Changes in consumption for the Pakistan tractor project (based on data assumed in Chapter 8)

Category (group)	Number of households	Change in average household consumption	Consumption change for group
Big farmers	202	+18.163	+3,668.9
Small farmers	879	−1.322	−1,162.0
Full-time workers becoming casual	496	−.560	−277.8
Full-time workers becoming unemployed	828	−1.004	−831.3

The formula for β was given in Chapter 3 as

$$\beta = \frac{M + X}{M (1 + t_m) + X (1 - t_x)} \qquad (13.2)$$

We were told that during the project period, Pakistan had a trade balance. With $M = X$ substituted into equation (13.2), the formula for β simplifies to

$$\beta = \frac{2}{(1 + t_m) + (1 - t_x)} \qquad (13.3)$$

where t_m was said to be 0.4 and t_x was set at 0.2. When these tax values are inserted into equation (13.3), we obtain the value $\beta = 0.9091$.

The iso-elastic distribution weighting function that we presented in Chapter 3 applies to small (marginal) changes in consumption. However, given the large changes in consumption behaviour by all four groups, Tyler thought that it would be more appropriate to use S & T's non-marginal weighting formula that appears in their appendix (for the case where $n = 1$). We follow Tyler and use for the ds

$$d = \bar{c} \left[\log_e (c_2/c_1) \right]/(c_2 - c_1) \qquad (13.4^*)$$

where the numbers 1 and 2 attached to the per capita consumption levels refer to the situations before and after the project, respectively; c_1 and c_2 are obtained by dividing the average household consumption levels in Table 8.3 by the household size. Using these values for c_1 and c_2, and noting that c was given as 0.552 (remember that we are making all our calculations in thousands of rupees), we find the values for the distribution weights in column 6 of Table 13.4 by dividing column 4 by column 5.

The importance given by the Pakistan government to its own income relative to that at the average consumption level (i.e. v) varied over the period. At times v was 1.5, while on other occasions it was equal to 4.

Table 13.4   Calculating the distribution weights for the Pakistan tractor project using equation (13.4)

Category (group)	c_2	c_1	$0.552 \log_e(c_2/c_1)$	$c_2 - c_1$	d
Big farmers	2.9627	0.8259	0.7051	2.1368	0.3300
Small farmers	0.1000	0.3938	−0.7569	−0.2938	2.5762
Full-time workers becoming casual	0.2110	0.3510	−0.2809	−0.1400	2.0066
Full-time workers becoming unemployed	0.1000	0.3510	−0.6931	−0.2510	2.7614

Table 13.5   Two sets of consumption weights for the Pakistan tractor project

Category (group)	d	d/v with $v = 1.5$	Weights with $v = 1.5$	d/v with $v = 4$	Weights with $v = 4$
Big farmers	0.3300	0.2200	+0.6891	0.0825	+0.8266
Small farmers	2.5762	1.7175	−0.8084	0.6441	+0.2650
Full-time workers becoming casual	2.0066	1.3377	−0.4286	0.5017	+0.4074
Full-time workers becoming unemployed	2.7614	1.8409	−0.9318	0.6904	+0.2187

These two values for v can be applied separately to form upper and lower bounds for ω (which is given by the ratio d/v).

Table 13.5 shows the two sets of consumption weights based on the formula $\beta - d/v$, using: the distribution weights from Table 13.4, the value of 0.9091 for β, and the two values for v. The two sets of consumption weights in Table 13.5 are combined with the consumption changes of Table 13.3 to produce the group and total weighted consumption changes presented in Table 13.6. This latter table indicates the distribution adjustment that needs to be made to the efficiency figure to form the social outcome. The social outcome is different for the two cases of v.

When $v = 1.5$, the weighted consumption change is 4,361.3 per annum. This represents the loss of welfare that the consumption has caused – remember that the consumption adjustment is minus C ($\beta - \omega$) in equation (13.1). Since this negative consumption effect swamps the per annum efficiency gain of 3,662.7, there is a net social loss in each year that the project operates. The NPV must be negative in this case, as there are no positive effects to offset the initial capital cost.

When $v = 4$, the weighted consumption change is 2,429.8 per annum. Subtracting this from the 3,662.7 efficiency gain produces a net social gain of 1,232.9 in each year of operation. The NPV for this case is shown in Table 13.7. We can see that when $v = 4$, the NPV for the Pakistan tractor project is positive and this time the project would pass the social criterion.

Table 13.6 The two sets of weighted consumption change for the Pakistan tractor project

Category (group)	Consumption change	Weighted consumption change with $v = 1.5$	Weighted consumption change with $v = 4$
Big farmers	+3,668.9	+2,528.2	+3,032.7
Small farmers	−1,162.0	+939.4	−307.9
Full-time workers becoming casual	−277.8	+119.1	−113.2
Full-time workers becoming unemployed	−831.3	+774.6	−181.8
Total weighted consumption change		+4,361.3	+2,429.8

Table 13.7 The social NPV for the Pakistan tractor project when $v = 4$

Year	Social net benefits (S)	Discount factor (at 10%)	Today's value (at 10%)
0	−5,231	1.000	−5,231
1	1,232.9	0.909	1,120.7
2	1,232.9	0.826	1,018.3
3	1,232.9	0.751	925.9
4	1,232.9	0.683	842.1
5	1,232.9	0.621	765.6
6	1,232.9	0.564	695.4
7	1,232.9	0.513	632.5
		NPV at 10% =	+769.5

Summary of the evaluation

The Pakistan tractor project had a high rate of return judged in efficiency terms. However, it did lead to large losses for all farmers and
workers, except the very rich big farmers. The rich farmers saved very
little of their increased income. Consequently, the loss of consumption
by the poorer farmers was more than offset by the increased consumption by the big farmers. If savings are valued highly, the distributional
adjustment caused by the increase in consumption leads to a negative
social outcome. But, if savings are not so highly valued, the social
outcome is positive. This is so even though the majority of Pakistan
farmers have been forced into poverty by the tractor project. It would
seem that using S & T's methods, which do allow for distributional
considerations, could nonetheless justify projects that many people
would judge to be clearly socially undesirable. It would certainly conflict with the World Bank's stated objective of promoting the welfare of

the poor. (This result, which I call the 'Tyler problem', will be referred to extensively in the next two sections.)

13.2 Main components

We will now reconsider separately some of the main components of the S & T methodology, starting with (intragenerational) distributional weights.

13.2.1 Distribution weights

It is possible to argue that one of the main reasons that the Pakistan tractor project was approved (when v was equal to 1.5) was because too 'low' a value was chosen for the distribution aversion parameter (n). The distributional weights were constructed on the basis of a value for n equal to unity. A value of $n = 2$ would be sufficient to turn around the positive outcome. However, only an infinite value for n (which is what the basic-needs approach of Scandizzo and Knudsen, 1980, effectively leads to) will ensure that in no situation will anyone be placed into poverty. The problem with an infinite weight is that one never knows the price (in terms of loss of output) that has to be paid in order that the distribution of income/consumption never be worsened. It could be that the price, if made explicit, may be considered to be too 'high'.

When looked at from the point of view of a group in poverty, large differences between the weights on the rich and the poor can be defended (though I do not, for the reasons explained in the next section, recommend this as the solution to the Tyler problem). A large weight to those in poverty means that you are concerned about keeping them alive. But this does not mean that one should advocate a high value for n in the S & T formula. This formula applies to all groups in society, and not all group differences are of social concern. (Do we really care if some millionaire farmers obtain larger gains than other millionaire farmers?)

Once one moves outside the realm of groups in poverty, the setting of the distribution parameter n should be much more restrained. Many people in project appraisal do not seem to understand what is a neutral position for n. Recall the S & T marginal weighting formula for distribution weights given by equation (3.14). When one group has five times as much consumption as another (the difference is only a factor of three for big farmers relative to the other farmers in the Pakistan study prior to the project), a value of $n = 1$ implies that the weight to a big farmer would be one-fifth that of a small farmer. With a value for $n = 2$, \$25 to a rich farmer would be treated as equal to \$1 to a small farmer. Surely that sort of differential weighting goes outside the realm of what the rich (or even a moderate egalitarian) would accept in order to help small farmers (assuming that the latter are above poverty levels)? For example, few would recommend (even in the absence of administrative costs and work disincentives) a marginal income tax rate of 96%, which is what such a weighting implies – but note the distinction between distributing in cash and kind made in Chapter 3 that this analogy ignores.

In the context of the gross inequalities in developing countries, it is possible (though highly unlikely, seeing that in Chapter 3 I advocate a figure of $n = \frac{1}{2}$) that I would actually recommend using a weight differential of 1 to 25. But the point is that if I did make such a recommendation for a particular country, I would have no illusion that this would constitute a 'neutral' set of weights. It would be extremely in favour of public projects that benefit the low income groups. Given this, it does a disservice (to those who wish to see project appraisal methods universally accepted throughout government) for one of the S & T authors to claim that (for Pakistan) a value for n 'should not be taken to be very large', and then set n equal to 2! (see Squire, Little and Durdag, 1979, pp. 29–30). If $n = 2$ were to be the norm, World Bank project appraisal studies would be largely ignored by everyone, irrespective of how competently the rest of the analysis was carried out.

13.2.2 Social discount rate

The choice of SDR is the most unsatisfactory part of the whole S & T methodology. Difficulties abound at both the practical and theoretical levels.

Practical difficulties

The basic approach recommended by S & T for the SDR is to use the rate of return on the marginal public investment project. The problem data on the SDR for the practice project appraisal (which I borrowed from Scott, MacArthur and Newberry, 1976) was therefore couched in those terms. Tyler does not even mention the SDR (he used the IRR criterion on its own), so I could not use his estimate of i. But, usually, such information will not be available. Note that it is the social rate on the marginal public project which is the relevant rate. Given that the World Bank has undertaken so few evaluations in any one country, it is likely that not only will the wrong type of rate be used (the average rather than the marginal), but also the basis used will be wrong (an efficiency rate rather than a social rate).

Difficulties with the theory

The fundamental problem with basing the SDR on the rate that rations public investment funds is that there is not a single marginal rate of return. External funds are more available for certain projects than for others. Kenya would not find it very easy to obtain outside funds for defence projects (which it may or may not want). But it would find it very easy to obtain finance for population control projects (which it does not seem to want).

The most satisfactory concept from the welfare economic point of view is the consumption rate of interest. The CRI is easy to calculate and includes provision for a concern over intergenerational issues (via ρ). In fact, as we saw in Chapter 4, when v does not vary over time (as S & T assume), i actually equals the CRI even in the S & T methodology. With investment (and not consumption) as their numeraire, S & T are reluctant to accept this conclusion (even though it is correct).

Overall, it is fair to say that S & T must find some way of utilising the CRI concept in order to improve both the theory and the practice involved with their choice of SDR.

13.2.3 Shadow prices

In keeping with the applied emphasis of this text, more attention was given to explaining and interpreting the use of world prices as shadow prices, rather than deriving the rule and producing new results. Nonetheless, it appears that the practical difficulties entailed in finding a unique world price from a myriad of statistical sources may be the main threat to the general adoption of the world price rule. The primary attraction of using world prices is its supposed simplicity. The objective is to have available a fixed valuation, and not be forced to resort to solving a complex mathematical formula comprising numerous elements which have to be estimated separately. But, when a large number of competing fixed valuations exist, some of the attraction of using world prices is lost.

The important point to remember with the use of world prices is that they are applicable only to tradable goods and services with infinite elasticities. Shadow prices for tradables with less than infinite elasticities, for non-tradables, and for labour services must all be estimated using alternative techniques. As is evident in a number of case studies, and in the practice project appraisal for the imported inputs, tradables have non-cost items attached to them which raise their domestic prices. This means that even tradables must be decomposed, which leads to accounting ratios different from unity. The S & T approach to shadow pricing is as much linked to using the decomposition procedure as simply relying on world prices.

Three reservations to the theory of using world prices as shadow prices were outlined in this book:

1. A project can make a country's balance of payments worse even though it makes a positive contribution to the free foreign exchange in the hands of the government. (Apart from the distinction between effects on the private and public sectors, one must remember that shadow prices are not prices that are actually received.) In these circumstances, the government needs to initiate some means of correcting the trade imbalance. If this is initiated in a neutral way (for example, by using an income tax) relative prices between tradables and non-tradables are unaffected. But if trade balance is brought about in a distortionary way (for example, by using tariffs or quotas) then relative prices will be affected. Domestic price and income repercussions would then need to be analysed.

2. For basic-needs projects (such as food projects supplying calories for those in poverty) the social demand exceeds the market demand. Even when no market distortions exist, and world prices are equal to market prices, the world price still undervalues the food output.

3. The use of world prices for project appraisal provides no guidance for the prices which need to be used for day-to-day management operations of a project once it is built. Nor does it recognise that there may be an incentive compatibility problem. If private persons are to be responsible for undertaking the project (as with the Kenya tea project), then there may be no incentive for them to proceed if the return at market prices dips well below that at world prices.

In addition, some criticisms of using world prices by Stewart (1978) need to be acknowledged. Sometimes projects have very specific (strategic) objectives in mind, such as the promotion of cash crop production, or 'Kenyanisation' (securing employment for Kenyans rather than expatriots). World prices do not recognise these objectives. Also, some projects produce indirect effects which do not accrue to the managers, but accrue to others. Examples are industrial pollution and learning effects in production. World prices focus on correcting for market distortions for activities that are internal to the project. They make no allowance for these 'external effects'.

13.3 Main themes

There are a number of issues which have recurred throughout the book and need to be highlighted. These recurring issues/themes identify the distinctive elements which help to define the subject area called project appraisal. We now examine three of these themes.

13.3.1 Individualistic versus imposed value judgements

In the introductory chapter, we pointed out that one difference between cost–benefit analysis and project appraisal its that the latter is more willing to contemplate non-individualistic elements in the evaluation. Developing countries (on the whole) have market imperfections and income inequalities on such a scale that individual preferences as revealed by the market (especially for food) seem to be out of line with their true preferences or needs. Whatever the reason for this divergence, let us uncover these extra-individual elements that were included in our account of project appraisal.

The first mention of an imposed element was with regard to the aversion to inequality parameter, n. Although a regard for income distribution may in fact be consistent with the altruistic preferences of the rich, project appraisal has not yet found a way of translating this regard into precise values for n.

Next came the rate of pure time preference, ρ, which played a part in the CRI. The higher the value placed on ρ, the greater is the priority to the consumption preferences of the present generation over the future generations. Giving an equal weight to all generations (by setting ρ equal to zero) has been called anti-democratic, because the votes of the existing generation presumably would be against this. But future generations will be comprised of individuals with preferences and votes. Again the difficulty is articulating these preferences.

Then came the social evaluation of an individual's unwillingness to work harder by moving to work in the towns, which was included as a part of the SWR; F was the proportion of an individual's evaluation that was valid from the social point of view, with $F = 1$ the consumer sovereignty assumption of cost–benefit analysis, and $F = 0$ the pro-testant work ethic assumption. This is the clearest example of a dif-ference in philosophy. When decision-makers set F equal to zero, they are actually overriding individual preferences, rather than, as in the other cases, giving articulation for individual preferences which are unknown at present.

Finally, we came across the social agent's demand for food (D_a), in the context of including basic needs into project appraisal. This was to be added to the private market demand for food by the poor to obtain the social demand. A construct of Scandizzo and Knudsen, D_a is the most sophisticated of the extra-individualistic approaches. It not only decides which set of preferences are to rule, individual or social, but also the outcome is different in different circumstances. When the poor consume the target levels of the basic needs good, their preferences are to count. On the other hand, when consumption is below the target, their revealed preferences are ignored and replaced by the social agent's specified consumption amount (equal to the target amount).

In all cases, S & T would seem to recommend that the latest development plan be used as the source for the extra-individualistic preferences. Only human beings can express preferences and not 'society' as such. Thus it is the planners who are to be mouthpieces for the social value judgements.

13.3.2 The control area for the project appraisal

Throughout the book, it was stressed that one needs to be explicit in what the person making the project appraisal is assuming about how the other agents of government are operating in the public policy field. Whatever aspects of the economy exist, and are assumed to be inviolate, are taken to be the constraints under which the project evaluator must operate. When there are no constraints (other than the production possibilities) the project decision-maker has full control. In this 'first-best' world, project appraisal would not be much different from a private investment decision. Market prices rule, and distribution and savings issues are dealt with by other government departments.

At all stages, we assumed that the project evaluator has no control of other government departments. S & T largely follow the same procedure (except for their discussion of the SER, where they refer to the free trade SER). The main cause of market imperfections would be tariffs and these are considered to be in existence for the whole life of the project. This necessitated the use of world prices to replace domestic prices. When urban wages were so large relative to rural wages, this was attributed to social/political factors. But there was no presumption that this wage differential could be removed by a government-imposed wages and incomes policy. The project evaluator accepts the fact that there will be income and consumption effects caused by high urban wages. The task is to analyse their distributional and savings effects, and see that they are weighted according to the implicit valuations that the constraints entail.

Because we took the stance that project appraisal should be undertaken with existing constraints as binding, we cannot go along with any of Tyler's remedies for the problem identified in the Pakistan tractor project. Tyler suggested two main solutions to the fact that certain groups were put into poverty by the introduction of tractors. First, he suggested that taxes be imposed on the big farmers to compensate the other groups. Then he recommended that projects especially in favour of the poor be initiated. Not only do we rule out the use of the tax/transfer system, we also recognise that the project evaluator (and even the World Bank itself) has no power to initiate projects of any kind. If poverty is to be considered a social issue, there is no alternative to including poverty as a separate factor that is part of project appraisal. It is not a consideration that we can assume will disappear by some other policy instrument being available and employed.

Sen (1974) is quite right to argue that there is no point in treating local employment as a benefit in a project appraisal, if we know that once the project has been accepted, skilled labour from overseas will, in fact, be hired to undertake construction (given the hiring practices in the past). But the issue here is really one of information. If we know the type of labour that will be employed (just as we think we know how large a money wage they will be paid) then just that type of labour should go into our calculations. Hiring practices should be treated just like any other constraint.

13.3.3 Project appraisal and the numbers effect

In Chapter 1, we argued that project appraisal would be more convincing if it included the numbers effect as a third social objective. Policy-makers do, in fact, make allowances for the numbers of people affected by a public expenditure decision. In addition, by including numbers as a separate social objective, project appraisal can overcome the basic welfare economic weakness of cost–benefit analysis. This subject has (for the most part) ignored the fact that any public investment decision would produce groups who would be net losers from the process. Since decisions cannot be Pareto optimal (lead to a situation where some gain and no one loses), it seems sensible to acknowledge that fact, and include the number of uncompensated losers as a (negative) component of the social objective function.

We saw that the numbers effect could be usefully included in three main areas of project appraisal. In each case, it would be supplying a missing ingredient. The areas were the CRI; the SWR; and basic needs. We cover each of these areas in turn.

1. CRI: the literature has already acknowledged the fact that the CRI may depend on the size of the population who live in a country at different times, p (the population growth rate), which is important because it reduces per capita consumption (for a given size growth rate of aggregate consumption). The size of p may be of social significance in its own right. In which case, one may not want to reduce the CRI by the full amount of the reduction in per capita income.

Following on from this type of reasoning, one may also want to allow for population in an intragenerational dimension (numbers of individuals at a given point in time). Many formulations have one individual's preferences to represent the group for the CRI. In particular, S & T use the person at the average level of consumption for this purpose. A simple extension would be to find out just how large a number (or proportion of the population) are at this level. One can then weight the individual's valuation by this number (proportion). This uses a multiplicative relation between numbers and the preference of the representative individual. As a final step, one could use numbers in an additive rather than a multiplicative fashion. It is the number of future losers that would now be involved. No matter whether numbers are added in an additive or a multiplicative form, the net result is that the CRI would be raised by the numbers effect.

2. SWR: the concept of uncompensated losers has a very obvious concrete counterpart in the context of the SWR. For there are workers who migrate to the towns and are unsuccessful in finding a job. The numbers newly unemployed are clearly losers stemming from the public project. Although seeking to reduce unemployment is often mentioned as a goal in project appraisal, it was never given special status as an objective in its own right. This is an obvious omission. It can be remedied by including a 'lost job' as the fourth component in the S & T SWR formula. This represents the social cost of unemployment created by the project. The higher this cost, the less encouragement should be given to urban projects which attract migrants. The SWR is therefore higher because of this effect.

3. Basic needs: Tyler correctly identifies his complaint with the outcome of the Pakistan tractor project in terms of the poverty that it generated. Since the Tyler problem involves a concern for poverty, it has a logical solution. That is, a concern for poverty should play a part in the project appraisal criterion. The issue then is how best to achieve this result.

The basic-needs approach from the outset has been defined as an anti-poverty strategy. The Scandizzo and Knudsen analysis, which incorporates the concern for poverty into the determination of the shadow price for food, is, therefore, one means of solving the Tyler problem. But it does combine the three social objectives of project appraisal (efficiency, distribution and the numbers effect) in a non-additive way. The weights in this formulation are implicit, and for certain ranges of output the weights are infinite. Project appraisal should always strive to clarify the trade-offs that are entailed with any public policy decision. By including numbers no longer in poverty into S & T's efficiency and distribution framework, one is forced to make the weight to the numbers effect explicit.

To conclude this discussion on the numbers effect, I will explain the reason that raising the distribution weights for those in poverty is not, in itself, the answer to the Tyler problem. One context in which distributional issues arise in project appraisal is where one group gains more than another. It is for the relative position of various groups that one wishes to make adjustments by using distributional weights (as currently conceived). However, there is another context in which distributional issues arise, and this is where one group gains and another group actually loses. This distributional issue is different because it is concerned with the absolute level of consumption (or satisfaction) of the losing group. So far, weights which allow for both differences and levels have been hard to construct. It would seem that introducing the numbers effect as a separate objective (in all its many guises) is one way of ensuring that absolute levels of well-being, and not just relative differences, are being included in project appraisal.

13.4 Problems

This is the stage to test one's overall understanding of project appraisal and S & T's methods. The practice project appraisal required one to understand the procedure through which one must go to carry out an evaluation, and checked that one could make the necessary calculations. In this way one was forced to deal with the specifics of project appraisal. In the essay questions which follow, the emphasis will be more on the conceptual basis of making a project evaluation.

Background information

The questions can be answered at a number of different levels. There are seven areas covered: shadow prices; distribution weights; the social discount rate; the shadow wage rate; a comparison of methods; risk; and basic needs.

Questions

(a) Under what circumstances would you consider it appropriate to use world prices as shadow prices? Outline any theoretical and practical reasons why one should not use world prices.

(b) Why does the fact that costless transfers from the rich to the poor are available imply that equal distribution weights should not be used in project appraisal? Assume that a particular group has a level of consumption which is one-quarter of the average. Examine the implications of using a value of $n = 1$ rather that $n = \frac{1}{2}$ or $n = 2$ for distributional weighting in the S & T framework, where n is the aversion to income equality parameter. Thus, how valid is it for S & T to recommend that $n = 1$ should be the presumed value for the distributional parameter?

(c) How is the possibility that future generations may be richer than those in the current generation incorporated in the consumption rate of interest (CRI). Does the CRI have any role to play in a method of project appraisal where consumption is not the numeraire? How would you go about putting a precise figure on the CRI in practice?

(d) Outline the main factors which should be considered in the shadow wage rate (SWR). Examine the role played by migration in the determination of the SWR.

(e) 'The domestic resource cost (DRC) is merely the switching value for the shadow exchange rate.' Explain the basis of this statement. By using the DRC, can one really avoid making an explicit calculation of the shadow exchange rate? Do you consider that the DRC procedure is a complete method for deciding the social merits of projects?

(f) 'When one considers the way that project appraisal deals with risk, one sees one of the few instances where analysing a project from a social viewpoint is simpler than carrying out the analysis from a private perspective.' Explain and evaluate this statement.

(g) When would you recommend using a cost-effectiveness analysis instead of undertaking a full project appraisal? Why is a cost-effectiveness analysis an inappropriate method for dealing with basic needs? How then should basic needs projects be evaluated?

References

Ahmed, S. (1983) 'Shadow prices for economic appraisal of projects', *World Bank Staff Working Papers* 609, Washington: World Bank.

Amin, G.A. (1978) 'Themes from the discussion at the symposium', special issue of *World Development*, **6**.

Arrow, K. and R.C. Lind (1970) 'Uncertainty and the evaluation of public investment decisions', *American Economic Review*, **60**.

Bacha, E. and L. Taylor (1971) 'Foreign exchange shadow prices: A critical review of current theories', *Quarterly Journal of Economics*, **85**.

Balassa, B. (1974) 'Estimating the shadow price of foreign exchange in project appraisal', *Oxford Economic Papers*, **26**.

Baum, W.C. (1978) 'The project cycle'. *Finance and Development*, **15**.

Baumol, W.J. (1972) *Economic Theory and Operations Analysis* (3rd edn), Hemel Hempstead: Prentice Hall.

Bell, C. and S. Devarajan (1983) 'Shadow prices for project evaluation under alternative macroeconomic specifications', *Quarterly Journal of Economics*, **87**.

Berlage, L. and R. Renard (1985) 'The discount rate in cost–benefit analysis and the choice of a numeraire', *Oxford Economic Papers*, **34**.

Bhagwati, J.N. and P. Desai (1970) *India: Planning for Industrialisation*, New York: Oxford University Press.

Bhagwati, J.N. and T.N. Srinivasan (1981) 'The evaluation of projects under trade distortions: Quantitative restrictions, monopoly power in trade and nontraded goods', *International Economic Review*, **22**.

Blitzer, C., Dasgupta, P. and J.E. Stiglitz (1981) 'Project appraisal and foreign exchange constraints', *Economic Journal*, **91**.

Boadway, R. (1975) 'Cost–benefit rules and general equilibrium', *Review of Economic Studies*, **42**.

Boadway, R. (1976) 'Integrating equity and efficiency in applied welfare economics', *Quarterly Journal of Economics*, **80**.

Brent, R.J. (1976) 'The Minister of Transport's social welfare function: A study of the factors behind railway closure decisions (1963–1970). Ph.D. thesis, University of Manchester.

Brent R.J. (1979) 'Imputing weights behind past railway closure decisions within a cost–benefit framework', *Applied Economics*, **16**.

Brent R.J. (1980) 'Distinguishing between money income and utility income in cost–benefit analysis', *Public Finance Quarterly*, **8**.

Brent R.J. (1984a) 'On the use of distributional weights in cost–benefit analysis: A survey of schools', *Public Finance Quarterly*, **12**.

Brent R.J. (1984b) 'A three objective social welfare function for cost–benefit analysis', *Applied Economics*, **16**.

Brent R.J. (1986a) 'An axiomatic basis for the three objective social welfare function within a poverty context', *Economics Letters*, **20**.

Brent R.J. (1986b) 'Lagged adjustments in short-run estimates of tax shifting in Kenya', *Journal of Development Economics*, **20**.

Brent R.J. (1987) 'The form of the social welfare function, the numbers effect and the social discount rate', Department of Economics, Fordham University.

Brent R.J. (1988) 'The cost–benefit analysis of government loans', Department of Economics, Fordham University.

Brent R.J. (1989) 'The shadow wage rate and the numbers effect', Department of Economics, Fordham University.

Brent R.J. (1990) 'On the choice of estimation technique to be used to reveal implicit government expenditure weights', *Applied Economics* (forthcoming).

Christiansen, V. and E.S. Jansen (1978) 'Implicit social preferences in the Norwegian system of indirect taxation', *Journal of Public Economics*, **10**.

Cleaver, K.M. (1980) 'Economic and social analysis of projects and of price policy: The Morocco fourth agricultural credit project', *World Bank Staff Working Paper*, 369, Washington: World Bank.

Dasgupta, A.K. (1972) *Cost–benefit analysis: Theory and Practice*, New York: Harper and Row.

Dasgupta, P. and J.E. Stiglitz (1974) 'Benefit-cost analysis and trade policies', *Journal of Political Economy*, **82**.

De Wolf, J. (1975) 'Fiscal incidence in developing countries: Survey and critique', *International Monetary Fund Staff Papers*, **22**.

Diamond, P. and J. Mirrlees (1971) 'On optimal taxation and public production, I and II', *American Economic Review*, **60**.

Dickey, J.W. and L.H. Miller (1984) *Road Project Appraisal for Developing Countries*, Chichester: John Wiley and Sons.

Dorfman, R. (1962) 'Decision rules under uncertainty', reprinted as chapter 15 of Richard Layard (1972) *Cost–benefit analysis*, London: Penguin.

Feldstein, M. (1972) 'Distributional equity and the optimal structure of public prices', *American Economic Review*, **62**.

Fields, G.S. (1977) 'Who benefits from economic development? A re-examination of Brazilian growth in the 1960s', *American Economic Review*, **67**.

Fields, G.S. (1982) *Poverty, Inequality and Development*, New York: Cambridge University Press.

FitzGerald, E.V.K. (1977) 'The public investment criterion and the role of the state', *Journal of Development Studies*, **13**.

Frey B.S. and F. Schneider (1986) 'Competing models of international lending activity', *Journal of Development Economics*, **20**.

Gittinger, J.P. (1984) *Compounding and Discounting Tables for Project Analysis*, 2nd edition (revised and expanded), Baltimore: Johns Hopkins.

Gramlich, E. (1981) *Benefit-cost Analysis of Government Programs*, New Jersey: Prentice Hall.

Guisinger, S. and D. Papageorgiou (1976) 'The selection of appropriate border prices in project evaluation', *Bulletin of Oxford University Institute of Statistics*, **38**.

Harberger, A.C. (1971) 'On measuring the social opportunity cost of labour', *International Labour Review*, **103**.

Harberger, A.C. (1978) 'On the use of distributional weights in social cost–benefit analysis', *Journal of Political Economy*, (supplement) **86**.

Harberger, A.C. (1984) 'Basic needs versus distributional weights in social cost–benefit analysis'. *Economic Development and Cultural Change*, **32**.

Harsanyi, J.C. (1955) 'Cardinal welfare, individualistic ethics and interpersonal comparisons of utility', *Journal of Political Economy*, **63**.

Heady, C.J. (1981) 'Shadow wages and induced migration', *Oxford Economic Papers*, **32**.

Heggie, I.G. (1976) 'Practical problems of implementing accounting prices', in Little, I.M.D. and M.FG. Scott (eds.) *Using Shadow Prices*, London: Heinemann.

Hicks, N. and P. Streeten (1979) 'Indicators of development: The search for a basic needs yardstick', *World Development*, **7**.

Hochman, H.M. and J.D. Rodgers (1971) 'Is efficiency a criterion for judging redistribution?' Public Finance, **26**.

Irvin, G. (1978) *Modern Cost–benefit Methods*, London: Macmillan.

Joshi, H. (1972) 'World prices as shadow prices: A critique', *Bulletin of Oxford University Institute of Statistics*, **34**.

Knight, F. (1921) *Risk, Uncertainty and Profit*, reprinted 1964, New York: Sentry Press.

Krueger, A.O. (1970) 'Some economic costs of exchange control: The Turkish case', *American Economic Review*, **60**.

Lal, D. (1973) 'Disutility of effort, migration and the shadow wage rate', *Oxford Economic Papers*, **25**.

Lal, D. (1974) 'Methods of project analysis: A review', *World Bank Staff Occasional Papers*, 16, Washington: World Bank.

Lal, D. (1978) 'Shadow pricing and wage and employment issues in national economic planning', *The Bangladesh Development Studies*, **6**. (Also reprinted under *World Bank Reprint Series*, no. 131.)

Layard, R. (1972) *Cost–benefit Analysis*, London: Penguin.

Lind, R.C. (1982) *Discounting for Time and Risk in Energy Policy*, Washington: Resources for the Future.

Little, I.M.D. and J.A. Mirrlees (1969) *Manual of Industrial Project Analysis in Developing Countries*, **2**, Paris: OECD.

Little, I.M.D. and J.A. Mirrlees (1974) *Project Appraisal and Planning for Developing Countries*, London: Heinemann.

Loury, G.C. (1983) 'Efficiency and equity impacts of natural gas deregulation', in R.H. Haveman and J. Margolis (eds). *Public Expenditure and Policy Analysis* (3rd edn) Boston: Houghton Mifflin.

MacArthur, J.D. (1978) 'Appraising the distributional aspects of rural development projects: A Kenyan case study', *World Development*, **6**.

Marglin, S. (1976) *Value and Price in the Labour-surplus Economy*, Oxford: Clarendon.

Mashayekhi, A. (1980) 'Shadow prices for project appraisal in Turkey', *World Bank Staff Working Paper*, 392, Washington: World Bank.

Mazumdar, D. (1975) 'The rural-urban wage gap, migration and the shadow wage rate'. *World Bank Staff Working Paper*, 197, Washington: World Bank.

Monson, T.D. and G.G. Pursell (1979) 'The use of DRCs to evaluate indigenisation programs', *Journal of Development Economics*, **6**.

Musgrave, R. (1969) 'Cost–benefit analysis and the theory of public finance', *Journal of Economic Literature*, **7**.

Musgrave, R.A. and P. Jarrett (1979) 'International redistribution', *Kyklos*, **32**.

Pouliquen, L. (1970) 'Risk analysis in project appraisal', *World Bank Staff Occasional Paper*, **11**, Washington: World Bank.

Rawls, J. (1971) *A theory of justice*, Cambridge, Mass: Harvard University Publisher.

Ray, A. (1984) *Cost–benefit Analysis*, Baltimore: Johns Hopkins.

Reutlinger, S. (1970) 'Techniques for project appraisal under uncertainty', *World Bank Staff Occasional Papers*, **10**, Washington: World Bank.

Reutlinger, S. and M. Selowsky (1976) 'Malnutrition and poverty: Magnitude and policy options', *World Bank Staff Occasional Paper*, 23, Washington: World Bank.

Scandizzo, P. and O.K. Knudsen (1980) 'The evaluation of the benefits of basic needs policies', *American Agricultural Economics Association*, **62**.

Scott, M.FG. (1974) 'How to use and estimate shadow exchange rates', *Oxford Economic Papers*, **26**.

Scott, M.FG., J. MacArthur and D.M.G. Newberry (1976) *Project Appraisal in Practice: The Little-Mirrlees method applied in Kenya*. London: Heinemann.

Sen, A.K. (1966) 'Peasants and dualism with and without surplus labour', *Journal of Political Economy*, **74**.

Sen, A.K. (1976) 'Poverty: An ordinal approach to measurement', *Econometrica*, **44**.

Sen, A.K. (1982) 'Approaches to the choice of discount rates for social benefit-cost analysis', In R.C. Lind (*op.cit*).

Squire, L., I. Little and M. Durdag (1979) 'Application of shadow pricing to country economic analysis with an illustration from Pakistan', *World Bank Staff Working Papers*, 330, Washington: World Bank.

Squire, L. and H. van der Tak (1975) Economic Analysis of Projects, Baltimore: Johns Hopkins.

Srinivasan, T.N. and J.N. Bhagwati (1978) 'Shadow prices for project selection in the presence of distortions: Effective rates of protection and domestic resource costs', *Journal of Political Economy*, **86**.

Stern, N.H. (1970) *An Appraisal of Smallholder Tea in Kenya*. OECD.

Stern, N.H. (1972) 'Experience with the use of the Little/Mirrlees method for an appraisal of small-holder tea in Kenya'. *Bulletin of Oxford University Institute of Statistics*, **34**.

Stern, N.H. (1977) 'Welfare weights and the elasticity of the marginal valuation of Income', in M.J. Artis and A.R. Nobay (eds.), *Studies in Modern Economic Analysis*; the proceedings of the AUTE Conference in Edinburgh, 1976. Oxford: Blackwell.

Stewart, F. (1975) 'A note on social cost benefit analysis and class conflict in LDCs', *World Development*, **3**.

Stewart, F. (1978) 'Social cost–benefit analysis in practice: Some reflections in the light of case studies using Little-Mirrlees techniques', *World Development*, **6**.

Sugden, R. and A. Williams (1978) *Practical Cost–benefit Analysis*, Oxford:

Oxford University Press.

Todaro, M.P. (1969) 'A model of labour migration and urban unemployment in less developed countries', *American Economic Review*, **58**.

Tower, E. and G. Purcel (1986) 'On shadow pricing', *World Bank Staff Working Papers*, 792, Washington: World Bank.

Toye, J. (1976) 'Review of Little and Mirrlees (1974)', *Journal of Development Studies*, **12**.

Tresch, R. (1981) *Public Finance*, Texas: Business Publications.

Tyler, G.T. (1979) 'Poverty, income distribution and the analysis of agricultural projects', *International Labour Review*, **118**.

UNIDO (1972) *Guidelines for Project Evaluation*, New York: United Nations.

Warr, P.G. (1982) 'Shadow pricing rules for non-traded commodities', *Oxford Economic Papers*, **34**.

Warr, P.G. (1983) 'Domestic resource cost as an investment criterion', *Oxford Economic Papers*, **35**.

Weisbrod, B.A. (1968) 'Income redistribution effects and benefit–cost analysis', in S.B. Chase, Jun. (ed.) *Problems in Public Expenditure Analysis*, Washington: Brookings.

Yotopoulos, P.A. and J.B. Nugent (1976) *Economics of Development*, New York: Harper and Row.

Index